Change from your dollars

Stories of personal cause
and financial effect

Brett Heaton Juarez

For JB,
who saw the future before I did.

Contents

preface

All these stories are autobiographical. From early childhood memories to the present, they capture my raw personal reflections. Each vignette paints my feelings and details my observations from that time. Each is written from memory. I didn't go back and verify any conversations. I didn't double check what I said. After all, we are the sum of the memories we carry, not a database. What I remember dictates my choices today. In writing this, I generalize a lot. I do this because in my head I generalize. I'm often wrong, and my brain knows it, but cognitive science shows we take shortcuts all the time. I may be quoted and criticized and taken out of context, but that's the price of authenticity. Our memories are inevitably biased as we attempt to make sense of our lives. Perception of our past shapes our future reality.

My standard of accuracy in telling these stories is, say, much higher than a politician's testimony under oath but much lower than a PhD dissertation. In other words, I believe everything I've said to be true, but

I have not verified every detail directly. In the 21st century, people make shit up all the time, so rest assured this is not that. I try to isolate the impressions made at age 9, 19, or 29 using "I remember," "I thought," or "I felt." To my memories, I add my present-day perspective, with all the insights I have gleaned along the way. I have more money data and knowledge as a CERTIFIED FINANCIAL PLANNER™ professional and from other designations that help me navigate a complex financial system. I have a master's degree in educational psychology, with a concentration in learning and development. (Hunches are good when they are reinforced by science and data.) My undergraduate degree was in history and secondary (high school) education. Then, there are thousands of confidential interviews with clients aged 18–81, full of messy emotions, difficult decisions, trials, and triumph.

Each chapter can stand on its own. Why not share one that speaks to your experience so that you start opening up about your relationship with money? Send it to your girlfriend saying, "This is why I was pissed after dinner on Tuesday." Message your dad or your boss, and say, "This might help you see where I'm coming from."

Our voices won't always agree. Authenticity cannot be distilled enough to resonate with everyone. However, by seeing me unpack my shame, shock, and identity confusion around money, maybe you can too.

I mention nonprofit boards I serve on by name. Of course, I'm there for a reason. I love the organization, and part of my role is to promote them. This doesn't mean I don't volunteer elsewhere or think that my organizations are the only ones doing good work. With for-profit companies, I mention some by name because they are all over, and I hope it allows you to understand the context better. As a consumer, I have not thoroughly vetted their employment practices, nor do I own individual stock in any of them. (I do own them by default in retirement index and mutual funds, as you might too.) Their inclusion is not meant to disparage or promote, but merely to give relatable examples about how I and others interact with them. Corporations are not inherently good or evil: they exist to make a profit by providing services or products. They become better or worse in response to what consumers and stockholders demand.

I do refer to specific financial transactions and benchmarks in a few parts of the book. Again, my intent is not to promote any particular company or product. If one choice was right for everybody, eventually there would be only one choice. Every millionaire would have made identical money decisions. We tend to want a simple answer, and Western thinking favors the either/or decision. The unsatisfying answer to most financial questions is "it depends," so always talk to someone who (a) you think you can trust and (b) knows what they're talking about. We all want a simple cause and effect explanation, but financial planning is rooted in probability. Your cousin's good luck doesn't make them qualified to give you financial advice.

The financial services industry is vast, and only a portion of us professionals see clients. There are some product pushers and hustlers out there, but what any quality financial advisor or planner knows is this: it's not really about the money. It's about culture and values as much as anything else. Once again, I felt compelled to share these stories not because I'm a financial expert, but because I can connect some dots. I am writing to reach those who write off financial experts categorically.

The biggest variable in financial health and success in general will always be your own behavior. So, for starters, just acknowledge that money is an important tool in this modern world, and that every one of us has to resist the onslaught of ads and daily demands to focus on our own financial why.

In this book, I skip the "how to" money talk and instead dig into the messiness of life and mindset. You are not alone. Your peers are grappling with their own baggage, contradictions, and definition of success. My own inner monologue (in italics) hums in the background of these stories: judging, doubting, worrying. But I have to take on the sharp pain of growth to escape the dull pain of regret. There will always be tradeoffs, but we don't have to choose between hard work and personal responsibility or equity and safety nets. Everyone needs all four. Time to go a little deeper.

This book is not about financial advice. Most of what you find online falls into two categories. The first type is very dry and technical, written by experts having difficulty being accessible without condescension. My dad once astutely observed that instruction manuals often aren't helpful because they are written by the designer of the product, not the target user. They overestimate prior knowledge, which is why I feel stupid and overwhelmed replacing a SIM card on my iPhone. Articles will explain what you search for. They can't identify what you aren't aware of.

The second type is the "I made a million dollars in a week and here's how" genre. Now, I don't doubt that it happened. However, the bar is set too high too soon, luck was a major factor, and the author is typically a guy whose style will immediately rub many people the wrong way. Also, read those disclaimers ...

The internet is full of money information. This book is full of money *stories*, written by a person who never liked thinking seriously about money until he realized how important it is. Money is not the root of all evil. The love of money itself is. I have found writing this to be therapeutic. It is my sincere hope that reading it will be therapeutic for you too.

foreword

I grew up in a blue-collar neighborhood in Chicago. My parents were not the best role models. I learned hard work and discipline from them but nothing about the realities of life. One of those realities is the importance of how to manage money and finances.

Fortunately for me, 30 years ago, I chose a career in financial planning. It has not only changed my life, but given me the opportunity to work with clients, and give the gift of this amazing career to hundreds of others.

What have I learned?

People have great goals and aspirations, but they often don't know how to plan for them or have the self-discipline to save money for the long term. We either work our whole life for money or we have our money work for us—the strength of compounding.

In working with clients, I've learned that most people are too busy, and life gets in the way of planning, or they aren't educated and don't know who to turn to for advice. Just as a focus on physical health or mental health will improve our quality of life, working on financial health does too.

The life lessons about money Brett lays out in this book are timeless and valuable to everyone. I appreciate his willingness to be vulnerable and share his intimate experiences so that we can all learn how to have a better relationship with money.

Steve Holter, Managing Partner

introduction

This book addresses the creation of human value and dollar value. Every person can have a high value in one and a low value in another. A person can have tremendous value to the community and no money. Someone can have tremendous value to the marketplace, but be a rotten human being. When we falsely assign or claim human value proportionate to dollar value, our culture is in trouble, reinforcing a lie. A more accurate assessment is that those with significant money can perform well under pressure, or have a unique insight, idea, or ability, or had a head start inheritance from someone who did. That's it.

Money has the value we say it has. It's just a substitute for trading actual goods. When we think dollar value aligns with human value, then everyone is happy. Our brains search for a neat and tidy explanation. The stress comes from misalignment. When that happens, we need a new policy or mindset. Every human life has inherent value, but we all agree some of us are more valuable to the goals of humankind than others.

As I approached age 30, I was plainly asked for the first time: "What do you want for yourself and your family?" No one had ever asked me this before and expected a sincere answer. Perhaps they had asked, but there were clear acceptable answers, and they all involved tradeoffs.

So, what did I want for my family? By that time, I realized I wasn't going to be able to afford to give our son the childhood experiences I'd had if I carried on working 60 hours a week as a nonprofit youth program director. These are somber moments, times when you realize that maybe your parents were a little "boring" sometimes because they had kids and a mortgage. And wait a minute … now, we are those parents. In this watershed moment of growing up, I had to admit that idealism doesn't always pay the bills. As a very young man, I felt my work and my worth were one, that working for a nonprofit defined me more than my own character. I couldn't shake the feeling that pursuing a greater dollar value for my family meant diminishing my own human value. I agonized over it. I wanted to earn more money for my family without selling out or working nonstop.

You, the reader, have your own tradeoffs playing on a loop in your mind. *If I work so hard, why haven't I gotten a promotion? I want to prioritize my startup, but won't that mean I sacrifice my personal life? Google (and my mom) says save for retirement early, but shouldn't I live my best life before I start adulting and settle down? Everything from Bible scripture to the latest Disney movie says be brave and take risks, so is it bad I'm so cautious financially? My love for my child is infinite, so does that mean they should get the best of everything that I can afford? My parents need help, but I need to make it out of this neighborhood, too. Should I help a little now or a lot later? If all people are created equal, why are some countries so wealthy and others so poor, and how do I feel about this kitchen remodel cost knowing that?*

Finance is defined as "money management and the process of acquiring funds." Culture is defined as "customs, arts, social institutions and achievements of a particular nation, people or other social group." How can we possibly separate these two?

In therapy, it is not enough to visualize a brighter future. We may be able to picture what we want in one state of mind, but still be triggered again and again, continuing to stumble into the same limiting patterns of learned behavior. Money is our motivator and our trigger. Money is part of the story of our trauma-molded world, a story that is too often told through statistics. Have you heard a toddler ask for a bedtime statistic? Let's make our money story human again.

I want my spending, my giving, and my saving to have real purpose. And I want to do this not just because it's what adults do. Adults created the world we're living in, and I have some constructive criticism.

I am not alone. After talking to so many peers in confidential interviews as prospective or existing clients, I know that meaning and purpose matter. For most of us, life is not about the money—until it must be about the money. Shit can get real just as quickly for us, for all kinds of reasons. Some people scrape by financially their whole lives. I've seen obituaries and healthcare GoFundMe campaigns run by people who operate like that. Being broke can be cute, until you have a hole in your tooth, or you can't afford to fly across the country to see a dying relative. Therefore, ascribing meaning and purpose to every dollar—in good times—is a worthwhile pursuit. And for those who say, "I don't care about money," this is privilege personified.

Maximizing my time and talents for the good of others is the primary way I reconcile my privilege. I can't take back the fact my parents paid a lot for my club soccer, or that I went to a great college, or that I could study abroad, or that I avoided a great deal of prejudice as a straight, able-bodied, White male. I used to feel guilty about it, but that didn't help anybody. Now I take the energy saved from a life free of micro-aggressions and use it in a meaningful way.

Ignoring or failing to understand money is not a long-term solution. And caring about financial planning does not mean you are shutting the door on every YOLO scenario. Sometimes my clients will joke on the way out the door, "Okay, that's enough adulting for one day." I'll reply, "Something is better than nothing."

For most of us, the primary goal is to live life on our own terms. We look to the culture at large for examples of what we can aspire to or wish to avoid. Our society facilitates the spending of money better than the saving of it. We get help with shopping whether we like it or not, but the equivalent help for saving is the responsibility of the individual. Over the years, the systems for wanting and spending have given us an effortless user experience: credit card offers, product placement, one-click-to-buy. Society does not encourage living within our means. We can lead lives of rich experiences without riches. Our quiet desperation is the gulf in between.

Many of us spend and live like our parents did and our friends do, without any context of what they could—or we can—afford. We are oblivious to the mathematical opportunity that some have harnessed to their advantage, or we avoid the truth of credit card debt or pending poverty in old age, or we are so bothered by the state of the world and our lives that we just can't find an action today that nudges us toward a better future.

After 18 months as a financial advisor, I'd had so many personal conversations fitting this description that I needed to pause and consider how to proceed. Prioritizing the young and broke clientele would leave me aging and broke myself. It bears repeating: money is not the root of all evil. Money can be an exchange to share, nurture, inspire, and live to the fullest. The love of money without humanity is the root of all evil. The existential crisis is that we—every bit as much as Baby Boomers, Gen Xers, and the Gilded Age robber barons before them—just love to spend money. It simply doesn't feel so capitalist when it's "local" or "sustainable" but, uh …it's still buying things.

The love of money can be over the top, like Ebenezer Scrooge or King Midas, or it can be subtle, like having a yard sign and an opinion but using your COVID relief check on landscaping instead of giving to the cause on the yard sign. Many do not accept that acquiring wealth is meaningful, in and of itself. As an end to itself, that's too boring. I'm no different. Living in the same town, working pretty much the same jobs, successfully raising kids, sending them to college, being comfortable? I feel some guilt in saying so, but that isn't enough for me. And if I chose to start saving for "retirement," it felt like I had accepted that future already. *Sesame Street* said I could be anything I wanted, dammit.

Having all my basic needs met allowed me to want more. I got to age 30 and realized—not for the first time—that life is short. I also realized that, unless I reached for new adventures, the rest of my life was familial love and some predictable sensory pleasures. I felt the cognitive dissonance of rational responsibility and soulful resistance.

If I continued as a "traditional" financial advisor, I somehow felt that I would grow bored. *Why must you always resist the well-worn path.* I had finally accepted that I deserved financial wealth and well-being for my family. But I couldn't accept a soul-killing marathon of consumer decisions like which minivan was best and why. That just couldn't be my only purpose. I was overqualified for many of my clients, but I couldn't stomach the idea of moving on. With every story of struggle I heard, I wondered how I could help more people without working myself into the ground. Yet working toward equality of access for all who are willing to learn was fundamental to my professional and personal being. It was a theme in all my work, and my parents taught my sister and me to treat people fairly if nothing else. And why the hell was money advice so confusing and contradictory? As an amateur social scientist, I needed to unpack that too.

And that's when I decided to write this book. I knew I had to get this message out there since so many people were failing to reach their dreams because of the way they viewed money. I was sitting in the Green Door Tavern in Chicago, drinking a beer, and waiting to meet my friend KB. I had just finished the book *Think and Grow Rich* and was pondering what I could do that was aligned with my values and my value proposition.

Years earlier, I would have listened endlessly to a prospective client's version of what to prioritize, invest or buy. Now I just wanted to say, "Look, I've interviewed hundreds of people in this situation. Here is what tends to work and why. These are pros and cons. What do you want to do?"

I had enhanced expertise but earning trust cannot be rushed. I had organized knowledge, but I wanted to apply it faster. A book can share much to many at a pace of their choosing. You can't do that in a one-hour client meeting.

This book contains my cultural reflections on financial choices. It is not diagnostic financial advice; you won't find that here. Instead, you will see the nature of money revealed in the ebb and flow of one human life. Money is like water. Both can nourish or drown us, calm or excite us. A slow and steady current is surprisingly strong when deep, while a splash gets attention but is fleeting. They can evaporate or freeze without controls. They become more powerful and volatile under pressure. Both are deeply embedded in the human experience. Routinely in the background, taken for granted, and sometimes looming large, instilling joy or fear. Often all of this at once.

And many of us never get swimming lessons.

When structure is in place to protect physical and emotional safety of individuals, each person can experiment with choice. Creativity can flourish. Confidence can bloom. You can have fun in the ocean. But one bad experience kills trust. You can avoid swimming most places. You can't avoid money.

Once we cross into financial adulthood, we are left to figure it out, often because the adults in our lives aren't sure what to say. They, too, are conflicted. As we get older, we increasingly identify with our economic class and define ourselves and others financially. So, why does money just seem to find some people and elude others, no matter what they do?

The 21st century world is operating at a faster and faster pace, making us more interconnected and gratification more instant. Consumer spending makes up three-quarters of the US economy. My prosperity makes others prosper. My spending is my friend's earning, so I don't want to stop that. The pandemic shutdown showed us what happens when we do just stop. I want to spend with businesses and people I like. I want us to be aware and intentional. A healthy democracy demands it. Every dollar has a social impact. Your actions and mine are never neutral. If we can grasp the properties of money in a human context, we can better align our actions with our values.

And I want kind people to do well, grow their influence, and fulfill their potential. People who are kind have a ripple effect; I want them to be colleagues, parents, partners, and citizens to the fullest, unburdened by nagging money doubt. And I don't want to work for unkind people.

Writing this memoir is one way I can fulfill the vision I hold for those kind people. I want to talk openly about my personal experiences with money, for better or worse, so that you will talk openly about yours. Right now, you may be mystified by an investment statement in the mail, compulsively open your credit card app and scroll through what you already know, commiserate your student loans over wine at your friend's place, or look on Zillow and compare where you are to what you're looking for. And it usually stops there.

We are increasingly comfortable talking about sex, religion, and politics, but money is still taboo. I aim to change that, because earning money is not something that only rich people do. It's not something only old people do. It's something *you* do. And no matter how much or how little is spent, your money reflects—and projects—your desires, your fears, and your values.

"I try to be an observer of things."
— Mr. Bentivegna
freshman World History, Palatine High School

a person out of place

For children, highs can seem higher; lows lower. I have a memory of being young enough to experience everything in a visceral way, the way kids do with their unchecked superego, yet old enough to be struck by this new experience that was out of my frame of reference.

I doubt it was my first ride on the Metra to downtown Chicago with my dad, but it was my first time with knowing eyes. One of the many privileges I've been given was a childhood in which I never felt poor or wealthy. My suburb of Palatine was fairly middle class. At least, my side of town was. The other side of town and the suburbs beyond were some of the wealthiest in the country. So, while my feelings in this story were genuine, I know I may have felt differently if I had moved 20 minutes east or west. Of course, all cities highlight income disparity. My wife grew up in Compton and thought that police helicopters and gunshots were the norm. At any rate, as a kid, I thought of my experience as "average."

My dad worked in Chicago all his life, but I don't think he ever went there by choice unless it was a cultural experience for my sister Nora and me to the Field Museum or Shedd Aquarium. I'd seen the train go through Palatine countless times. Waiting at the station there and getting off at Ogilvie downtown was a transformation of sights, smells, sounds, and pace. *Why is everyone walking faster all of a sudden?* Even Dad did, which was odd because I thought we weren't late.

It was winter, windy, but not snowing. Cold enough that the prevailing sentiment on the street was "get me inside ASAP." Chins were burrowed behind collars. Those without a collar had that grimace of windburn. People rushed toward us, my dad herding us out of the way and onward to the kid-friendly environment of the aquarium.

I saw a man sitting on the sidewalk, leaning against a building, somewhat shielded from the wind. His clothes were worn. That's what my young mind registered first: that this man had simply been wearing these clothes for a long time. They were gray-blue, likely tinged with the colors of the sidewalks, alleys, and underpasses.

His eyes were empty.

As a child raised in a healthy home, when you look at another person, and they see you, you expect a response of some kind. We made eye contact, but his blank expression didn't change. And just like that, we moved on. He was sitting in a recessed nook at the base of a glittering skyscraper, a poetic contrast in hindsight. As I glanced back over my shoulder, all I could see were his legs from the knee down. The current of people continued to flow past. It seemed like only I had noticed him.

As a train commuter with a 10-minute walk to his building, my dad along with all the other adults acted accustomed to this. We never talked about it—and that's just it. It's much easier not to talk about it because this man didn't approach us. He didn't ask for bus money. His eyes were empty because he had become a part of the scenery.

I remember the encounter so vividly because it was so jarring for me as a child. What series of events in the man's life, left unchecked, could have led to that experience? I had support systems that kept me grounded, so witnessing another human being with no semblance of a support system contrasted my own experience and was surprising. Regardless of fault or blame, it just didn't feel right. On that day, it presented a sharp opposition to my daily life. I was attending a school in which we all followed the same rules, internalizing the *Sesame Street* 90s refrain of "you can grow up to be whatever you want to be," and following my parents' example of class, dignity, and respect for others. Now, of course, it feels normal.

I was raised in an environment based on sharing, kindness, and doing your best. I am grateful that my parents and teachers preserved some of my innocence so I could stretch my comfort zone in childhood, navigate team tryouts instead of temptations, and develop the confidence to succeed in adulthood. A promising future made me behave because I had plenty to lose.

That day on the street, I was confronted with the kind of scarcity not shown on *Mister Rogers*. A seed of doubt was planted because I had evidence that things did not work out for everyone. *Are adults not sharing and caring like I've been told? And if they are, was the man not doing his best and working hard?*

Growing up with scarcity is perhaps the greatest impediment of all for the body, mind, and spirit. In a nation with incredible wealth, who is complicit? Or is this inevitable? It depends on how we define our sphere of responsibility. We tell kids to share and work hard, but we also know people who take advantage.

When I first started working in downtown Milwaukee as a financial advisor, my route passed two intersections daily, which are prime spots for panhandlers. As a WASPy male, I thought I was approached for money a lot before. Then I started wearing a suit, and the number of asks tripled. Why? Because the suit signaled money? *I'm more broke than ever, buddy, sorry.* I mean, a suit was not expected in our local Walgreens down the block, let me tell you.

About once a month, I get the feeling I'm living in the movie *The Matrix* because I see something that is awful but common enough to be accepted. The binary code behind *The Matrix* governed parameters for economics, civil war, and religion. In our world, systems aren't broken. We haven't entered new codes to get new outcomes. Homelessness is one of those things we accept. Someone who doesn't often go into a city finds stark inequality difficult to absorb emotionally because they haven't been conditioned to being asked a question by a weary, desperate person, seemingly without shame. When leaving the station, the urban commuter may not even notice this living part of the scenery. Sometimes there is more shame in the car from Barrington exiting the Kennedy on the way to Wrigley Field, trying not to make eye contact with the human being 10 feet away.

A person asking another person for money brings all our feelings about humans and money to the surface. *Why don't we give them money? I saw some in Dad's wallet. They'll just buy drugs. So sad. Why don't they get a job? It makes my day to help another. My job promotes addiction. The least I can do is give them a few bucks. The kids are watching me. Hmm, what to do …*

We may feel worlds apart, but that human is just trying to make a living, worn down by a full-time job—a shared experience with the driver fidgeting while they wait for the light to change. The job was facing repeated rejection for the occasional affirmation.

Before you scorn the homeless for asking for change, know that they use a formula employed by nonprofit fundraisers, telemarketers, and financial advisors alike: *If you ask x number of people, you'll get acknowledged y times and get a donation/sale/account z times.* The diligence and consistency of the panhandler might not require skill, but it does require discipline. It's not hard at all to get an entry-level sales job. However, it is hard to keep one and succeed. Repeatedly asking and stomaching the painful rejection is a proven path to making enough.

I always try to acknowledge the people who do ask. I make eye contact, say hello. Sometimes I'm not even asked. In my junior year of college, I went on a service-learning trip through Alternative Spring Break. We were hosted by the National Coalition for the Homeless in Washington, D.C. The message from those living on the street at the time, or those who had in the past, was the human acknowledgment was often more helpful than the money.

You know the feeling after a vacation of settling in back home, and everything is familiar and just so? Your coffee maker, your thermostat, your TV settings? After acknowledging that 90% of the world doesn't take vacations, and that they are a luxury, much as they can wear you out, imagine you could never go home, always on the move, no refuge.

The National Coalition for the Homeless put on the "Urban Plunge," a 48-hour experience of living on the streets of Washington, D.C. We had a meeting place each night where we met our guide, who made sure we didn't take someone's spot or get in trouble overnight. Our guide was an art student diagnosed with schizophrenia who couldn't hold a job because of his mental health and didn't have health insurance through his work. That's a downward spiral of mounting bills.

Partnered with one other student, Alli, I wandered the city, asking for money. We were not given food or shelter for the full two days, and it was amazing how quickly I felt detached from the community of humans who hurried by with things to do. A few folks stepped out of the mid-day sidewalk traffic to ask us what happened and where we were from. We were so young. We seemed like a glitch in the matrix. We weren't Vietnam veterans or heroin addicts. We made enough to eat by panhandling, but the human toll of rejection mounted after just two days.

After my wife Rebeca and I had been together a few years, I told her about this experience of pretending to be homeless for two days. It was very fake to her, but very real to me. We did sleep in a concrete nook next to some federal building and had to wake at 5:00 am to leave before the guard's rounds. We wore old, plain clothes, whatever we thought looked "appropriate." Even though we didn't start with money or a phone, we knew that two days later, we'd go back to our own lives. Her first reaction was to mock me—a privileged college kid with bright prospects taking an insensitive field trip in poverty. I lashed back, "And where were you? Clubbing?" I called her cynical. *I knew I shouldn't have told her.* And we were both right.

Any experience can be seen through many different eyes. The same phrase said by two different people will be taken differently. When our oldest son Roque was four, we were at a red light, and about 20 feet away, a man was sitting on the ground next to a dumpster. I could see my son staring at him intently, and I wondered what he would say. "Why is nobody helping him?" he asked. The next day at the same light, he asked where the man was. His own money memory was made. Children may need simple vocabulary, but they spot hypocrisy better than we do. Seeing the world again through a child's eyes made me question how I could believe in a financial system with such deep, human flaws.

the seen and the unseen

It was rare for my mother to make a statement about money (other than the offhand "that's ridiculous for a pair of jeans" comment). I had reached the age in which material comparisons become important: clothes, hair, shoes, house, and by association, parents' clothes, hair, shoes.

There was a family down the block that had a very large house and a BMW convertible. I thought the BMW was cool because it was obviously impractical, and no one else in our neighborhood had one that I could see. I said something to my mom like, "Can we afford a car like that?"

After a fleeting look of annoyance and surprise, my mom said, "We could get cars like that anytime if we wanted to." And then—mic drop, mind blown—she went about her business folding laundry. It was no surprise that my parents didn't buy a car like that. Still, if they could afford it, I assumed they would at least have spent an equivalent amount on something else, like a private reserve for birdwatching or an original

Charles Dickens manuscript. My working worldview at the time was that all money earned was spent on tangible things, like houses, cars, clothes, travel, TVs, whatever. The idea of earning money beyond that and just keeping it somewhere was a novel one.

The family with the BMW may have been house-rich and cash-poor. I have no idea. But that's the point. They chose to make a statement, and I bought it, as did many of the adults in the neighborhood. I get the impression my comment stung my mother a little bit. She may have thought, *"We're going to cover his college tuition, and he wants a convertible, fantastic …"* People are social creatures. If we aren't careful, we may succumb to the trap of keeping up with the Joneses, losing sight of our own core values and priorities.

We don't think back fondly on the leather interior in our childhood car or have a wave of nostalgia for that magnificent guest bedroom in our fifth-grade house. I've never heard someone refer to their exclusive gated community with any trace of emotion, if at all. "My best memories were formed in the Oakwood Estates. I'm so glad I wasn't in an 'unlabeled' block of homes somewhere." What? No.

Your memories were formed while playing hide and seek with your friend down the street or on summer nights catching fireflies, wherever that may have happened. I remember board games and inside jokes, roller hockey and Kool-Aid in the driveway.

Financial security is felt strongly by the child. My parents made an impression by focusing on remarkable consistency in my upbringing, not the car in the driveway. I remember the few times I heard my parents argue. I wouldn't trade a BMW for more arguing.

I cherish my childhood relationships and experiences. My parents bought new reliable Toyota cars in cash. Along with travel, soccer for two kids, a vacation or two to national parks each year, an unlimited number of books, and anything else they felt was of value to our development.

I never made a meaningful ask that was turned down because they couldn't afford it. I was turned down often because I asked on a whim or wanted something inappropriate or dumb. My parents' house was never the biggest. Thanks for saying no to three BMWs, Mom and Dad.

The house remains the benchmark many people use for assessing wealth, which is awfully oversimplified, especially as the sharing economy accelerates in the 21st century. That phrase we may hear, "house-rich, cash-poor," means that fixed expenses like car payments and mortgages take up too much of our earned income, leaving very little for eating out, travel, or fun. For someone who is house-rich and cash-poor, fun should be showcasing your house and car at every opportunity. Some people do that and don't spend much on travel or restaurants, which is fine. It's tempting to window shop homes like in that *Saturday Night Live* sketch on "Zillow porn." It's just so tangible and shareable.

The paradox of giving financial advice to most Millennials is the total detachment between the purpose of a home or reasons to buy a home and the actual lifestyle they want to lead. (Or I should say that "we want to lead," as this totally applies to me. I blame my kids.)

Here's what I mean:

The client says, "I'd like to be a homeowner in the next few years."

I ask, "Why is that important to you?"

"I'm throwing my money away on rent. I want to own something and be responsible."

"What do you like to do for fun? What does your ideal lifestyle look like?"

"I want the freedom to change careers. I want to be able to travel. I love being out, seeing shows, and going to restaurants. I like to be spontaneous and experience as many different places and things as I can."

In other words, you want to enjoy a lack of responsibility while you still can.

None of these statements promote homeownership. Let me rephrase. None of that promotes owning the home that you live in. Income properties could provide a win-win for you and prospective tenants. If nicer things are motivating, by all means, do what makes you happy. Nothing wrong with buying a better car. Yet there is a diminishing return on luxury. Eventually, we go for the Aston Martin over the Mercedes, and that is driven primarily by ego, validating our worth with a tangible comparison to others. *I got this, which proves that I can.* But the cost to the owner behind the scenes is not discussed. The expensive car is a cultural marker of wealth, the most visible thing other than clothes. Whether the owner is truly wealthy is unclear.

Luxury cars may feel good in public and bad in private. You may get behind on the note. I see the Escalade with the temp license tag in the window, and it makes me wonder … The driver doesn't own it until the bank is paid back, after all. And Jay-Z isn't sweating out the credit check in the back room at the Bentley dealer.

From Magic Johnson to my wife, I hear people talk about hand-me-downs as a sign they weren't given much, a sign that their family had limited means. Societally, this is a painful memory. Yet, hand-me-downs make so much sense financially. Do you remember the shirts you wore when you were five? Of course not. So, as parents, what if we kept hand-me-downs, avoided the new stuff, and instead give our kids an experience they will remember, like a trip to a waterpark or the ocean? The memory can be painful for children raised this way, but now that we are adults, we can expand our definition by recycling and repurposing toddler clothing dollars into experiences. "Kids, we choose this over that." Like my parents, I wear clothes that are 15 years old. *Should I post our family ski day to show I can afford it? No, don't go down that path.*

I read that advertising dollars targeting toddlers has increased twentyfold in the last 20 years. There is no end to stuff that will excite kids for 15 minutes until either (a) they lose interest or (b) it breaks. How we spend money on our kids causes me to doubt myself a lot of the time. Just because we can afford it and it makes them happy doesn't mean we should always get it for them, right? That temptation to spoil our children, or spare them from pain, is embedded in our own narrative. "My winter coat didn't fit. My child will have a new one." In our home, I don't mind a tear in our 7-year-old's winter coat because I've never had a teacher assume I can't afford a new one. As a woman of color, Rebeca reminds me she doesn't always get that treatment.

It is easier for me to save because I have less to prove by spending. As a White male, I have less pressure to prove my worth. I wake up in the morning with a tailwind. An executive person of color may feel the need to demonstrate their belonging through tangible markers. I was born with my marker of belonging. Every time I've spent on something I cannot afford, it has been to mark my belonging to peers and clients or demonstrate abundance for my children. Some of us are spending to find belonging.

My parents did own our house. I would guess they followed a rule of thumb shared by a high-net-worth advisor in my office: buy a home worth no more than two times your household income. With a lower mortgage, they could seize other opportunities with less stress. By not giving a f**k about "the Joneses," they built an environment in which nothing deeply appreciated was unaffordable. And they never sacrificed their responsibility as parents because of financial stress. They knew who they were and aligned their money actions with their human values.

In conversation and workshops with colleagues, I hear and admittedly use the phrase "my best client." How is this measured? By income? By fulfillment? Coachability? Balance? If not stated outright, it's implied that "best" means more money in absolute dollar amounts. Our compensation as advisors is linked to these definitions, so it monetarily makes sense. We look for big houses and BMWs. Big dollars being spent means dollars are coming in.

In the context of dollar percentages, my best client is a 25-year-old Deferred Action for Childhood Arrivals (DACA) visa holder, a temporary legal status given to undocumented adults who were brought here as children. She saved about 40% of her income while helping her parents. She was a retail manager and made about $25,000 a year, before taxes. She couldn't borrow money for college because of her visa status. But she can pay taxes, which is bogus. She now earns $40,000 in a corporate job and owns a home.

If her habits continue as she earns more and is given a path to citizenship, her utility or growth per dollar will represent the maximization of the American Dream, more than any other client of mine so far. Her net worth ratio in 10, 20, or 30 years will be remarkable, especially when her income, challenges, and barriers to entry are factored in. She may be average when measured in dollars, but she'll remain my best client if she saves that percentage of income. More impressive, she is delaying gratification while her peers think short term, showing faith in a country that hasn't given her citizenship.

So, she doesn't drive a BMW. Yet. But she is creating generational wealth, as my parents did. That always happens behind the scenes, not parked in the driveway.

chapter three

a tale of two grandfathers

I knew my grandfathers better than I knew my grandmothers.

My Grandma Heaton passed away at 68 when I was nine years old. A low-risk operation went wrong, and she died from an infection as a result. I remember her as warm and loving, eager to play and bake cookies, and spoil my little sister and me. She was also quiet and submissive in a way, content to be in the background. My Grandpa Heaton had a big personality, so that made sense.

My Grandma Wilbrandt's mental condition started to deteriorate when I was in middle school and worsened until she passed about eight years later. I could tell she was very proud and refined. Even if she didn't recognize my face, she had a certain dignity about her. While we spent many weekend afternoons together, she became a shell of her former self.

My grandfathers were, by most measures used by most people, successful men. They were blue-collar and white-collar symbols of the Greatest Generation. Children in the Great Depression, young men in World War II, galvanizing the economy in the 1950s, and starting Baby Boomer families. They seemed to have mutual respect, despite being drastically different in personality and action. There is more than one pathway to a legacy.

Grandpa Heaton served in the Pacific Theater on an aircraft carrier. Returning home, he began work in the construction industry in an era when construction was booming. He built bridges, holding jobs that lasted a few months to a few years, so his family of four traveled with him. My dad said Grandpa Heaton would leave the house before dawn and came home exhausted, eating dinner, reading the paper, and going to bed. He became a foreman and eventually the general superintendent of a regional construction firm. His knack for problem-solving was clear. As he would tinker around the house in old age, me trailing behind, he seemed to create home improvement projects and their corresponding problems for the sheer joy of figuring out the solution. Combined with the guts to deliver tough messages and the charisma to motivate people, it was fitting that he had overseen large-scale construction projects.

Once, he told me that he poured the curb and pavement surrounding Buckingham Fountain in Chicago. Another time, my dad mentioned that his mother had taken him to the job site as a baby, and my grandpa, with his infant son in one arm, had walked out onto a single beam over a large drop to a riverbed to check on something.

And you know those concrete blocks that are about three feet high and divide freeways in urban areas? Grandpa Heaton even invented the slip-form concrete machine, designed to create those medians, barriers, and curbs more efficiently on site, instead of shipping them from somewhere else. As a kid, I found original designs submitted to the patent office, along with "modern shop theory" and lots of sophisticated books on machinery. Apparently, the year this invention would be sold, another guy who had been hanging around the job site watching it in use copied his design and beat him to the market, essentially stealing his invention.

That same year, however, my father's brother was killed suddenly at age 20, which may be why Grandpa Heaton never took the other guy to court. Another reason was perhaps his devout Catholic faith. Maybe he just turned the other cheek.

I share all this to show his potential to be much wealthier had things gone differently.

Grandpa and Grandma Heaton, when she was alive, were younger, more energetic, and generally more "fun" than Grandpa and Grandma Wilbrandt. We were also their only grandchildren, while the Wilbrandt side had eight. Grandpa Heaton lived in the moment. He was always positive, always smiling, and always lively. He would repeatedly tell the same joke over and over, and you would laugh because he still thought it was funny. *Here it comes.* "Workin' hard or hardly workin'?!"

We all know people who live in the moment, but that quality isn't always good. He was easily distracted and forgetful, but when I would help him out with a project at his house or mine, I could see that glimmer of genius from time to time. He was happiest when he was *MacGyver-ing*. His basement and garage were overflowing with tools. And when he couldn't find what he needed, which was at least twice a day, he would buy another one. So, next week, there were five more tools cluttering the room that held the next needed tool. And because he was so focused on the task at hand, he always threw it on the pile with no rhyme or reason. Like in the movies, brilliant minds rarely appear organized. It doesn't diminish their gift, but it certainly can be a drag on their time and money.

Whether it was handing him tools or mowing his lawn, he always paid well. Mowing his small suburban lawn took a little less than an hour and was easy work, but he still gave me $20. Who wouldn't want to see him every weekend? If the lawn didn't need mowing, he'd pay me anyway for some made-up tasks that may have been easier. And my sister would do the dusting inside his modest ranch house.

On days we didn't have school, Nora and I would often go to my grandparents' place, because my mom worked nearby at my other grandpa's law firm. Working the system like any kids our age, we would disagree on Taco Bell or Burger King, and so he would take us to both, allowing me to get a Rodeo Burger, chicken tenders, *and* two Baja chalupas. (Remember, this was the mid-90s before eating organic or even healthy was mainstream.) He would travel with us on vacation, go out to eat with us on special occasions, and come over on Sundays to watch the Bulls and other NBA games.

He spent his money on his family, church, and love of fixing things. Some people think of financial peace of mind as being able to buy anything you want without thinking twice about the price tag, and that seemed to be what he did. I can't remember him ever exercising restraint on anything. He didn't have expensive taste, but he never thought twice about dropping $20 either. For him, money was a thing to be used, rightly or wrongly, to live life. My parents once said he would be broke if he weren't with my grandma. He'd give away every dollar. But seeing the look on my face while getting a $20 bill was priceless to him.

Maybe being poor as a child, or having his house flattened by a tornado, or having his wife and one of his sons killed unexpectedly meant he wouldn't turn out a careful planner. Maybe it was having faith that his true riches—and family—were waiting in heaven. Or maybe it was just that he was charming and bold enough to BS his way through some sticky situations. A man who worked all his life with his hands, money likely never seemed real enough to give much thought as long as he could get the bill. Leaving $10,000 in a forgotten savings account for decades was a costly mistake given the potential interest earned, but it was not a priority. Then again, had he remembered, perhaps he would simply have spent it.

When Grandpa Heaton passed, his estate was organized in the same fashion as his tool piles. At the time, I was busy starting my own adult life in Milwaukee. Yet the friction between my bubbly, spontaneous grandfather and my reserved, meticulous father may have been at its peak after his death in 2008. He had seemingly random bank accounts all over, handwritten notes about this or that, no passwords or statements, and a house full of *things*. Other than a hip replacement, he was active until shortly before he passed, so he never downsized. Everything from priceless family heirlooms to four shelves of half-used cans of paint had to be sorted, deliberated upon, and then stored, sold, donated, recycled, or thrown out. It was a lot of work. If you think spring cleaning your basement is hard, imagine combing through every possession your parent acquired over decades and trying to separate the meaningful, the useful, and the trash.

My other grandpa, Grandpa Wilbrandt, was stoic. Already through law school before World War II, an injury kept him home from the war. He lived in Crystal Lake, Illinois from then on, maybe the longest residency in the town, my mom thought. My mom also said that her parents were always working. They had five children and a giant house with a huge yard. My Grandpa Wilbrandt embodied that German Protestant work ethic. As a result, my mom sometimes said, "I'll rest when I'm dead." Pretty intense.

To get to work, he would take the train into downtown Chicago, the lead attorney for the prominent department store Marshall Field & Company. When prompted, he would tell stories of when the "elephant got loose" or the lawsuit of "the Crying Amgees" with great detail. He and my grandmother went on vacation to Mexico from time to time.

Grandma Wilbrandt was always cooking, cleaning, and sewing, but went to her bowling league once a week. My mom and aunt said she could be judgmental, the "Slavic Queen." I imagine their life to be like Don and Betty Draper's from *Mad Men*, only more boring and ethical.

Grandpa Wilbrandt would mow the expansive lawn, tend to the orchard, and do yard work all weekend. Having a stressful white-collar job myself now, I get it. Focusing on a tangible outdoor task like weeding helps calm the mind. On some weekends, he would "go see the widows," as he put it, checking in on his clients to do estate planning.

From that "side hustle," he opened his own law firm adjacent to his house and the two rental properties he owned over half a city block. By the time I was born, two of my uncles had joined him as attorneys. The third uncle had an office there for his landscaping business. It can be strange to think back on things that appeared normal and realize, "Wait a minute, most people don't do that." About half of that lot was forested, and yours truly would pick up sticks from time to time. For a few hours of work, bending up and down, putting them in piles, carting them to the curb, he would give me $5. *Really?* Before I had ever heard the word, I recall thinking that surely inflation must not have been accounted for since his 1920s era of stick-picking-up.

My mom would "treat" her parents on the weekend by grabbing McDonald's on the way. It was a treat because they otherwise would eat a TV dinner. And our visits consisted of sitting in their living room. And I do mean sitting. Talking was optional. My grandpa was rail thin except for a sizable potbelly. His home wardrobe was almost entirely slacks, suspenders, and stained white undershirts. He didn't spend much time in public in his eighties, so whatever.

He had a vacation home west of Wisconsin Dells, then later downsized and bought a plot of farmland and a mobile home in a small town of about 200 people. We would drive up there many weekends in summer and camp in a state park. We hiked and swam at Devil's Lake and walked down the street to the gas station to buy ice cream. I live in Wisconsin these days, so I know now that we were "f**kin' Illinois bastards" (FIBs) in every sense of the word. Those memories are priceless, FIB or not.

His estate was always to be divided into equal fifths for his children. Estate planning is about fairness. However, life being what it is, fairness is elusive. Equality of the dollar may not capture equity in the family. And how could anyone itemize the actions of each child? *But they all know deep down my mom did more than anyone else. Who cares about life circumstances? She didn't have to go all the time, yet she did.*

When he passed, the liquidation of my grandfather's assets, properties, and business interests was very contentious, given how his children's relationships with their parents changed over the years: caregiver, business partner, executor, medical advocate, errand-runner. For all the effort my Grandpa Wilbrandt put into building something of lasting value for his children, he probably didn't show his love often enough, at least not in the way each child wanted to feel it. He maybe didn't ever say it. He understood money, he delayed gratification, and through corporate and estate law, he maximized money for a living. He understood in his bones what most people never grasp: investments in businesses and real estate tend to grow in value, and everything else loses it. He knew the system, but true equality is a theory, not a realistic goal. The more that is at stake, the harder it is to satisfy all parties.

Who am I to say which approach was better? Both are right, and both are wrong. As one grandchild of eight, I don't know much of the story, and I've only shared what I could observe as a child and young adult. My parents never shared any dollar amounts about their money situation, nor would I expect them to do so. Is love better expressed through acts of service? Through kind words and deeds? Through a legacy of experiences? Or through dollars? We do our best with what we know.

If you're lucky enough to know your grandparents, this is a golden opportunity. Our grandparents are a window into the past, an insight into our parents. Having the opportunity to know my grandparents shaped my character in ways I'll probably never fully appreciate. By observation or osmosis, they taught me a lot. I try to live joyfully in the moment, as Grandpa Heaton did, with the power of action. And I try to strategize well into the future, like Grandpa Wilbrandt did, with the power of wisdom.

I believe in the importance of grandkids knowing their grandparents well. There are issues as families grow apart, especially higher-income families. Lower-income families tend to stay close to support each other, and oftentimes hardship brings people together. There is tremendous social capital in having extended family under one roof. We gave up the lush mountains of Seattle to give our kids a meaningful relationship with their grandparents. I want to be nearby when they get older because that's what they did for their parents. I consider it my duty to pay that forward.

Estate planning is extremely difficult. It is often not done at all because we suppress the thought. We avoid the conversations and the preparation process as if thinking on it will usher it in the door. Death takes some unexpectedly and creeps up on others while their families are across the state or across the world. After death, sometimes money changes hands very quickly or very slowly, depending on the documents and people involved. These people are all at once coping with loss and managing an intricate web of possessions, people, and accounts. The people closest to the deceased are usually doing all this. A member of our family had to decide to take his mother off life support. I asked my mother to make sure her wishes are in writing in a living will. In the moment, I'm not sure I could carry them out.

It's true you can't take money with you. Even with none, death brings financial transactions to families. Transactions without intention are soulless. But every plan has an energy; every gift has a spirit.

Only the coldest beneficiary views an inheritance as free money to be spent randomly, like a tax refund. With Grandpa Wilbrandt and

Grandpa Heaton, money from them never felt like an allowance given just because. Instead, Grandpa Wilbrandt's pay felt like an honor. Like, "I could pay a professional to pick up sticks, but I am giving you the opportunity to begin climbing the ladder of success yourself, Grandson." There was something dignified about it. A lesson was learned at the end of the stick-picking-up: beggars can't be choosers. *He has the money, so I guess he decides how much.* He handed me a five, and that was it. The pay was for service—no substitute for hard work.

I would do things for Grandpa Heaton, like mowing the lawn and being his gopher on projects. So, I did work for him, but it had the spirit of a gift. If it was hot, or he didn't feel like painting the basement that day, he would pay anyway. He was all about doing things himself to save a buck but gladly gave money away to his family. And not just that, but he would give me a twenty. The pay was playful and joyful—no substitute for affirmation.

When we would eat out together, I remember Grandpa Heaton and my dad used to both stand up to snatch the checkout of the server's hand before the other: Grandpa eager to give; Dad willfully independent. The blue-collar mantra seems to be more about thrift than financial strategy. And the financial strategy was the dominion of the other side, the white-collars like Grandpa Wilbrandt.

No doubt Grandpa Heaton wasted lots of money by not capturing interest, reading contracts fully, or returning every unused piece of hardware. Easy to criticize, but then again, can you put a price tag on the ability to (seemingly) not worry or care about money? That's liberating. It made him happier around others, lifting their spirits.

Grandpa Wilbrandt, on the other hand, may have seen so many missed opportunities doing estate planning for the widows on weekends that he vowed to get it right for his children. I have no idea. People are shaped by life experiences.

The life stage we refer to as "retirement" may be a destination, but it will not change who you are. It's a culmination. Grandpa Wilbrandt hung out in his office with impressive books and organized assets, and Grandpa Heaton was fixing things and hitting up Dairy Queen. As they had been doing for decades.

Fulfillment comes from authenticity and choice, by meeting our own unique potential. And we also should seek trusted support for our shortcomings. Our spending and giving, saving and planning, are reflections of our values. Leaving property in a trust to avoid probate to create more generational wealth or buying a second ice cream because your grandson just loves ice cream? Well, both show love. And both leave a legacy.

we can't afford that

I never heard this as a child. What a privilege. It's a phrase that I recall from movies and novels, although I couldn't quote one for you. It sure wasn't my mother's style. I've heard it from parents as a youth program director and a financial advisor. For a good parent in a tough position, how painful it is to say out loud.

As a White suburban middle-class kid growing up in the 90s, things seemed pretty good. The Chicago Bulls were in dynasty-mode, the economy was strong, and the internet was starting to catch on. People of all stripes, on average, seemed to have some momentum. Our family tradition was to go out on Friday night. "Going out" meant going to eat at a mid-range, family-friendly restaurant, then going shopping after.

Dinner was usually Barnaby's or Fuddruckers, occasionally Portillo's. As far as food went, we were creatures of habit, not adventurous. Shopping usually meant the same stretch of Golf Road in Schaumburg surrounding Woodfield Mall. This area had everything. Sports Authority was usually in there for me, my mom's favorite, the Container Store, was nearby, and we would often get Ben & Jerry's ice cream afterward. The one staple was Borders bookstore, at the time comparable to Barnes & Noble. Borders had something for all four of us: books downstairs, music upstairs. So, if Nora or I had money of our own, we could buy a CD or two. Books were always free.

What do I mean by free? I mean my parents would buy us books. Flimsy paperbacks or beautiful photography collections, it didn't matter. My dad would shop mostly in natural sciences, my mom classical literature. Nora and I would have phases. In high school, I was acquiring many classic works of political science and philosophy, which I read in class. I was also getting coffee table books featuring *National Geographic*'s portraits, Frank Lloyd Wright's sketches, and the best of the Impressionist period. I still have all of them.

At the register, I remember the total could cross the $100 mark. And that was just Borders, not counting other stores. And that was just one week. And that was in the late 1990s. My mom and dad were able to promote their own values and our development by supporting our curiosity. How lucky we were. The inflation-adjusted equivalent of their choices today could push $1,000 a month, just on things that directly fueled our intellect and physical health. That doesn't count the ice cream after Borders, or the pizza before, or the cost of travel, soccer, or college tuition.

They also said no all the time. To clothes and curfews alike, we often heard "we aren't doing that" when things didn't meet their development standard. *Mom, I know you don't care, but this is seventh grade. This is important!* The decision was always value-based, not money-based. My parents were intentional. Whether they were able to pay was irrelevant. Why is this *thing* so important? That was the question that mattered.

This is an important distinction, regardless of family income, although, of course, it gets harder when people have less. Things that are acquired cheaply are perceived to be cheap, even if they aren't. All financial transactions are imbued with an energy. By including me in the decision, the effect of the purchase was amplified. I wore my new soccer cleats in my room, the way a new homeowner shares pictures of their kitchen on Instagram.

That was the significance of the books …price was no object. All that mattered was that I picked them out, and they were nurturing our young minds. To this day, I love to read. My parents molded my sister and me by spending freely on what they felt was important, and mercilessly cutting out and saying no to what wasn't. All consumers and all parents act as a referee. Make a rulebook if you don't have one, so you don't rely on emotion in the moment. My parents' clothes may have been decades old, but their values will last generations.

In the summer of 2015, my own family of three was invited to tag along on vacation in Orlando with my sister-in-law. Nothing extravagant, we just had to say no. Saying we can't fly to Fiji or buy a Mercedes is not the same, because luxury goods and experiences are outside the norm for most people. Saying we couldn't afford that trip was the first time I felt that I had dropped out of middle-class income. I had to deny an experience to my son because I wasn't earning enough.

Is it better to buy your kid a $20 toy every month at Target, or to ask your kid every month what they would like to do or have with $240 at the end of the year? Every parent can answer that differently. There is so much uncertainty in our lives that delaying is difficult. That aside, teaching the child to dream and focus and wait for the $240 would help them more long term. They would think about it, weigh their options. But when life is hard, a night of joyful distraction is worth it. When basic needs are met, parents have a bit more willpower. What's left over each month dictates price ceiling. If that ceiling is low, we tend to fill it each month with cheaper things that have faster but fleeting value, versus delaying gratification to get the desired thing. (Like my Lego pirate ship.)

My approach as a parent, and how I model decision-making on screens, toys, experiences, and food has a lot to do with not voicing my inner thought, *"How much does it cost?"* Instead, I ask myself, sometimes aloud in front of Roque, "How much do you want it? How will you use it? Why do you want it? How will it exercise your body or your brain?" Imagination, creativity, and curiosity compound over time, just like money can. When a child reads a book, they are transported to a place, time or activity that can ignite a flame.

It is so hard for us to say no in the 21st century. We are more and more aware of all the awesome things we could be doing, parents and kids alike. But most "success manuals" will point to saying no as key. Steve Jobs spoke about how cutting products from Apple's offerings was key to their success. Less is more. So, when Roque comes with me to Target for deodorant and diapers and asks for yet another Thomas the Train, I can look him in the eye and say, "You just went to the ocean, and felt the waves and sand, and saw dolphins swim by. No more toys." *That woman down the aisle is judging me, f**k.* A vacation, the memory of running ahead of an incoming wave, appreciates in value. A plastic toy made in China does not.

All those books my parents bought—some of which are dated, yes— are still filled with beautiful words and pictures. I flip through wildlife photography collections with Roque today. Will he read the one about the politics behind the Iraq War? Probably not, but my 18-year-old curiosity was reinforced.

That being said, OMG is it fun to buy things. *Why are you looking at off-road SUVs? You aren't a professional driver on a closed course. When the streets aren't plowed, schools close anyway.* I knew my parents could afford something, and they said no anyway. And every time they did, they strengthened our family's financial safety net. How many times do you say, "Less than $10? Whatever." 10 times a month? That's $100 a month, $1,200 a year, $12,000 a decade. Do that for three decades, that's $36,000. Invested long term, that would very likely triple in value. Saying no to little Brett at age 40 means another $100,000 or more at age 70. Decide based on values, not on capacity. A little *no* now means more *yes* later. Money, like our discipline, compounds over time.

chapter five

I like girls who wear Abercrombie & Fitch

Whether you grew up calling it middle school or junior high, it's an emotionally charged time in our lives. Dragging your mother to Abercrombie & Fitch to stand by while you shop in front of larger-than-life half-naked photos of models only exacerbates this emotional clusterf**k.

Middle school is when most of us start to make material comparisons. With the right shoes or the right haircut, you could go far in popularity at this age. With the wrong one, ridicule. Personally, I don't recall thinking of much more than who was good at sports relative to me, and which hot girls were sitting by me in my next class. Our junior high was the most racially diverse in the area with a little under half of the student body being of color. I determined early on that FUBU, while cool, wasn't an option for me. So, I settled for A&F, and under dire circumstances, American Eagle.

Things change so rapidly in adolescent taste. I was an early bloomer as far as puberty goes, and so my acne arrived on the scene in full force in seventh grade. With that going against me, clothing was something I could control. I did have choices with my hair, but it still sucked for some reason.

I told my mom that I had to have Abercrombie clothes. So, we went down to Woodfield Mall to check it out. My mom, stoic as ever, bravely followed me into the store. The house music was bumping, the lights were low, and the first thing we saw upon crossing the threshold were two beautiful sets of six-pack abs. Actually, "bravely" is my narrative. My mom clearly didn't give a shit, nor should she. She correctly understood that this was important to me. And because my parents are rational people who believe in research, she no doubt knew that I was having identity issues and that complete resistance was futile.

So, when I finally found the jeans that would inevitably vault me to the top of the Winston Campus Junior High social hierarchy, I was ecstatic but dreaded showing her the price tag. She surprised me with an elegant solution. "We'll pay for what a regular pair of jeans costs, and you can pay the rest." *Oh, put your money where your mouth is ...*

At age 12 or 13 in 1998, Abercrombie price minus Lee price at K-Mart equaled $25 that I'd have to find. So, at 14, I started working because I needed to increase my limited cash flow from Grandpa Heaton's handouts and the occasional hard-fought chore compensation from Grandpa Wilbrandt. Older now, she did me a great favor by empowering me to decide what these pre-distressed jeans were worth. Not an outright no or yes, but rather, "How badly do you want it?"

As a parent now myself, I am constantly faced with our kids' demands and witness other parents fielding them too. A yes or no is simple, concise, and neatly tied off. There isn't an immediate tally or record; from the parent's perspective, we move on. But every yes or no, however insignificant in isolation, compounds with the other thousands of requests. Together, they build in our minds, shape our values, and set parameters around what we think is reasonable or even possible for us. I carry this "Mom/Dad would approve/disapprove" reference to this day.

I chose to pay the $25. Choice is a form of agency and developing agency in children is so important. The $25 jeans, $2.50 snack, $250 tablet—whatever is meaningful and doable in your family—gives children the opportunity to flex that agency muscle.

After that initial visit, my mom and I went back again and again with the same deal in place. I was a good kid around my parents because they had integrity. They kept their word, which was a little scary because there was no such thing as an idle threat in the Heaton Society. (Credit to my BFF Sean Bunce, who coined Heaton Society during a car ride in which I suggested my mom take us somewhere, and she suggested I give her gas money.) Although strict, they respected my sister and me enough to give us the choice. All-or-nothing thinking is a hallmark of dissatisfaction and often depression. Most choices are a shade of gray.

About four years later, my parents made a similar offer around something of much more consequence: college. They told me they would pay for four years of state university tuition. So, I applied for early admission to the University of Illinois (U of I) at Urbana-Champaign, where I knew I would get in. That was the only college application I did. (Four years later, my parents, mindful of fairness, gave my sister the same support. She worked harder to save money and earn scholarships, and paid the difference between out-of-state and in-state tuition to join the University of Iowa Writer's Workshop. She, as I did, made a choice about value.)

So, I went to Champaign, which was the largest and, I believe, best public institution in the state. It was close enough to go home for the weekend, far enough to feel "apart" and avoid a parent drop-in (which was not their style anyway).

This arrangement included my room and board. My freshman and sophomore years were dorm life. In my junior and senior years, they set limits on my off-campus rent. Additionally, they would audit my spending to a degree. I don't remember the details, but throughout my time in Champaign, their thrift was very much at the forefront of my mind. It was an unspoken expectation. I knew I would have to apply the Abercrombie jeans formula to my college lifestyle. They provided a grocery stipend of sorts, but beer money was my own. I worked throughout college because working was an expectation, not a necessity. My parents never said I had to, but I knew they wouldn't fund my social life either, especially because their own college social life didn't go far beyond dorm room pizza and cards.

As an unproven freshman, my parents agreed to pay about $1,800 for my three-week winter study-abroad experience in India. Hooked on travel from a young age, I was fixated on going overseas again. Knowing I had a four-year limit to my college experience, I had to, or chose to (again, not sure which, or both at once), study in the UK because every credit I took there could count as transferable credit toward my history major. I would have gone to Peru or Japan or Italy otherwise. Ever the opportunist, I made the most of my time in Europe but failed my physical geography course, which was 100% final exam grade. Consequently, I concluded my undergrad degree with that course in summer school after full-time student-teaching, finishing not with a bang but with a whimper. Every credit counts. Without the time limit, I would have been like so many other undergrads, putting it on the proverbial "credit card" and dealing with it later.

I continue to be passionate about youth work because youth and young adulthood is the best time to build good habits! Ah, the power of childhood habits! Do you doubt how much they shape our lives? Then try to begin flossing as an adult. I didn't floss as a kid, and damn it is hard to add that step now.

Childhood, or lack of a childhood, is the ultimate first impression of life. First impression bias means that initial advice is more heavily weighted than subsequent advice. I would guess that some of the first advice new parents hear is "better start saving for their college." College is likely something they remember enjoying, so they get started.

How my parents "funded" jeans was the framework of decision-making. In their mind, the extra cost was for status, not function. They approached our college funding that way. I approach many things that way today. When it came to college, I went with the Kohl's option instead of Abercrombie & Fitch. As a result, I remember the decisions around clothes in seventh grade more clearly than my decision on which college to attend. Although it cost like 10,000 times more, my money wasn't involved.

What parents want is to give their children the best possible chance of success. How this is done is an art, not a science. Saving for college is a science: the rates of inflation, the tuition increases, the rates of return on the funds used to grow savings, and the amount of time to get there are all measurable. How well that money is used is an art because we are parenting for work ethic and responsibility. Telling your kids, "You're going here," versus respecting their own opinion of where they'll thrive may undermine their agency. Telling them art history is an interest "not a career" is wrong. Telling them "Art history can be a career, but it's difficult to get started, and you'll have to provide tremendous insight to make it" is more accurate. There's a difference between wanting to study something because you like it and being passionate about it. The most prominent art historian in residence at the Louvre is indeed a career and an enviable one. An average student in art history at a mediocre college who works at Walmart during their summers is a wasted investment. And you saved the money for them regardless, right?

The economy is more scientific than we'd like to believe. We can research average starting salaries, competition for acting roles, and number of hours engineering students must study to get A grades. My friends at U of I College of Engineering studied way harder than I did. Their tuition was a bit more, and their starting salaries were a lot more.

Perhaps the question to ask your 19-year-old is this: "Is it more important you have a job that meets your need for identity and purpose, or that you have an extra $700 a month to spend on whatever you like, and your job is …okay?" The question to ask *yourself* is: "Am I willing to subsidize the discrepancy in their judgment and the gap in their cash flow?" And then follow up with: "If not, can I stand by and watch them struggle financially?"

I have seen parents' college savings (529 plan distributions) become the classic example of the sunk-cost effect, where we spend on something just because we planned to, even though it isn't worth it anymore, like the Vietnam War. My concern as a parent is that I'll save for something that one day is subsidized by the government. Or instead of taking walks across the leafy quad like I did, my kids will log in from their beds, dozing off there instead of in a cavernous musty lecture hall. Is their version inherently worse or more likely? I don't know. I do know, with absolute certainty, that I would like to have more money than social security provides in old age, and I don't want to depend on my kids for money or them hauling me to the bathroom when I can't do it myself. So, I'll start there.

I am grateful that my parents paid for my college, but I didn't for a second believe it was a blank check. We may decide that one or all our kids need to feel the pressure of a student loan for a while to help them focus, or budget, or grow the f**k up. But there is no reason why a surprise gift of $30,000 when they turn 30 would be less appreciated than their freshman-year tuition, room, and board. Financial choices, from college to jeans, are rarely all or nothing. By forcing them to be, we create a win-lose proposition about parental priorities versus adolescent autonomy. We forfeit an opportunity to have a meaningful conversation about what things are worth to us and why.

the value of a penalty kick

When I was 14, I started to work as a soccer referee for the Palatine Park District. That year, I was given 7- and 8-year-old "house league," AKA park district, no-tryouts, recreational games. This is the age where the goalie does somersaults while the ball is at the other end, and the ball rarely moves much faster than a 14-year-old can walk. The difficulty in refereeing this age group was discerning fouls like tripping from "unforced errors" like, well, tripping.

I wanted to be a referee because I loved soccer, I liked being outside, and I didn't want to work that many hours. This job paid $20 an hour, which was awesome, and I usually had two or three-hour-long games on Saturday or Sunday. So, why could I earn that much? I wasn't sure.

I soon found that many parents bring the same fanatic behavior to 7-year-old park district soccer that I'd expect at the World Cup. At least once or twice a week, I was publicly berated for a "bad call" and "not watching the game." *Oh my God, he's coming onto the field. Shit, shit. Do I look at him? Or look away? Shit.* Some of these coaches paced the sideline, spittle flying, willing their booger-picking, daydreaming sons and daughters to dig deep and find the soul of a champion on the field. They looked for any conceivable barrier holding back their team, and that often meant a fall was really a foul.

At age 14, adult disapproval was still significant. And the adults on the sidelines were, in many cases, finally fulfilling a long-harbored fantasy of coaching their child to victory on the field of battle. They brought the fan/player/referee script they saw on TV the day before. *This age group doesn't even have playoff games.* As the season went on, and subsequent seasons, I started refereeing older age groups, and my ref school cohort began to drop out. By the time I stopped refereeing in the spring before college, I had served as a linesman in travel soccer club games and was the lead official for park district playoff games, even the U14 championship game. I called an excellent match down to the wire, with parents screaming on both sides. It was a rush and a challenge. I had to be focused enough to make a judgment in a second, then a minute later look a glaring grown man in the eyes, and calmly tell him to step back off the field.

So, why did refereeing park district games pay well as a 14-year-old? Not many of my peers could maintain their composure and bear the brunt of adult criticism. I've always been a calm and quick thinker. *I actually like this.* Making the right call when one side was bound to disagree was a value the league needed. They needed a kid who wouldn't cave to the more obnoxious coach or quit. For many of my peers, the $20 wasn't worth the abuse or pressure. And the weather could be 70 degrees and sunny, but sometimes it was 35 degrees with sleet. College kids were gone, and most parents were with their own kids on Saturday afternoons.

Much of the time, we make decisions based on *price*. A price is neat and quantifiable. "I'm willing to pay this much, but not that much." It's a reference point for comparisons. The irony is that we often go for low prices in lieu of assessing value.

Correctly identifying the *value* of an object we aren't familiar with is difficult. Price is only one component of value. You can be taken for a ride with auto repair, spending a fortune on cosmetic fixes when your budget allows for only the essentials. You also could ask your friend who knows a guy who knows a guy who does work for cheap, but over time you may pay more for related and repeated work because of taking a shortcut for cost.

The cheap referee solution would have been a parent volunteer or something. But yelling at the referee is such a fundamental element of any sport. The beauty of competition is built on the transparency of rules. Some of those dads wanted to yell at their boss on Friday but transferred their anger to me on Saturday. I had value as a referee because I was tied to the hopes of every kid, parent, and coach. The kids practiced in hopes of winning. The parents and coaches wanted their team to be happy, validated, confident, and successful. There are a lot of life lessons in team sports. When something is important, what we are hoping for is value. Good value is not always the same as buying something on sale. The sale is a gimmick to unload overripe fruit; the value bears fruit over time.

Positions that pay well generally either: (a) require unique or specialized skills or abilities that others don't have (like best-in-the-world soccer players) or (b) force you to do things that other people don't want to do. And go figure, to get to (a), often you must endure years of (b). Those athletes must train and avoid eating dessert. They take penalty kicks in front of an audience of millions. Most people don't want to do that. The world is full of people (I meet them all the time) who expect a raise but cannot articulate their own value.

Not everyone can delay so much gratification for a chance at success on a high level. Medical school is demanding. There is a shortage of skilled labor in the US because most people want to go to college and drop $30,000 tuition on a $30,000-a-year job after graduation. They could spend a fraction—if anything at all—on licensing to be a semi-truck driver and start making $60,000 before their friends even graduate. Why does trucking pay well? Most people don't want to do it. Even without a desire to be close to friends and family and sleep in your own bed, there is pressure. We often hear or say, "Don't fold under pressure." Remember, pressure makes diamonds sometimes.

Should top surgeons make $600,000 a year? Well, that's not for me to say. I overhear people saying, "I've got a headache and just don't feel like working today," or "I'm distracted because my dog is sick," and other similar things. But consider this: when a patient is scheduled for surgery to remove a tumor or transplant a kidney, the cost is not an issue, time doesn't wait, and the surgeon must show up ready.

As a parent, I cannot wait to coach. John Wooden, perhaps the most respected basketball coach of all time, said he was happiest with the highest level of play, not wins. If you play your own best, then wins will come. Top performers focus on inputs. I did that as an athlete. I focused on my best abilities and the value I brought to the team. I didn't try to score goals in soccer. I knew I was good at reading other players, so I managed the spacing of the field, directing my teammates and holding it down from center-back. I was a team captain, and I was a role player. By accepting that I wasn't a flashy player, being a starter and captain came naturally. Championship teams are filled with players who know their roles.

And after months of preparation and determination, the championship can be decided by a referee. The referee is the one variable (other than player health) the coaches can't control. The referee's role is to show up ready and keep their composure. *That's a penalty kick. Can't let that one go. Shit, against that coach's team in a tie game second half. Here we go, call it. And 3, 2, 1 …*

"YOU CALL THAT A FOUL, REF?!!"

The pathway to greater dollar value starts with honoring your own human value. My self-esteem (not to mention height, skin color, and gender) allowed me to perform well under pressure in this role. I perform best under pressure, and this early feedback helped me realize I'd enjoy client-facing financial planning, another performance-under-pressure profession. Running a summer camp was too.

Today, when I attempt to see trends between wealthy and broke behavior—which has little correlation with income and is not the same as flashy versus modest—I notice that the empowered shop for value and the floundering fixate on price. As consumers, the price we pay reflects a blend of three elements: quality, convenience, and service. As consumers, we generally look for as much quality as we can afford. Convenience is more context-dependent. And service is all over the map. Value is the sum of these.

We were at Walmart on vacation in the Outer Banks, North Carolina, with our then-four-year-old and his new infant little brother, buying sunscreen and some other stuff we forgot. While there, I got a bottle of wine and a shirt, each for $3 plus change. Yes, I got a $3 shirt. Walmart responds to consumer demand for low prices. Was the wine very good? Of course not, but everything is cheap and in one place. Lower prices reduce profit margins when goods are sold. And cheap things are priced to sell, not to last. Generally, you get what you pay for.

Afterward, we stopped at McDonald's on the way to the beach. *Ick, they put mayo on, but what service can I expect from a minimum-wage employee assembling a $1 sandwich?* The price for a sandwich went up at the beach, because convenience improved for us and worsened for the seller.

As for service fees, they are everywhere. The question isn't the fee structure; it's the value. The broke person will walk away from stellar service and quality because the convenience and the price aren't right. Avoid fees to pay interest, save $1 today, and owe $2 more tomorrow. The scarcity mindset of not enough today is the opposite of what is needed to attract wealth—an abundance mentality. Faithfully honor your own human worth, and dollar worth is more likely follow.

At the beach, we set up in front of the lifeguard tower. She was super-hot, of course, and I was glad when Rebeca brought it up first. Google says lifeguards there make $12–16 per hour. A lot more than down the street at Walmart or McDonald's, doing unpleasant work daily. Newport Beach permanent lifeguards make $58,000 a year and higher. It sounds like a lot for what we typically see lifeguards doing: chilling and looking super-hot while moms and dads chase their kids around.

Here, again, it is critical that the service be performed well every time. Qualifications are non-negotiable. At the ocean, they must be ready to act under pressure, no matter how easy they make it look. The best always make it look easy, but value is revealed in the toughest moments. Still, it's never easy to be the best. The McDonald's assembly line seems harder than tanning, but the pressure of water rescue is heavier than the pressure of mayo mistakes. I guess the value of calling a penalty kick in 7 year-old soccer is somewhere in between.

new freedom, no boundaries

I *love* **to drive. If it** were carbon neutral and I had the time, one of my hobbies would be driving to new random places and back again. I did that quite a bit when I was in high school and college.

When I was amped on hormonal frustration with my girlfriend or filled with angst over how fake our social circle and "society" could be, I would drive to downtown Chicago. This was often around 11:00 pm when traffic was light or nonexistent coming back. I loved the freedom of the nearly vacant Kennedy expressway. I loved the solitude of six lanes engineered to ebb and flow, straightaway and curve, as I passed under the streetlights bright and dim, bright and dim through the windshield.

At 80–90 miles per hour, the scenery passed quickly: IKEA, Rosemont Horizon, O'Hare Airport, then the skyline waiting. Reaching the lakefront and circling Grant Park, the Shedd, and the Field was so calming. There is something about the irony of iconic urban places being empty. I would park by the Adler Planetarium and look out over the water, the orange city light fading to black. After pondering the meaning of life, and with balance restored, I would head back.

Four or five years later, every Sunday morning, I would take a drive through the small towns and cropland of central Illinois. I was student-teaching at the time, five sections of high school juniors, and I was overwhelmed. My cooperating teacher even took two weeks of family leave. My grandpa was dying, but I couldn't quit and still graduate with a teaching degree. I couldn't coast either. I had real students earning real grades. Two classes were advanced placement US history, and the students were cramming to test out of college coursework. My other three classes were co-taught with a special education teacher, as there were many students with learning disabilities. It was the most exhausting five months of my life. When I had to get away from people, I'd drive to Starbucks in downtown Urbana by the county courthouse, buy an expensive "FML" style drink, and keep driving.

Central Illinois is flat with a stark beauty. You can see the weather coming from a long way off. I'd be driving in the sunshine and see sheets of rain falling from a chain of clouds in the distance. Lots of 90-degree turns, no center stripe or curb, the rows of soybeans starting a few feet from the road.

I would not take a map or keep track of where I was going. I would get out at small cemeteries, no bigger than a front yard. Some lying there had passed in the 19th century, and I would wonder what that was like, homesteading near Abraham Lincoln. No destination, just rebalance, space, solitude, and perspective. Driving gave me these things, plus privacy with my own music, and agency to turn right, left, or not at all. Without a car, I could have taken long walks or rides, but I wanted to get as far away as possible.

When I was 16, I headed home after school with one of my best and oldest friends, Bunce. When we got there, a new car was in the driveway. But my dad's old car was still there. *Does this mean? Could it be? Ohhhhhhh, yes!* More choices, more speed, and more independence. The elation was so vivid it I remember like it was yesterday.

The "Black Pearl," a 1995 Toyota Camry, first set sail with yours truly as captain sometime in the spring of 2002. It was passed to me with 94,000 miles on it and became my trusted companion through all the highs and lows until August 2010, when we moved to Seattle. It was laid to rest after adding another 180,000 miles of my own.

Like my father and his father, I love being in cars. I don't like or know how to fix them. I don't know much about different models. Yet I am perfectly happy driving. My personal best was 13 consecutive driving hours from Joplin, Mississippi to somewhere in New Mexico. Having a car allowed me to spend more time with friends and less time coordinating pick-up or bus logistics. Having a car allowed me to test boundaries by hitting 120 mph on the 53 near Woodfield. (There's a great article in *National Geographic* on how teenage risk behavior is adaptive. So, it was okay right?)

As I grew older, having a car challenged my parents and me to stretch our comfort zones gradually. It broadened my horizons, figuratively and literally. The times described above were emotionally significant, but mostly I went to fun places in my car, like our bro-time camping trip to Warren Dunes. Driving more meant I saw more things, met more people, and gained more knowledge. In the critical period of young adulthood, I had the freedom to explore instead of work to make my car payment.

In the psychology of development, there is a big difference between packing bags in your own car, deciding you want to hit the road or when to pull over for the restroom or a soda, and being dropped off somewhere and having those decisions made for you. In college, as senior staff at a summer program for young people, I would occasionally make the three-hour round trip to pick up a counselor from the bus stop in Madison. They tended to be a little sheepish, especially if the bus arrived late. Contrast that to my experience as a counselor at that age: triumphantly arriving in the Black Pearl while blasting Third Eye Blind on my own terms.

What implications does that have on our psychology of dependence? In Milwaukee, taking the bus is still more associated with poverty than environmentalism. When a mother with an infant is waiting at the bus stop in winter, and her eyes lock with the Marquette freshman idling at the red light, in a car his family paid for, what is she thinking? What is he thinking?

When individual behavior is average, then wealth tends to be generational, broadly meaning that the perks, privileges, discipline, and career path of the parent(s) will be emulated by the child(ren). The gift of a car at age 16 changed my life. Even in its used condition, I could not have afforded that car until I was 22 and working full-time. Six formative years could have looked very different. I wouldn't have gone on nearly as many weekend camping trips with friends or had an off-campus job or been able to have the volunteer experiences I had, like taking my friend with Down's Syndrome to Taco Bell and playing his favorite, Billy Ray Cyrus, on the way. In fact, I stopped being a volunteer mentor with Big Brothers Big Sisters after one semester of my freshman year because the bus ride to his school was 50 minutes one way. Not proud of that, but access matters.

At age 24, when we were engaged, Rebeca and I moved to Seattle. My parents had since given my sister an older car of theirs and now generously offered me my grandpa's car, a 2003 Ford Taurus. At the time, it was seven years old (like the Black Pearl when I got it) with only 60,000 miles or so. The difference here was that I hated this one. It was not fun to drive, being clunky, too big, and too "beige" for my liking. Especially in Seattle, it stood out as the kind of car a Midwestern grandpa would drive. Go figure. But my free car existence was extended once again, while my fiancé's car note was generously covered by her parents. That bulky V6 gas guzzler towed all our belongings there and back again, including my motorcycle.

There is no other consumer product as common, as visible, or as expensive as a car. The car is a staple of American culture, even in the 21st century. Granted, a lot of my friends now live in Chicago and don't have or need one, and those readers in New York City may not identify with this, but the fact remains the car is common.

Common because, in most of the country, not having a car is a serious impediment. Metro areas and small cities may have a bus system, but it is far from efficient or perfect. Subject to delays, a bus may be the difference between making it to daycare on time or being six minutes late and paying a steep fine. In the Midwest (outside of Chicago), if you can afford a car, you have one. Taking the bus or Uber by choice is not the same as depending on them.

Visible because, unlike your 700-square-foot apartment or 7,000-square-foot mansion, you cannot control who sees you in it. It is the most visible marker of success or struggle. Your home is invite-only. Yes, there can be judgment when asked where you live, a fleeting opportunity to flex or deflect. However, a car is ostensibly yours when you arrive somewhere. It is an immediate indicator of your station in life. Most cars on the road fall within the normal distribution; they are not luxurious nor decrepit. Cosmetic repairs are made in higher-income neighborhoods. In neighborhoods with lower socioeconomic status (SES) like ours? If it runs, we're good. No bumper? No problem. *At least I'm not driving that.*

This observation is top of mind because I drove my grandpa's car until I was 32. Comparing car value to income, my best year ever was at age 16. My worst year car-wise was when I was a 31-year-old financial advisor driving a rusting 14-year-old mid-price sedan. I am just starting to leave the normal distribution of cars on the road, mostly because the cars and I are "aging out," and there is a big dent on the passenger side. My brother-in-law said that when I get out of this car wearing a suit, I look like a con artist. But you know what? I'm hanging on.

A few years ago, when the car was starting to lurch occasionally, my parents, continuing their generosity, put in $3,000 worth of repairs. *C'mon I was so close to unloading this guilt-free.* Kelley Blue Book valued the car at about $4,000 at the time, but they understood the value of a reliable car. *You also said that potential clients would judge me if I'm seen in this car, so why extend my misery?* The car is a daily reminder of how my parents and my grandpa took care of their vehicles to pass them on. The car now runs beautifully and only has 140,000 miles. It's old enough to be depreciating slowly and holding great utility in our lives. Considering what a replacement would cost, keeping it is a no-brainer. Except it's so …visible.

Expensive because, other than a house and maybe higher education, a car is the single most expensive purchase most Americans make. The more you think about what a car really is, the more your mind is blown. They should be expensive.

At age 18 or 20, if I had to buy a car comparable to the estimated $9,000 car I was given by my parents at age 16, my options would have been: (a) save every dime of my personal income from my time as a soccer referee, brief stints as a carpenter's lackey, and summer soccer camp coach, plus relying on the U of I dining services for three years, and not spending on anything else in that time or (b) take out a loan for the car. Assuming I put $1,000 down and borrowed $8,000 at 12% interest (generous for an unmarried, 20-year-old male with no credit history and no money), the actual price would be $11,677 with a monthly payment of $177 for five years. Big difference. And that was for one car. Do that math again for another car at age 24. Inheriting reliable cars meant I was basically given about $25,000 of spending money in emerging adulthood instead of a payment.

As it was, I spent that money getting the most I could out of my life: friends, travel, dating, learning, and competing. Sometimes spending foolishly, sometimes wisely, but always remaining cognizant of my future and exploring who I wanted to become.

That's the direct cost, the price tag. But let's say I saved all that money and put it in a stock market fund Roth IRA between ages 16–24. A $1,000 down payment, plus $177 per month for five years (the Black Pearl's hypothetical loan) equals $13,759 at age 21 (assuming 6% compound interest, no fees), $16,465 by age 24 (with no car payment or saving ages 21–24), then repeat that first scenario from ages 24–29 (using the hypothetical loan on Grandpa's car) and I get $34,619 in a Roth IRA before my 30th birthday. If I didn't put another dollar in from age 30 to 70, a reasonable estimate is an ending value of $379,336. And if left alone to age 80, $500,000 is likely.

This is the time value of money expressed in cars.

This is how generational wealth works: take away the boundaries of a payment, and the freedom of a clean slate is passed on.

Before we continue, an update on my consecutive drive time personal best: 18 hours, from Milwaukee on the way to Avon, Colorado. Motivation? Covering as much ground as possible while the antsy three-year-old was asleep, and traffic was nonexistent.

My car saga continues. Yes, I drive it. But despite my best efforts to accelerate "normal wear and tear," I don't drive the 2003 Ford Taurus that much. When I do, it's for a boring errand, my ten-minute office commute once or twice a week, or a jaunt to go camping or to buy stuff at Menards, where I couldn't care less about appearances. Having a car you don't care about preserving is very liberating at times. Is the seat muddy? Who cares! But you never know who you'll see. And there was at least one time I wished I was wearing a disguise.

I did have an experience where a young couple, referred to me as prospective clients by a friend, saw me get out of it walking into their meeting. *Shit, they saw it.* You know, the meeting where I would tell them how to get it together and become wealthy. So, I brought it up on purpose as a lesson in delayed gratification. I said, "I have an old Taurus that was my grandpa's and has no payment…It runs great, and I barely drive it, and by waiting, I can be more strategic, blah, blah, blah."

By living below our means (which I wasn't at the time, but that's what I wanted them to believe), we can make significant financial progress. The more extreme we get, the faster we can turn things around and the greater the risk of rejection. *Okay, that's the address. Let's park around the corner out of view.* The drumbeat of consumerism whispers in our ear: *more, more, more, now, now, now.* And the hardest habit for me to develop in a client is spending less when they don't have to spend less.

There are a lot of luxuries I don't need. A nice car is something I would *really* enjoy. I will absolutely get a hybrid or electric car, so do I get a Prius now or a Tesla in a few years? *Don't lie to yourself…You know what's better for the environment than buying a new electric vehicle? Reduce new car production, reuse the car you've been given and recycle the dollars saved into something else.* I read many years ago that the most efficient way to use a car is to buy a gently used vehicle, one to three years old, and drive it as long as you can. That same article said the most common vehicle owned by millionaires is the Ford F-150 pickup.

Remember that car payment math? Factor in this, too: cars lose resale value fast. I read an article in *Forbes* about car models that depreciate the fastest—some luxury cars go for half the new purchase price after three to four years. So, is that new car smell worth $25,000? In other words, can you accept a Mercedes or BMW with 40,000 miles on it for $25,000 or do you "need" a new one?

Most of us struggle with first impressions. The car price is no secret as that's how we send a message that we've arrived. In Mexico, the new truck on the ranch is a sign that the family has turned the corner. With culture being powerful, Mexican families in our neighborhood are driving mammoth-sized trucks and SUVs. Not towing or bouncing through the fields, just trying to fit through the crowded alleys and parallel parking in their urban environment.

Rebeca and I went to a friend's wedding in Destin, Florida. We stayed in a resort on the beach and didn't rent a car. The breakfast spot was about a mile away. Captain Eco-Friendly here proclaimed, "We shall walk! We have two legs and our health. Let's enjoy the sunshine and get some exercise too!" So, with our second child Rio, who was four months old at the time, in a baby carrier, we headed off. You know the feeling you get when you're walking in an area where no one typically walks? There was a sidewalk, but it was along a four-lane busy state highway lined with gated community access points and strip malls. About halfway there, I was sweaty and starting to question my plan as Rebeca was getting grumpy.

At breakfast, she made a point that I had heard before but forgotten once again. She had to take the bus or wait for the family car as a kid. Now, as a person of color in this affluent area, she felt like everyone assumed that her car had broken down or she couldn't afford one. Or at least she was triggered by the childhood memory.

This is the money paradox for the first generation moving out of poverty: wanting to spend to prove you aren't broke. So many times, after a client meeting in a coffee shop, the Ford Taurus stared at me through the windowpane—my scarlet letter. "I'm staying a bit," I'd lie so they wouldn't see my walk of shame to *that* car. That was before I knew I belonged. As a new financial advisor, I was scraping by financially and felt insecure as a result. Maybe that's how Rebeca felt her entire childhood.

I've come to terms with keeping my car until it needs a major repair. I've thought about donating it to charity or renting it out. But I've embraced my vision, my values, and my math. This takes a lot of conviction and discipline. The things I am prioritizing before a car payment are: (1) reinvesting in my business through education, systems, and software; (2) writing a book; (3) spending more time with my kids; (4) taking more vacations and time off; (5) preparing for a larger payment on a used Tesla Model S when the Ford craps out.

What do these five things have in common? They are all focused on my legacy, joy, and well-being. It's hard to do that in survival mode. It takes mustering self-esteem when you feel less-than. It takes self-esteem in the face of comparison. There's money to be made for those strong enough to handle it.

Since writing this, I sold the car for $1,800 cash. A weight was lifted. A mathematical gift became an emotional burden. By letting go, I became a full-time bike commuter, which saved money. Most days, it was fun, plus I lost weight. After two years of that, with a third child on the way and cognizant of the time value of money, I bought a gently used, reliable car like the practical, informed financial planner I was. *How sad, you boring dad. Ugh. Wait, wait! You chose a black Toyota Camry, a reminder of the new freedom given at 16 and the boundaries you've explored since. Recapture that spirit, and you'll drive this one until your son is 16. That's a better story.*

chapter eight

balloon ball

In my early twenties, my three remaining grandparents all passed away.

This chapter tells the story of my Grandma Wilbrandt.

As I mentioned earlier, I didn't know her very well because, by the time I reached my teenage years, her mind was fading. By my own memory and all other accounts, she was a dignified person, haughty even. In the nursing home, she would glance at her neighbors with disdain. My grandpa, who was a wonderful storyteller, referred to her once as the "Slavic Jewel" with a smirk. My mom said that she was high-class and dressed to impress. As an adult, my mom would often be greeted with the remark, "When are you going to change your hair?" Grandma Wilbrandt's other daughter and daughters-in-law didn't fare much better.

Long before me, Grandma Wilbrandt was a tireless worker and ran what sounded like a happy household of five kids. Summer camp, three square meals a day, kids ready for college, etc. Her children didn't seem close to her, but they all gave her respect. She didn't seem to want affection anyway. She was not our grandma or nana. She was Grandma Wilbrandt. Capitalized.

She started to lose her memory in her early seventies, as far as I understand. Maybe my mom realized that life is short, and our window for really knowing our grandparents was closing. At any rate, visiting them wasn't "fun" in any sense, but we went. My Grandpa Heaton was having the time of his life doing whatever we wanted and was generally more active, so a day at his house was like a party. We even got to watch TV! *Mr. Belvedere*! *Maury*! He'd take us to breakfast, and I'd order a plate of French toast and a Western omelet. It was fantastic. A visit to Grandpa and Grandma Wilbrandt's, on the other hand, felt like we were hosting them in their own house. My mom diligently started conversations, which weren't sustained without continuous effort. My grandpa, his head full of memory, knowledge, and wisdom, would often look at some faraway point in the distance. My mom would say, "So, Dad, we were thinking about cleaning out the basement sometime this spring," to which he would reply, "Oooohh …" with the intonation rising at the end, not falling. It was like this suggestion had to echo back through the halls of time before resurfacing in the present.

My grandma began to struggle to follow along. Mental illness is uncomfortable for most of us. Something you can't see is harder to define and wrap your head around. Mental illness can't be solved by the individual because "your mind is where the problem started in the first place" (taken from the film *A Beautiful Mind*), just like "tough it out" isn't an answer to disease.

In my adolescent years, our visits became more frequent. My mom's conversation shifted to my grandma to keep her mind active and exercising. We would play "balloon ball," which is just what it sounds like:

the five of us sitting in the living room trying to keep a balloon in the air without leaving our seats. We would play bingo to practice recalling numbers. Grandma would forget what decade she was in. And she would accuse my grandpa of things out of nowhere, which I know hurt his feelings. I've learned since that psychosis and paranoia is common with Alzheimer's patients, but that didn't make it easier.

Grandpa Wilbrandt was mentally sharp, but physically very frail, so my mom would do little things for them. My uncle, raising teenagers and running his own business, would stop by to change hard-to-reach light bulbs. And my grandpa's growing dependency on his children was frustrating to him, with nothing to do but sit and wait for them to arrive.

After a few years of receiving daytime home health aide, Grandma Wilbrandt moved to a home for people with Alzheimer's and other forms of dementia. It was a nice home, clean and beautiful. There was a passcode on the doors to prevent people from wandering away. Eventually, when we would visit, she wouldn't even remember our names. She couldn't form words, leading my mom to wonder if she had Parkinson's. But she said the dimple in my chin would get me the girls, which at least made that visit worth the hour's drive each way.

My mom and her siblings began to drift. All five of them had different relationships with their parents. Different webs of history. Different versions of what supporting them meant. Different barriers (real or perceived) to giving more support: distance, emotional baggage, or career. The reasons we all give. My mother, whose love language is acts of service, would drive over there every Saturday and Sunday. She still wasn't always greeted warmly, but she was there, almost always away from her kids, in a sterile home surrounded by gloomy men and women pondering meaning, love, and loss as they approached the end.

By that point, it seemed like Nora and I had lots of activities, keeping our own lives full. Walking in to visit Grandma was always a somber affair. Then she was moved into skilled nursing care at the adjacent nursing home. That move was uncomfortable for me. Our culture doesn't handle aging and death well.

Some of my mom's siblings may have been given more than others. So much of life and relationships is not quantifiable, no matter how hard we try. Life is not fair. One person's best efforts may be another's worst. And to whom much is given, much is asked. My mom was there.

We spend our money in accordance with our values. And I have no idea how much my grandmother's care cost, but it was a lot. It was as high-class as she could get, I think. If my third of the college rent was $350 in Urbana, then a well-maintained and decorated room in Woodstock, with 24/7 care, would have cost a lot.

As I reflected on it in college, I recall thinking I wouldn't need all that. Now I know, if I'm a good father, how would my kids be able to deny me the dignity of quality care if I need it? They only would if they couldn't afford it or if I couldn't. (My Grandpa Heaton went from home to nursing home to hospital in months without me visiting. Student-teaching was consuming my life, but not seeing his last living spaces made closure harder. That's also how he wanted it: in my last memory of him, he was living, not dying.)

We spend our time in accordance with our values. Humans are social creatures, and we judge each other based on how we spend our time and money. I don't expect that will ever change if both are finite. I am grateful that I knew my grandmother. She passed in 2007, and my Grandpa Wilbrandt passed less than a year later. Technically, he died of cancer. But like in Ben Folds' song "The Luckiest," "that's a strange way to tell you that I know we're in love." If Rebeca were to pass away when we are 90, I might wilt. Emotion is infinite. It keeps us going. And for Grandpa Wilbrandt, he hadn't spoken to the woman he knew and married through the last 10 years of her life. Instead, he visited with a shell of her former self. The chance of a reunion after death, no matter how remote, could be more appealing than slogging on alone.

A rift in the family widened. My grandpa's estate was split five ways. My mom said that was always the way it was going to be. Frankly, that's all I knew about it. He was wealthy, and drama ensued. My mom was neutral in the disputes. She was there when no one was looking. There was no financial reward. And the fifth wasn't increasing. Whatever happened and whatever was said, the family is now distant. No more get-togethers on the Fourth of July or Christmas Eve. No more shared knowledge, shared connections, or shared memories. Some relationships won't be repaired until one of their generation is dying, if at all.

I carry my mom's steadfast objectivity. I want to reconnect with our cousins and give my son a childhood memory that I had: extended family crammed into a living room or parlor, replete with corny jokes, stories we heard last year, awkward questions to significant others, and traditions that bring us together even if they're stupid. Money got in the way.

I'm not sure whether it was disheartening or reassuring to find out how common sibling drama is when parents pass away or need long-term care. It's reassuring to know that my relatives and mom weren't crazy, but disheartening that this scenario is so difficult and traumatic for many, yet few plan ahead, and many don't have the capacity to prepare. It's a universal experience and resources abound, but most aren't ready. Once it happens, families will do whatever it takes. It's just that a little foresight could lessen what it takes.

As a financial planner, I've learned what I need to know to plan finances. That means thinking ahead. Industry designations, webinars, and stories all reinforce the need to talk about this before it happens. We all want to assume our parents won't need memory care, but if we realize they do, the ideal time to talk has passed. Everyone is already on their heels, forced into reaction instead of action.

Planning for negative events doesn't make you a negative person. Controlling what you can makes you a realist. Taking simple steps, however uncomfortable now, allows you to chase positives with more energy and peace of mind.

I have a few clients my age who are dealing with parents in the early phases of dementia. It's not easy. There is an entire legal specialty devoted to Medicaid planning, which is how to shift assets and savings out of the person's name and into ownership by children or other family members. The problem that arises suddenly is that all your savings—401k, IRA, bank accounts—must be used to pay bills for custodial care before Medicaid kicks in. Medicare pays for acute care, which is hospital stays, medications, surgery, ER, and doctor visits. It does not pay for a home healthcare worker to help your dad get dressed or use the toilet. As I write, current estimates are that memory care, like my grandmother's, costs about $60,000 a year. Her stays in the nursing home would have been more. If your parents have a lot of savings, shifting assets for long-term care insurance will help. Long-term care insurance is expensive because the probability of using it is high.

In contrast, if your parents don't have any savings, they will go straight to government-sponsored care. Their 401k, their life savings, could be gone before you know it and be taxed on the way out, too. But like other forms of welfare, it keeps them off the street. I'm not saying this is fair, but this is reality. Call your senator. I'm guessing your dad won't take comfort in you telling him that universal healthcare works in Sweden because he's here and can't watch the Packers in Sweden. In much of the world, putting an elderly family member in a home is unthinkable, even if it is possible. If this isn't your path, then start thinking about where your mom will stay in 10 years. Does your home have an extra bedroom? Will your mom be willing to move out of her home of 40 years?

With younger generations living far away from their parents, this is a growing issue. The issue is made worse by many parents, with their paternalistic responses to their children's questions. "Do you have a durable financial power of attorney?" "Oh, don't worry about us, honey." This discussion means the young professional who asked needs to accept two difficult truths at once: your parents are mortal and getting older, and they don't always know best. Or they will protect you at all costs, as they always have until they . . . can't.

Ask them: "Which is more of a burden to you: (a) shorting some of my college tuition and giving me a $30,000 loan to pay off for now and maybe pitching in later, or (b) moving in with me when I'm 35, raising kids of my own, growing my career, and asking me for a hand lifting your pants when you're done on the toilet?"

There is peace of mind waiting on the other side of a painful conversation. With money and relationships, risking rejection can lead to new growth and clarity. My grandmother's experience was one path of many. Long after she could express her wishes verbally, her eyes made me wonder if that was the path she would have chosen.

the "Pride of Palatine"

In the fall of my senior year, I played arguably the best soccer game of my life. To be in the zone for this game meant even more.

My senior year was interrupted early on by breaking my nose in a contested header. After six games out and a game or two with a Will Purdue-style face mask, I was back in action. I was beginning to grasp the reality that I was reaching the pinnacle of my competitive soccer career. I wasn't good enough to play competitive D1 college soccer, nor did I want to dedicate my college experience to intense training (although it was hard to say which led to the other).

I was a captain of the varsity team in my senior year. During my junior year in 2003, the varsity team almost went to the state championship, but the 2004 team was young. Of the starters that year, only four of us were seniors, and many on the bench were sophomores. We were roughly half-Latino, half-White, and had two Black guys. Another co-captain was a phenomenally talented Latino striker. A four-year varsity starter, he led the team in scoring, had a great smile, and loved to laugh. He was not a vocal leader but was obsessed with the game, very fast (when running in a straight line), and quick (able to turn on a dime). He was just plain fun to watch.

As a center-back (the anchor of the defense), I was hard-working, disciplined, responsible, and fundamentally sound, but not a natural talent, though probably more humble than I could have been. Consequently, I played a safe style of soccer. Very likely, I was no fun to watch. In other words, Lalo and I were representatives of our teammates, our school, and our side of town.

Every year, Palatine High School and Fremd High School had a cross-town match-up. They called it the Celtic Cup. It drew a crowd beyond the players' families and girlfriends. In my senior year, it filled the bleachers on both sides with probably a few thousand people. It was an event like high school football every week. This year, we played at Fremd.

In suburban Chicago, or I guess in most neighborhoods, you can gauge wealth by the quality of the car being driven. A Fremd High School senior drove a car on par with a Palatine High School parent. The bus pulled into the lot, and we walked toward the field while the Fremd players were loosely kicking the ball around. In the spring season, my club soccer team drew players from the entire Village of Palatine, about 80,000 people at the time, and some from neighboring Inverness and Barrington. So, I knew a lot of the guys on the Fremd team. Some I liked personally, others not so much. A lot of them I'd played with for years. Huddled up during wins and losses, November wind and May mud, they were teammates.

They warmed up in black t-shirts with a custom-printed design I couldn't make out at first. I was expecting the standard Adidas or Nike warm-up clothes in school colors, so this was odd. Then as I took to the field, I could finally read it: "Fremd High School: The Pride of Palatine."

Instantly, I was fuming, whereas I've always had a slow fuse. The Pride of Palatine? How could that be construed as anything but a taunt at best and thinly veiled classism and racism at worst? There were *two* public high schools in Palatine. Ours was *called* "Palatine" High School. Whose idea was this? A player's? A coach's? A parent's? Who could be so arrogant or oblivious to pitch this? Occasionally, I was invited to a get-together at someone's house that went to Fremd, so I knew they could be smug. And a lot of the club soccer parents on Nora's and my teams could be, too. *But how could my own teammates in the spring wear this message in the fall?*

The feeling of that t-shirt still stings when I think about it. I don't know how the Latinos on the team felt. Maybe they thought it was just White people nonsense. For those who didn't play club soccer or didn't have friends on that side of town, maybe it just felt like another away game. After all, this was just a game and wasn't even a playoff game. But the idea that wealth somehow equated to them being better or the pride of our town was hard to swallow. Like others, I felt let down by the "adults" who let this fly. *What was their agenda?*

As I was reading *Newsweek* and Rousseau in school by this point, I knew that adults were mortal and often made it up as they went along. Some of my teachers and coaches, who we perceived as sages at the time, were younger than I am now. And as an adult, I know how socioeconomic status divides people. Basic psychology, the attribution theory, lets us know that those with money credit their own attributes for that wealth and external factors for the failures along the way. I've been privileged all my life. As a straight, White male, I could don a t-shirt of my own: "The Pride of America." That night was my first deep imprint of being dismissed based on my category alone, a feeling most Americans absorb daily: racism, sexism, and classism.

I had an incredible game. Some key stops on defense, winning balls in the air, and crisp touch in the midfield. Down by one goal with 15 minutes left, I sent a beautiful shot just inches over the crossbar. I fantasized about that shot going in the net for months after. My photo would have been in the paper. I would have been the hero of the game and garnered extra female attention at school. But most of all, it would have wiped those smug smiles off their faces.

Seeing Fremd players wearing that shirt is a vivid memory for me. Fourteen years later, I was invited to the home of a prospective client a few blocks away from Fremd High School. This client was a long-time classmate of mine from Winston Elementary through Palatine High School. As we began talking, she said she was happy to live near Fremd so her kids would go to "the better school." For a split second, I was fuming. *Traitor! She's turning her back on her own past.* Then I caught myself. I obsess about which school in Milwaukee is best. I don't even live in Palatine anymore. Why do I care? Why do so many of us care about these ranking lists?

People wouldn't care so much about sports if they were only about the game. Let's start there. Sports are often a proxy and outlet for class and cultural conflict. That's why we see the heroification of athletes and intense rivalries, often regional but sometimes between the coasts and flyover country. Having a harder time expressing their feelings, when men say, "Yankees suck," they are really saying, "New York snobs who think they're better than us suck; the Yankees are only good because of their salary cap." It can be thinly veiled prejudice sometimes.

This story may be part of why I rooted for the Cleveland Cavaliers over the Golden State Warriors in the NBA Finals. A Rust Belt city, the humble roots hometown of star Lebron James, and an underdog team defeated the heavily favored team from the wealthy Bay Area. Steph Curry seems delightful, but *c'mon* his dad was in the NBA. Do you think there is a connection? When the Cavaliers won, I was so pumped I drove to Taco Bell and dropped $16.

Milwaukee is an underdog, too. To be fair, I love and hate Milwaukee. Milwaukee is home. But just like how we love and hate family: *I* can critique them, but *you* can't without a damn good reason. I know them. I am loyal to them. And I am hardest on those I care about. I have moments wishing for Chicago culture, and I have moments of deep appreciation for the loyalty and humility of Milwaukeeans, too. We contain multitudes.

Contrast this with our time living in Seattle. I was drawn by a fixed mindset: Seattle is cool, progressive, and outdoorsy, so if I live there, I will be too.

Sports and money show how fixed and growth mindsets still confound expert predictions of the favorite and the underdog. I had read Dr. Carol Dweck's bestseller *Mindset: The New Psychology of Success* when I was in youth work, then read more of her peer-reviewed articles in my Educational Psychology master's program. Examples of the fixed mindset: "My child will be successful because she went to Fremd High School," or "My child will only beat Fremd's team if they get lucky because they are major underdogs." An example of the growth mindset: "My child's education is my responsibility; as an involved parent, I can supplement and advocate where I think the school is falling short. My child and his team will have to be extremely focused, disciplined, and determined to beat this talented Fremd team, and I know that's possible."

The fixed versus growth mindset may help us understand how we see ourselves in America's pecking order. In sports, no one remembers who came in second. In life, there's never really a finish line. So, we scheme and strive to create our own. Money, like the score, can be measured. More people compete than can finish first, so by definition, there are far fewer "favorites" than underdogs. We see the champion as a finished product, but don't buy tickets to watch them train. To achieve success at the highest level, we need to identify what we are good at and enjoy putting ourselves in a position to leverage our strengths and love the work we do as much as possible. We also need to apply daily discipline and consistent effort to put ourselves in a position to win.

Take the tortoise and the hare. The highest performers are both. They have some hare ability and apply tortoise focus. The world is full of hares: potential unfulfilled.

The trick is to have faith you are the favorite while applying the effort of the underdog. We don't identify with the underdog, but we do root for them. Everyone is happy for Rudy and Rocky, but we don't really want to be them. Did you see Rocky's apartment? After all, they were called underdogs for a reason. We want to be the favorite, the effortless winner. Money can bestow confidence, and confidence is needed to compete.

First-generation wealth is a progression. Imagine your future to motivate your present sacrifice. It's no coincidence that two middle-class couples I work with, both in their late fifties, great savers, and sent kids to private schools, both have sizable retirement savings. They also have modest homes, clothes, and spending habits. Not flashy star habits, but now, after consistent discipline, they could buy beach houses and be just fine. They looked within for their definition of success.

On the other hand, I have young professional clients who identify as being of the upper middle class simply because they grew up in that stratum. Ahem, no, your parents are upper middle class. You are broke and on the way to bankruptcy with an upper-middle-class support system. It works for now, but you carry your past habits into a present that cannot sustain them. You will be eclipsed by an underdog.

Money, like the score, is quantifiable. It lets us know who won and who lost. I was a good athlete because my parents allowed me to be, by giving me ample time and resources. That was my relative advantage. A good athlete without similar family support is more remarkable. Adults apply a dollar score without considering how each athlete gets different coaching, different amounts of practice time, and different amounts of head trash like "The Pride of Palatine" t-shirts to overcome.

In sports, we search for how the odds were beaten or upheld on a level playing field. But money moves the starting line. It always has and always will. Life isn't fair, and I'm not suggesting we have two World Cups for colonized and colonizer countries, even though nothing is truly fair in a post-colonial world. *That's why I love it. There's only one winner.* The least we could do is acknowledge that all children have a right to thrive. We should invest in that foundation, then be proud of their choices. Not their neighborhood.

optimism

In my senior year in high school, I took a class called Leadership for Life, which was offered to freshmen, sophomores, juniors, and seniors, honor roll students and students with learning and physical disabilities, jocks and artsy kids, shy and loud, everyone you can imagine. The diversity was by design. I didn't even know about it; I was approached by the teacher to sign up.

Up to this point, I'd been spending all my time with my advanced placement course classmates and varsity sports teammates. I recognized other faces, but nothing deeper. Sitting at a desk next to a student with an obvious learning disability was a new experience. I was lifted from the fog of *Essays on Inequality* and *In Praise of Folly* and whatever I'd been reading during the period before.

The course was designed to open our eyes to the potential in others and ourselves. We wrote self-reflections, went to a high-ropes course together, and, more importantly, were given the emotional space to process feelings and opinions as a group. Imagine having non-STEM or reading time during the school day. We had room for authentic conversation.

This course had a profound impact on me. My very Christian then-girlfriend wasn't a very good Christian, which made me more atheist. And unchecked nationalism in the wake of the 9/11 attacks, government corruption, and White-washed history made me even more negative. Big feelings teenagers have. Yes, I could be such a delightful party guest. The idea that people were inherently good, which our Leadership for Life teacher seemed to believe, was very disruptive to my worldview. In theory, I felt that being nice was asking to be taken advantage of. I'd seen it in history, politics, and relationships. But in spirit, I was the nice guy. At least, I thought I was. *No, all you do is talk shit.* In my own little bubble, my friends and I had so much in common. We would mock everyone in school for being dumb, unathletic, awkward, lame; you name it. I was fairly kind to others in person but mean behind their backs. By the impossibly low moral standards of high school, I don't know where I fell. I know now that my then-bubble met all my needs for comradery, identity, and security.

I had a wake-up call through Leadership for Life. For the first time in a while, a classmate might speak to me as just another human, not as a high school alpha. The class was co-taught, meaning a second teacher was present to support the many students with physical and/or cognitive disabilities. That spring, my last in high school, one of the Special Education teachers presented an opportunity to our class: volunteering for a week at an overnight camp as counselors serving children and young adults with muscular dystrophy. I had no other plans, I liked new experiences, and my earlier ex-girlfriend, who was still fun and still hot, was going.

The Muscular Dystrophy Association (MDA) runs these camps all over the country. Three other girls from my school volunteered with me, along with others from all over the state. We sang songs, had themed parties, and did lots of typical summer camp stuff. It was a joyous place. So much so that I felt comfortable being joyous myself.

I learned there that optimism is important. Hope is not a sign of weakness. The camper I was paired with was physically very high functioning. Many others at the camp were paraplegic or quadriplegic. All of them had a genetic disease through no choice or fault of their own. All of them were like other kids in many respects: they wanted to swim, liked to hang out with friends, and liked to laugh. Most of them knew their lifespan was limited, but their attitude was not.

Their joy in the little things seemed infinite. I witnessed the excitement of being in a swimming pool. (Pools accessible by ramp or motorized lift are rare.) I saw how some people cherished sitting at a table with a group of peers. (Most houses don't have a room big enough to accommodate five wheelchairs.) And here I was at age 18, sulking over the military-industrial complex and judging others for their positive attitude. For a "nice guy," I wasn't doing enough with the abilities and upbringing I'd been given. What a dick.

I regained some humility. Despite our high school being a district magnet for kids with disabilities, living with them, however briefly, was an eye-opener. I stayed in a cabin with boys that were all about 10 years old, with varying degrees of physical impairments caused by muscular dystrophy. It took a long time to get ready, to get anywhere. *It's about them. Don't look at your watch. Stop fidgeting.*

Being a caregiver wasn't just a responsibility. Caring for children with special needs can be a full-time job, not to mention the medical equipment and the time. Time is money, right? Life is fleeting and finite. The clock is ticking for all of us, but that doesn't mean the answer is to hurry up.

I had spent too much time living in the past or the future. Any time I spent in the present, I was in my bubble. My approach to my income, my education, and my future goals had been, "How do I maximize my skills and abilities in the context of what I already know that I like?" This approach got me accepted into college and led me to pursue teaching. I had a steady girlfriend and great friends. I was a two-sport varsity captain, got good enough grades, and was generally well-liked. I was clinging to what was working versus seeking what was best. MDA Camp showed me that there was a world beyond what I knew. I just had to be humble enough to look for it. Like Leadership for Life class, it grounded me in the present and what I could contribute to the world instead of complaining.

I know now that healthcare costs and the opportunity cost of care-giving must amount to tens of thousands of dollars a year. It's not just the deductible or copays. It's how much the parent could make if they could pursue all career options. Travel, meeting deadlines, and long hours are harder or impossible when raising a child with disabilities. I went into the week at MDA Camp thinking this was a wonderful getaway for the kids. I didn't realize it was also a respite for the parents. Caring for someone with a chronic health impairment is a full-time job. Some long-term care insurance contracts have a "caregiver respite" feature because caring for a loved one is so taxing that time away is needed.

When someone is born into a tough situation, we are more sym-pathetic. Down's syndrome is genetic. It was not a choice. When some of us are dealt a hand that others avoid by no merit of their own, what is society's role in supporting this inequity? The Americans with Disabilities Act (ADA) is a start. Considering how astronomical the cost is, after that, it's a matter of knowing how to navigate the system. The Centers for Medicare and Medicaid Services (CMS) sets the rules for who gets what assistance. Family income, age of the insured, type of disability, length of disability, and family assets—all these things affect the out-of-pocket cost. The interplay of variables is so complex that attorneys are often involved.

Government policy tends to most affect people on the fringes: the very powerful who can lobby and the very dependent who rely on policies for the basics. Unfortunately, the very dependent often have things that are more urgent and feel more important than voting and lobbying. When I meet a client who is truly on the cusp of poverty, it's not a financial planning case. It's an advocacy case. I try to make connections to reputable resources and people who can make sense of the endless forms.

I began to learn more about this when I connected two people with each other:

The first was my Leadership for Life teacher. She became a client of mine when she semi-retired in her sixties. For years, she generously gave her time and money to others. Now her feelings about what was "responsible" were deeply conflicted. She retired from Palatine High School, but ran a Special Needs Ministry at church. She gave tirelessly and knew how overwhelming life was for a family with special needs.

The second person was Tom Canale, a financial planner in Chicago. I heard him speak at an event. His depth of character struck me, and his niche expertise was something I'd never encountered: special needs trust planning. A trust is a form of ownership that offers limited access for certain people, which can protect assets from CMS and allow children to qualify for assistance. Families willing to make any sacrifice for the benefit of their child can lose thousands of dollars in the absence of a strategy.

When I connected these two in Tom's office near O'Hare Airport, it was very emotional. My teacher, a tireless human advocate for decades, discovered within an hour how an expert navigating these systems could protect or grow financial resources for a family simply through the reorganization of dollars. It was a striking example of how knowing the rulebook makes all the difference. I have since earned the Chartered Special Needs Consultant® designation from the American College to be an expert in these rules. Does charging your adult child rent for living in your house sound logical? Not really, but it helps families get more support under current rules. Know the rulebook.

In the 21st century, health insurance linked to employment is archaic, and it stifles innovation. A parent considering freelance work for the flexibility needed to be a caregiver shouldn't be discouraged by giving up their quality corporate health insurance plan to keep a child well-covered.

Shouldn't we group healthcare plans based on need instead of an employer? Oh, wait, big employers want us to need their benevolent employment. The quality of care for the child shouldn't be dictated by a parent's employer. And the quality of public education shouldn't be dictated by their home address.

The framework of costs and rights is a result of decades of negotiation. There are many costs at stake, and nothing seems to fall into place automatically. My clients who are raising children with special needs have more on their plates. For that reason alone, they can be harder to work with. Time is scarce and overwhelm is common. They have to advocate for their child at the school's Individual Education Plan meeting, and then battle for the adequate support promised under ADA. They have nothing left for an evening talk with me about long-term planning. And I understand that. Taking life one day at a time makes it difficult to make more time for a meeting with some finance guy who will just tell them something they already know or say they need to save more money in a condescending way. Why risk it?

What my teacher learned from Tom is that specialized knowledge is a powerful thing. When the universe connects a specific problem with a specific solution, new things become possible. Suddenly, 1 + 1 = 3. And expertise is an exponent. Mix it with effort, and the results can be more than imagined.

Ultimately, this remains a story of optimism. I learned that optimism is not a sign of weakness or naivety. Sometimes optimism is the only answer. Pessimism adds nothing of value to a person with a degenerative disease. Negativity is easy. My buddies and I would hash out the events of the day at Wendy's, ruthlessly cutting down others and each other. Optimism, in the face of uncertainty, requires supreme mental effort.

I joined the Best Buddies program in college, which is a national non-profit that creates opportunities for one-to-one friendships and inclusive living for people with intellectual and developmental disabilities. I keep in touch with my buddy Alex to this day. Hanging out with him is so much fun. His childlike enthusiasm brings me joy and gratitude. MDA Camp gave me optimism that the human spirit can thrive in unlikely places. Emotions are infinite. When we nurture a relationship or an idea, we find room in our hearts we didn't know was there. You'll never know how you'll feel until you put yourself out there.

Having this experience right after high school graduation brought me out of my bubble. I had been looking for meaning in books. Then, a decade after MDA Camp, I saw on a motivational calendar in the check-out line: "Stop looking for meaning, but instead try to come alive." Volunteering at MDA Camp did that for me.

chapter eleven

Global Studies

When I was 18, I crossed the globe. The University of Illinois had a Global Studies program that included a three-week study-abroad opportunity following a semester-long course. My parents (the good savers) said they would pay for me to go, for $1,800, as I recall. (The plane ticket for a 24-hour flight was about $1,300. And $500 goes a long way in some parts of the world.)

I chose the option the most different and furthest away from everything I knew: Mumbai, India. The course, including the time in India, was taught by Professor of Sociology (and Mumbai native) Dr. Manisha Desai. The coursework in India focused on three elements of globalization: Bollywood cinema, the IT call center industry, and housing rights. I went to India with about 15 other students, ranging from freshmen to doctoral candidates. Our typical day was a group outing into the city pertaining to the coursework (and the occasional monument or vista), followed by a few hours of group discussion.

I had two initial impressions of Mumbai. The first was that many buildings and streets were very dirty (I went in the dry season), yet the city was full of vibrant color, much of it from clothing. The second was it was full of children. Years later, the movie *Slumdog Millionaire* rang true to this American tourist. I did see blinded children singing for donations.

The streets have layers: the physical storefronts, followed by a line of mobile street vendors selling everything imaginable, followed by throngs of people walking along the street, children running in and out of the alleys, and a jumble of traffic in the middle. The entire city feels like one organism. The air, the dust, the heat (and, in my case, the sweat) all mingled together. The idea of "personal space" was nonexistent outside of your home. I think Americans forget just how spacious our country is.

One day, our group was walking toward the Gateway of India, a monument towering over the sea of humanity. I too had a great vantage point, as I appeared to be the tallest person in the subcontinent at the time of my visit. We stopped in the Taj Mahal Hotel for a bit (later, the site of a terrorist attack, but a landmark hotel even then). In many places where rich and poor mingled, we noticed that security and police carried wooden sticks that were routinely used to threaten kids on the street.

As we approached the building, the crowd of about 20 children that had swarmed us for a few blocks suddenly vanished. Then, we walked into air-conditioning. And the lobby was beautiful. It was like we had teleported to Switzerland or Manhattan or something. It was serene, clean, and minimalist. *If each one of the children outside were permitted to enter just once, it could change them forever. Some of them, at least.* Travel broadens the mind. It has for me. Crossing that forbidden threshold for one of those kids might be like flying across the world for me. Money can buy stuff and experiences, but the impact of money is most keenly felt in terms of access.

On another day, we visited one of the largest slums in the city. It was several square miles and devoid of any municipal services. One of the themes of the course was the inequitable allocation of resources. Access, again. The view of the community from a distance was much like the *National Geographic* images that Americans have seen: the patchwork of sheet metal roofing and the large pipelines carrying drinking water through this community to the affluent. Entering the slum, the streets were about 15 feet across, just wide enough for rickshaws to navigate. The "streets," as I'm calling them, were not a product of city planning, but simply where the housing stopped and there was space between dwellings. There were no curbs, no stop lights, no traffic markings of any kind. And those streets were crowded and full of life.

We were meeting a community organizer of some kind. Stepping inside, the interior of his home and office was immaculate. As were the other private offices and homes we visited, as if the only way to maintain dignity within the squalor outside was to assert control over the environment in your own dwelling. Our host explained how the residents of this slum, tens of thousands of people, were rigging their own electricity and engineering their own plumbing in the absence of government support. The alternative was not to have them in any form. We were told rural poverty was even more difficult, and all the other land within the greater Mumbai area was already privately owned.

My lasting impression of this visit was that people would do what they must to survive. A stark contrast between the US and much of the world is that the US government provides some minimum protections. I've been told by homeless advocates that no one will starve in Milwaukee. In much of the world, you might well starve without some hustle. We forget that.

On the other hand, the US stifles entrepreneurship with regulation. You don't need a food truck license in Mumbai. You just go out and do it. In much of the world, the powers-that-be hand out nothing, but if you want to sell bootleg phones and watches on the street, they won't stop you. I don't know which system is better. In this slum, people lived independently from government support. They also ran the risk of their neighborhood being bulldozed for luxury condos. I had to cross the world to appreciate my civil rights as an American citizen.

It is harder to voice your frustration over not having the latest iPhone when you know not everyone has clean drinking water. Ironically, my time in India made asking for a raise much more difficult five years later, but that's another story. Everything is relative. I would like more to spend, to save, and to give, but #firstworldproblems.

And what makes us "*first* world" anyway? Better at colonizing? Ugh. The American exceptionalism we grow up learning in school implies that we are a wealthy country because we are the brightest. If anything, the most incredible ingenuity was on display when I visited India. As a student of history, I had read *Guns, Germs and Steel* by Jared Diamond by this time, a broad analysis of the geographic factors that allowed some people from some parts of the world to conquer and colonize others. Not above critique, the book nonetheless outlines theories that have merit, unlike cultural or genetic superiority. But a Western tourist abroad must wonder, "Why are things so much more comfortable where I'm from? Why is that?" Domesticable species for livestock improved farming and immunity to disease, latitudinal geography suited trade, and the lack of a dominant empire fueled eternal war among European nation-states, in turn accelerating weapons technology.

All financial success and struggle have a current. The engineers in the slum were succeeding in swimming against the current, but only to stay in place. The headwaters of those currents originated centuries earlier when the British invaded with better weapons and stole natural resources. The ability to survive was more impressive under the circumstances than a third-generation American college graduate getting a job making $50,000. With that relative advantage, that's the least they could do. When an American visits Mumbai, they may believe they have worked harder because they have more. Money doesn't work that way though. They slipped your boat into the river at the ideal spot, and you were whisked along. When the engineer from the slum gets a visa to study in the United States, they work their ass off because they understand that the economic bottom rung is lower than their American-born classmates realize.

The United States has always been a country defined by laws and immigration. Many immigrants are often unaccustomed to so many laws. In India, things don't happen unless you know the right people. The "law" is the human web of connection. Regulation in the United States does make entrepreneurship harder. Street vendors need licenses, and most people won't buy a watch on a street corner anyway. There is a safety net here, but you have to navigate the system.

The up-and-comer wants a "free" market where every vendor follows the rules. But free markets are free in theory only. In a Mumbai alley or Manhattan courtroom, the bullies usually win. The corporation wants to lobby the referee to swing the rules in their favor. I had a financial app idea for years, and in researching intellectual property law, I basically had to let it go or quit my job and lawyer up to take on big tech. This may be getting worse because we are so litigious: the hustle in America is in knowing the financial and legal web as much as working hard. (Look at what some people have been able to do with a team of lawyers.) So, when I hear a story about not trusting banks or Wall Street, I acknowledge the cultural and historical context. And I know that trying to thrive in America without leveraging these systems is like playing soccer with ankle weights. A good player can still score but after more effort.

The legal barriers to small businesses are created by big businesses lobbying the government to make it so. It's nice to be able to get out of my car in Wisconsin and not be swarmed by children peddling necklaces. But it's also bad that many children are stuck inside with TV since they have no hustle available to them; here, children need to be "supervised." It is hard for children to support meager family incomes, too. Not sure which is better. Neither is good. Which does more for a child's cognitive development? Hazardous street hustle? Or the "safety" of a screen?

Many immigrants don't want handouts. I know this because there is no safety net in many countries, so people originating from those countries are not conditioned to expect them. This is an American assumption based on our perspective. When my father-in-law fled El Salvador as a teenager after the government began to gun down his friends in the street, his first thought in Los Angeles wasn't to seek government assistance. Many immigrants hit the US economy with a clean slate, so to speak. Work, spend, save, and sacrifice. While America was far from perfect, my in-laws could leave their pain behind and have a fresh start. Over time, they regained basic security, which allowed them to focus on earning, and now they can send money back to their family in El Salvador. They plan to spend most of their old age there because home is where the heart is, but they'll be the first to tell you that the opportunity is in America. We're far from perfect, but immigrants keep coming so it can't be all bad.

When you have experienced serious risks to your safety, you realize that smaller risks are worth taking. With a billion people in India, I saw children run into traffic, fleeing the police. I saw four adults on a 500cc motorcycle. I saw men climb onto the train car roof and ride there. When you accept that help isn't coming, you tap into reserves of human innovation and resilience hidden from the psyche of the comfortable. People make decisions by comparing the worst-case scenario and the best-case. When that tradeoff is clear, we can act. When it's murky, we pause. Survival forces us to act quickly. Privilege allows us to pause for years.

In my naive, sheltered way, I took a risk choosing India. No one I knew well had been there. I got tropical disease vaccinations from the biggest needle I'd ever seen and limped my way around the dorm afterward. I didn't know anyone else who was going. I knew I would get stares traveling in public as a light-skinned giant. And it could have been an uncomfortable and unfulfilling three weeks. Unknowns are risky.

But my risk was rewarded because I discovered I was naive and sheltered. I met new friends who didn't look or think like my high school crowd. I ate an unprocessed, sugarless meal at a yoga institute. *I eat more sugar than I thought because this is awful.* I hung out of the open door of a speeding train to feel the breeze. I experienced what it feels like to be looked at and have people wondering why you are there. I discovered a rich culture and returned with more nuanced appreciation—and concern—about my own instead of accepting it as "the way." The more a person sees, the harder it becomes to judge anyone for anything. My identity became less fixed. I became kinder. My parents afforded me an experience that appreciates in value to this day, a gift that keeps on giving.

A Marcel Proust quote goes, "The real voyage of discovery consists not in seeking new landscapes, but in having new eyes." That's true, but in this case, it took a trip to new landscapes to return home with new eyes. I went to learn and absorb something about the wide world. Often people travel by carefully curating an experience that reinforces their "eyes" and costs a hell of a lot more, too. We stay in the hotel, instead of walking the street. Nothing ventured, nothing gained.

In my Milwaukee office overlooking Lake Michigan, a photo I took of a girl hangs on the wall. The blue of her dress is somehow reflected off the ocean water into her dark brown eyes, which search the camera. She followed me along the narrow walkway out to Haji Ali Dargah, a mosque in the bay. In moments of doubt, I look at her photo as a reminder that curiosity opens doors and to always see those who have had a different experience.

chapter twelve

"you gonna eat that?"

Wasting food has always bothered me. I have a fuzzy image of spitting out broccoli as a toddler, but since then, wasting food has *always* bothered me. To be fair, I have always had a pretty fast metabolism, and until my mid-twenties, I exercised a *lot*. I remember going through the high school cafeteria main line and then moving on to the "snack" type line in the middle, which was more packaged items like Pop-Tarts and then to the dessert line on the far right. My tray was heaped with items. It must have been like 10,000 calories, too.

Growing up, me in my teens and Nora four years younger, we went through a gallon of milk each day. I would have a bowl of cereal each morning and three pints with dinner. Thanks for not cutting me off, Mom. I've never been picky either: Wendy's, Hamburger Helper, California Pizza Kitchen, carrots, and any combination of toppings—I'll take it. Nora, on the other hand, would come home from school, microwave Home Run Inn pizzas, and remove all the cheese and toppings.

WTF? Being the 1990s and us having so many after-school activities, we ate a lot of processed food. One of my fondest childhood memories is returning from soccer practice on a cold, wet night in late fall or early spring, and demolishing a can of SpaghettiOs, from shelf to saucepan to mouth in 10 minutes.

Maybe I used to burn calories at such a rate that I thought of all of it as "fuel," anyway. I know my parents thought that way. My mother has been heard to say, "I wish I were a scarecrow, so I didn't have to eat or sleep. Such a waste of time." Logically, yes, I agree. You could get a lot done. Then without bathroom breaks? Wow. But not eating or sleeping?! My dad, while he hasn't been quoted in a comparable way, does perceive eating as a means to an end. In high school, he and I took a trip to Rocky Mountain National Park. It was an amazing trip, and we would eat Subway twice a day. No joke. Stop at Subway in Estes Park in the morning, order a sandwich, eat half then, and save half for lunch up in the mountains. Frankly, my two-foot sub was all I needed. I wanted to focus on hiking, driving, and exploring. We travel well together, focused on what we came for: the mountains.

Coming out of this family environment, I met Rebeca, Queen of Cravings. To this day, I have to breathe deeply and check my inner monologue when she says, "I want [oysters/McDonald's/Thai/ZOURS]" right when I'm about to sit down. I have moods, yes, but cravings? *Well, that's probably how she feels when I rub her shoulders, and she knows I'm after more than that …* That accounts for the craving, but what about the waste?

For every action, there is an equal and opposite reaction. The craving makes the purchase, and the body makes the final call. Like many dads, I eat the table scraps: bread crusts, soggy pancakes, etc. I truly am the bottom feeder of our household. I scrutinize the fridge for looming expiration dates. And I find them: sustenance met, container discarded.

My frustration with food waste is so extreme that I sacrifice my health for it, in two ways. First, I will eat well beyond satiation. "Are you full?" "Well, yeah, I've eaten a shit-ton of food." *But that's irrelevant! If the food is going to be wasted, then I will eat it.* Guilt around food waste has been repackaged into some version of bleeding-heart liberal gluttony. The second is eating beyond the expiration date. Expiration dates seem like a guess anyway, right? (Jerry Seinfeld did a great standup bit where the dairy cow calls back to the farmer milking her, "Juulyyy Thirrrrd.") So, yes, I occasionally spend more time in the bathroom than necessary, and I am 20 pounds overweight because I feel compelled to finish what we have paid for.

Our behavior as consumers is defined by the categories to which we apply this ideology and those we don't. For example, regarding food, Rebeca's group says, "Why stress? It isn't useful, and if it is, I don't want it anyway. Life is too short to stress throwing out 37 cents worth of chicken nuggets." This group does waste, but they also avoid the burden of excess. By contrast, when I hear people saying, "Well, you could do this, but you'd be living on ramen," I always think, *"Yes! I want to live on ramen so I can spend on all the other stuff!"*

In economics, the concept of durable versus nondurable goods is helpful. I tend to value the utility of durable goods. *We got those rock-climbing shoes seven years ago at a discount. They are in great condition. Renting shoes costs so much, but these will always "work," and therefore, we are not giving them away.* Rebeca, on the other hand? *Toss 'em.* She threw out an old ratty pair of my shoes without my permission, and I was pissed. From her perspective, it's hoarding. I am painting her as excessive, but we balance each other out. She is not high maintenance when it comes to clothes, home decor, and cars, to name a few. It's all funneled into food.

Food is cheap in the continental US. From its inception, our country has benefited economically and politically from exceptional physical geography. When studying in Europe in 2006, it caught me off guard that you have to *pay* for drinking water, and refills aren't free. In fact, beer was often cheaper than water.

Rebeca would justifiably criticize me when I would spend on alcohol. And I would criticize her when we would go out to eat for the third time that week because the total tab equaled another pair of rock-climbing shoes. This was a contentious issue but a central one to how people experience the world, and, more importantly, how we show our appreciation for others. She wanted me to know what excellent Thai tasted like. I wanted her to be dry when we went camping. We were both right.

Not all nondurable goods and services make it into the "meaningful experiences" category. Not all nondurable spending is memorable. I felt, and still feel, that getting buzzed on alcohol is worth it sometimes. It may bring people closer together, as sharing a drink lowers inhibitions, which may elevate authenticity. More than that, it can stimulate creative thinking (and disease and destruction, too). Even so, I've spent a lot on booze *just because.* The first time I did a budget, after rent, alcohol was my biggest monthly expense. It was a sobering moment, considering that a monthly budget is nothing but a reflection of values and a summary of habits. And spending is a transfer of energy. We can act out of fear and distraction or joy and optimism.

Much of the Millennial money stress is wrapped up in meaning.

"How can I waste food when people are starving?" I asked.

(The caricature of a Baby Boomer parent scolding "there are children starving in Africa" is rooted in reality, as all caricatures are.)

Rebeca asked, "How can you spend money on these extreme hobbies when you don't even do them that much?"

"At least I'm not actively wasting things like food!"

"It's such a luxury to just keep expensive things that you might use one day, knowing you'll never have them taken away."

And so on.

How can I buy an $11 cocktail when a pound of grain costs less? And how can I not finish my complimentary ice water when mothers walk two hours each day for clean drinking water? Sometimes I do, and sometimes I don't.

When I lived in Urbana-Champaign, the heart of the American breadbasket, and surrounded by corn and soybeans as far as the eye can see, I went to town on dorm food. Mainly because my freshman and sophomore dorm meal plans were three square meals a day, buffet-style. The sunk-cost effect is real: it is free, so my parents already sort of paid for it, so I will get their money's worth. I also worked in the kitchen and used to leave my late-night shift carrying a bag of cheeseburgers that would've been thrown out. When I'd see a homeless person, I'd give some away. Not all of them, come to think of it. My last undergrad course was in physical geography, and the professor anticipated burning through central Illinois topsoil completely by the mid-21st century, fueled mostly by the demand for cheap beef. But whatever, I *had* to get another burger. I mean, it was "free."

American portions and American consumption are fueled by excess. Preachy as I can be about food waste, I am too. The money lesson to be learned is that what is cheap is perceived to have less value. If I walked two hours a day for my water, I'd cherish it. If my meal plan said you could eat unlimited cheeseburgers, then I won't savor them. I studied abroad in England for a semester. I walked more, food cost more, and portions were smaller. Lo and behold, I lost weight. My relationship with food was improved by higher prices.

We spend on what we value. We value what we can see, hear, touch, taste, smell, fear, or desire. Are the last two senses? Not sure, but desire and fear are catalysts for behavior change. Their distilled cousins, want and worry, leave us in a rut. I want food more than I worry about the cost.

The fear is distant, but the desire is now. In the breadbasket of America, we are pushing carbs in large quantities. American commercial farmers produce a lot, and the market needs to figure out a way to use all that. Cheap food is full of the same ingredients used to fatten livestock for slaughter and is made addictive by very well-compensated chemists. It's beefing us up too, and, not unlike cows, we eat mindlessly and in excess. But why? Out of boredom? Ease of access? Unhealthy distraction from pain? There is so much money to be made in food. The seller just needs to spark the craving long enough and have it ready to go. They have no responsibility for long-term health outcomes. For most Americans, eating processed food is the most dangerous voluntary action they make.

We have plenty of food in this country. Unfortunately, the supply chain is pretty complex. I've seen students, family, and myself throw food away because it's hard to keep. Whether or not we can afford it is irrelevant. I bet a lot of well-to-do folks let their Whole Foods produce expire. The fresh cilantro looks great misting on the shelf and on the enchiladas that night, but what about next week when it is brown and leaking onto the lemons? *What recipe calls for a whole bunch of cilantro?* It's just harder to stomach waste when our cash is tight. Beyond that, wasting versus saving is a choice.

In my career, I haven't seen a correlation between income and a person's conviction to use things they paid for. Instead, small actions compound their effect over time. I have seen a strong correlation between financial outcomes and the focus on buying only what you'll use and using what you buy. That daily discipline of deliberate, intentional choices builds momentum on a $10,000 a month income or $1,000.

I've also been to business events and fundraisers where the waste from one meal must be hundreds of pounds of food. The structure of the event has as much to do with tax law and publicity as conscious generosity. Spend money to make money: an excellent entrée or open bar equals more donations. I know next to nothing about the hospitality industry other than that. And that a lot goes into crafting a memorable experience, including many items wasted. I do know that businesses can deduct unused food as an expense and avoid paying taxes on it. So, the financial system pushes them to focus on filling the room instead of predicting consumption.

Rebeca approaches food as most people do: after it's on her plate, it is a sunk cost. A sunk cost in business is defined as one already incurred and cannot be recovered. *The food is here, and I can't get my money back, so I can do as I wish.* I approach food with the sunk-cost effect, defined in psychology as the tendency to continue the fruitless endeavor if the resources have already been spent. *I paid for it, so I will clean my plate at all costs.* Both are sloppy effects of market-based decisions.

What if an innovator were to figure out how to reduce waste? David McCullough's biography *Truman* tells the story of a tireless worker, molded by hardship, who cared deeply about people. Before he became president, Harry Truman oversaw a government agency that prevented waste in the supply chain for World War II. He knew we needed to defeat the Nazis, but he hustled to prevent waste along the way, not wanting to let taxpayers' dollars evaporate into grift and inefficiency since they had sacrificed so much already. His State of the Union Address in 1949 included the powerful line, "Poverty is just as wasteful and just as unnecessary as preventable disease."

In the 21st century, the people who can influence others or devise an algorithm to predict consumption and redistribute will have a profound impact on our world and will be compensated financially when a larger business, or the government, can fund and scale the model. If health and wealth have a compounding effect, then let's problem-solve what's coming instead of consuming what is.

Is food too perishable to respond to changing market demands, though? The UN airdrops bags of grain and wheat, not the cheeseburgers remaining at closing time. The college buffet is a classic example of a sunk cost. College kids are too immature not to waste, hungover or not. Working in that kitchen, I would throw out all the burgers, French toast, and chicken; you name it. It was in my job description. Think of all the water needed for the beef cattle. Think of malnourished children in drought-stricken places. The most fundamental human need is completely out of balance because of market value forces. There isn't a strong financial incentive to redistribute food. *If I'm paid to throw it out, why can't I be paid to hand it out?*

A decade later in Beijing, my friend and I stayed in the business district at the Ritz Carlton, where there were few tourists, especially in winter. The breakfast buffet was unreal. Dumplings and sushi—and I can't do it justice as a non-foodie. It was decadent, spectacular, and all the more so as a buffet. Food consumption, being an experience as well as a necessity, is hard to predict. How much will we need? Will they like it? Breaking bread is a real thing. Every person on Earth needs to eat. But this decadence was on another level. Often, we observe a transaction as easy, but the work always happens first, to be ready just in case.

Relaxing in the Ritz—enjoying strong coffee in the morning, tea in the afternoon, and cocktails at night—I felt spoiled. Day by day, I began to shift my feelings from guilt to worthiness. In that nourishing environment, I read *On Writing* by Stephen King. I thought about how I would finish writing this book, a scary endeavor. The luxurious surroundings and attentive staff made me feel worthy. My self-esteem was buoyed by afternoon tea brought to me in a soft leather chair, surrounded by abundance. How might my self-esteem be affected if my grain bag was thrown off the back of a United Nations truck?

Access to that excess made me feel…wonderful. *I'm so confused. Is this awesome or not?*

Bearing witness to staggering inequality takes an emotional toll. We can deal with avoidance or create a causal story about why some are more deserving than others. Fixing the problem should give humanity an equivalent emotional boost.

Of course, it's complicated and will require some experimentation to figure out. Capitalism's need to follow the money created inequality. Socialism can redirect money to capitalists who solve problems. Governments need foundations and startups to troubleshoot first because they don't want to put taxpayer money toward a failure. But failures are often necessary to find a success.

As a culture, we seem to care about food quality now. The next step is food waste, followed by waste of all kinds. Instead of sending stuff to a landfill, can we ship it somewhere else? If we are to cut back, we need to rebrand hand-me-downs. Not rich or poor, but caring, passing memories. It's not fair to tell the growing middle class in India, China, and Brazil that they should eat less meat and buy fewer things. Some things you have to try yourself in order to know if it's worth it. Including hollow consumerism. Jim Carrey said he wished everyone could be rich and famous just so they would know that it alone is not enough to be fulfilled.

The thing about food is that our relationship with it, for better or worse, is a constant. It's a relationship we can't opt out of, and our interactions happen daily. In psychology, the frequency of an action will diminish our perception of its significance. But any daily action repeated often enough has tremendous impacts over time. Twenty minutes of daily aerobic activity. Ten minutes of mindful meditation. One hour of mindless social media. I'll never get back the time I spent inventing a use for half an onion at the eleventh hour. What is the dollar value of the food that expires in our fridge each year? Until very recently, I've been scared to estimate. But $100 a month of reduced food spending for four decades, set aside monthly into an investment account earning 6% interest on average, would amount to $200,000. Little things add up.

Confusing things further is that food can be very cheap or very expensive, taste very good or very bad, and be prepared very easily or be very time-consuming. Food is a refuge; food is a need; food is an addiction; food is a joy. Without a doubt, that a McChicken is available everywhere, tastes awesome, exactly resembles the last one the customer ate, and costs them $1, this is a remarkable capitalist feat. So, it is no surprise the corporation is doing quite well. They are meeting market demand. But what's the energy in the drive-thru? Either: (a) I'm in a rush, (b) I want to eat out, and this is my price range, (c) I'm craving this (or my kids are), and I know exactly what my fix will do for me, or (d) I'm distracting myself. Compare this to driving a thousand miles for a family reunion, where your uncle has been smoking the meat since yesterday, your grandmother almost shares her famous secret recipe, and you sit down with loved ones. All actions are imbued with a spirit, and we accept food made by a machine instead of a person at a cost.

Rebeca and I have met halfway on the food issue. After ten years of marriage and meal plan trial and error, we don't waste as much, and we eat better than before. For something that we will continue doing as long as we breathe, ten years of struggle is well worth it physically and financially. She has acknowledged her sugar problem, and I have admitted that gastrointestinal reflux disease isn't thrifty if I end up getting cancer. When we eat food that nourishes us, it makes us feel better, gives us more energy, and helps our financial and parenting outcomes.

Ice cream is the exception. That's always worth it.

chapter thirteen

SOC 100

My love of history has never waned throughout my life. My freshman year at the University of Illinois gave me a window into true scholarship. I had wonderful teachers in high school, but now I could have wonderful teachers that spoke from a century-old stage in Lincoln Hall, at a land-grant university founded in 1867. The history was palpable. I've always been in tune with a sense of place. I spent much of college wandering through campus, listening to Death Cab for Cutie (nighttime) or Guster (daytime). The sycamore trees were sprawling and majestic, and the wrought-iron lamp posts flooded the quad with warm yellow light from incandescent bulbs. I could feel the idealism and ambition of my peers and me taking shape. I could sense the expectation for our future. I was grateful to spend four years as a college student. A young employee who takes some classes at night doesn't have the same experience.

I took Sociology 100 in Altgeld Hall. The professor was excellent.

How much unsung praise do we owe teachers? I knew I would love the course because I've always loved psychoanalyzing everybody. I took a basic psych and economics course in high school, but sociology was new. I didn't know what to expect. Looking back on it, what an enormous undertaking. This was a concert hall. It probably held a few thousand people and looked about half full the first day of class. Pretty much the whole College of Liberal Arts and Sciences had to take it. U of I was fairly segregated socially, meaning that most dorms attracted by reputation predominantly students of color, engineering majors, artists, or athletes. In the Union and on the street, underclassmen groups self-selected. But this course had everyone: rich/poor, farm country/Chicago, every shade of skin color, and many different majors. The professor, in a personable, thoughtful, and tactful way, gave weekly lectures to around a thousand 19-year-olds explaining some of the ways the great-grandparents of some of us exploited the great-grandparents of others of us.

Through this class I was introduced to statistics. I had a lot of ideas to shape my worldview but not a lot of data. Like most people, regardless of age, I equated financial health with income. Make more money, then buy a better house, better clothes, more vacations, etc. Less income equaled less wealth equaled less power. And more equaled more equaled more.

This liberal arts course, not my economics courses, overturned that simplistic assumption. I didn't understand assets. I didn't understand how the transfer of assets had a greater impact on wealth than income. (My dad giving me his car for free didn't click until then.) The transfer of assets and the competition for scarce resources is what turns the wheel of history in Westeros and in our world. Innovation and creativity aim to make the wheel non-violent.

Most media messages tell us to make more money, so in turn we can spend more money. The point of college is to go and learn so that we can get a job, and apply our knowledge and skills in exchange for compensation. For a 19-year-old like me, income was the only focus, the only measurable in close enough proximity to care. Property values, retirement funds, and estate planning didn't exist for me. If I had a concrete professional track like teaching, with transferable skills like teaching, then I knew I would find a job earning something. With my parents earning "enough," I didn't really think about what salary was "enough" for me alone. I wouldn't have student loans or a car payment. My memory of that time is that my friends and I talked a lot about what we wanted to be but very little about what we wanted to earn. (I observe with new clients that a focus on earning, for most people, comes once they take on commitments.)

Back to assets … What I didn't understand at the time was how my Black and Latino classmates would have such a harder time climbing the ladder to wealth than I would. After all, we were getting the same education, right? Well, yes, but it wasn't free, and schools are always eager to take tuition dollars. In job interviews, discrimination was real. I knew that. I also knew that women made less doing the same work. And now I'm hearing that assets are the real story.

Take real estate. "Real property" is, by definition, any property that is "affixed to the land." The land is valuable, right? The Gold Rush, The Homestead Act, Plymouth Rock, or 40 acres and a mule, you name it, people are very motivated to acquire land. But was access to land always equal? No, of course not. Schools today are defunding social studies because kids are falling behind in math and reading. I'd say that if the kids had a better understanding of social studies, they'd be more moti-vated to improve their math and reading.

Centuries ago, if you had the balls, the money, and/or the firepower, you could just steal land. Three hundred years ago, European powers began to realize that the amount of land was finite. The colonization of Africa began, and speculators left en masse for the so-called New World. Two hundred years ago, most people were either: (a) subsistence farmers, eking out a living on crummy land that rich people didn't want, or (b) earning wages or basic room and board to tend and enrich the land of the wealthy, aptly named "landed gentry." One hundred years ago, the American West was finally starting to fill up, and the *Downton Abbey* lifestyle was in decline. The Industrial Revolution made fortunes for the "titans of industry" or "robber barons" (depending on which newspaper you read). Those who could continued to acquire land and property.

I learned back in high school about "Manifest Destiny," or the idea that the United States should expand control, democracy, and capitalism across the entire North American continent at all costs *because God said so*. Manifest Destiny *is* American history. That ideology drove the accumulation of *stuff*. Pre-stock market, the most valuable *stuff* you could have was land. It had grass to graze cattle, which could feed you and other people. It might have had minerals like copper or natural resources like timber. If you operated in an economy of scarcity, supply, and demand, you understood that owning land meant leverage. And if you had the firepower, you could create leverage where none existed.

Take this example. In the movie *3:10 to Yuma* (the new version), railroad thugs force Christian Bale off his land. They dam the river upstream, preventing it from flowing onto his land. (This crazy water policy is still in effect.) His character moved there in the first place because his son had respiratory issues or something, and needed a dry climate. (Healthcare has always been expensive, see?)

On top of that, some land is simply nicer than others. The *Planet Earth* miniseries made it pretty clear that much of Earth's land can't support permanent human life. Even less is farmable, which is the primary sustenance or revenue generator. Other land, like beaches or mountaintops, is scenic or exceptional, meaning you can charge people a lot to see it or live there. Water is valuable because it's nice and because it's good for shipping. The Illinois Canal, from Peoria to Chicago, brought major cash to the Midwest because a barge could go from New York to Chicago to New Orleans, making deliveries along the way. Manifest Destiny was propaganda as well because the backbreaking and dangerous work of claiming and clearing forests in (justifiably) hostile Indian Territory was done by those who didn't have a better, safer option back east. And, as always, immigrants. They cleared the way for the "free" markets that propelled industrial growth.

The Dutch purchased the island of Manhattan for something like $24, which, adjusted for inflation, would be only $1,143 as I write this. The narrative could be that the local tribes were suckers. More likely, they didn't conceive that people could really "buy" the Earth, nor realize that, by sheer historical accident, European-borne disease would wipe out 90% of their population.

Today, Indigenous peoples of the Americas have been relegated to the forgotten corners of the country. The Black Hills of South Dakota are sacred to the Lakota tribes, so the American government, in a total f**k-you move, built Mount Rushmore right in the middle. There's a fee to see Mount Rushmore and to go to Custer State Park. After we claimed the land for ourselves, we exiled Indigenous peoples to empty grazing land with little access to services or a livelihood.

I made a service trip in college to the Cheyenne River Reservation. The town of Dupree, South Dakota was weighted with sad resignation, severed from their land in spirit and conferred "ownership" in the White man's way. Being removed from the mainstream public eye by hundreds of miles of empty space and a chasm of cultural identity, rural poverty on reservations is different than urban poverty. This is a loss of identity that I'll never fully appreciate. The guilty conscience of US government policymakers pushed Indigenous peoples deep into the dark corners of collective memory as if hoping Americans wouldn't realize our "exceptionalism" came from good ol' fashioned bullying on a brutal scale. Residents of Dupree have to drive hours to even get to a large retail store. *So, if you don't work at the gas station/mini food mart, where could you work?*

The Southwestern third of the present-day United States once belonged to Mexico and was won by military conquest. The Mexican-American War, the Civil War's less-noble contemporary, shifted millions of acres from Mexico to the US, a transfer of assets that dictates trade negotiations and international influence in our favor to this day. The US has always been a nation of immigrants; for many, not by choice.

The capture, enslavement, and import of Africans propelled American industry. Assets dictate history. In hindsight, it may seem that the Confederacy was horrific for moral reasons alone and was motivated to maintain the system of slavery for purely selfish reasons. *How the hell could people do that?*

Given the value of assets, let me challenge the 21st-century perspective a bit. Let's say you're 35 in the 1860s. You have three kids, and you earn a middle-class living, with about $1,000 a month after your bills are paid, to save long term, buy a new sofa, eat out, whatever. You own a home worth $150,000. You own slaves worth $100,000. They were inherited from your mother's family; you haven't purchased any new human property. Legislation from Washington decrees that your slaves are free.

Might you create a narrative that makes it easier to hold on to $100,000 worth of property? Would it be easier to "believe" that your slaves are happy? Easier to hate the Northern industrialists far away who think they know best? Even Abraham Lincoln, a man who valued fairness, wasn't in favor of racial equality as we understand it today. He was opposed to the expansion of slavery. He was not in favor of emancipation until he felt it was an effective military move and realized how intractable the South was.

What if we developed AI robots that can perform all the tasks of judgment that humans can? You buy one for $100,000, then ten years later, the government rules that AI robots have feelings and must be released. Is that easier to imagine?

Transfer of assets, indeed. African Americans, given freedom in 1865 (in theory), faced legal barriers to homeownership in many neighborhoods (called redlining) for another 100 years and institutional discrimination to this day. My grandfathers both bought houses after World War II. They could buy where they wanted. Price point was the only barrier. They weren't given a higher interest on their mortgage. In the neighborhood where my parents grew up, homes increased in value as they became more desirable when more people moved into the area. The value of these homes factored into my grandparents' estate in some way, and that legacy was passed to my parents, who now have a home themselves that is appreciating in value. They live in Palatine, Illinois, a suburb of Chicago.

A house comparable to theirs in a Black neighborhood in Milwaukee is worth about a third as much. For the same home.

So, the brother sitting a few seats down the aisle from me in that dimly lit, musty-smelling Sociology 100 lecture hall might have the same grades as me, and his parents might have earned the same amount as mine do. But his grandfather's home was more modest because back then job prospects were limited for people like his grandfather. His grandfather's home also did not appreciate in value at the same rate as my grandparents' homes because Black folks tend to remain in Black neighborhoods, which were devalued by public policy divestment and racial profiling. If he sold his home for less than he bought it for, he couldn't deduct the loss on his income taxes, even though losses on other types of investments are allowed. Just a kick-'em-when-they're-down tax rule I first heard about from an interview with law professor Dorothy Brown. The public school he attended was funded by property taxes, which are, generally speaking, proportional to property values. So, his school had to stretch every dollar further in order to keep up with mine. Adjusted for sociology, his grades are now far better than mine.

That class taught me that assets are concentrated in the hands of a few. Assets typically appreciate, freeing more capital to buy more assets, compounding the trend. Asset disparity, not income disparity, is the argument for reparations.

At 11:50 am, the lecture ended, and all of us streamed toward the exit back onto the vista of the main quad, filled with the frisbee, tanning, and loitering of youth. The brother down the aisle may have looked out and thought, "They have no idea. This is so unfair." The weight of our ancestors is heavy on the shoulders of a teenager. I was able to push it out of my mind, looking at beautiful girls and thinking about where I would get drunk that night, promising to revisit this troublesome issue when I had the inclination and the time.

Fortunately, it seems that more people are becoming aware of racism in recent years. Unfortunately, the pattern of oppression is the same old story. Partly by circumstance and partly by the choices I've made, I've been exposed to a lot more than some peers. Middle-class childhood, close relationships with wealthy and poor people, multiracial school, and work community, this all makes code-switching easier, and my advice more in context and accessible. If ignorance is bliss, then is awareness sobering? Once you take SOC 100, an introduction to the study of social problems, you are either unaffected and complicit, or you are ... what? I don't know, but there's no going back.

Our country has done things that are really f**ked up, *and* it has created an environment where many find abundance. We contain multitudes. The financial math does not discriminate. Access to it does. We can't look at Sweden's public policy and how everyone there seems to magically love sharing and think we can replicate it, given our nation's traumatic history.

We can seek to understand trauma moving forward, but our nation's original sin of slavery cannot be undone. As a culture, we are mired in that false narrative that the more you lose, the more I win. If others get more, I must be missing something. Not true. Wealth is not a zero-sum game, but a scarcity mentality makes it so. Those consciously seeking to uphold racist policies are generally in two camps: the elite who stand to lose a lot financially from improved labor standards (from the Confederate slaver to the modern meat-packing corporation) and the struggling, marginalized Whites that have nothing to cling to except the fact that at least they aren't Black or Brown. Our history is the elite Whites using the marginalized Whites to perpetuate a culture war of scarcity to draw attention away from the real battle for power: the one for assets. They whisper, "If we can keep them arguing over race and religion-based culture wars, we can fortify our culture by growing wealth behind the scenes." When we come together long enough, we realize everybody is just trying to get through the day and do their thing. Even "foreign invaders" buy groceries and buckle their toddlers' seat belts. Exposure softens the fear.

But fear sells. Legal contracts do not. And if you've listened to a victim of trauma, you know that logic doesn't always carry the day.

Dissent is patriotic. If some liberals continue to be so politically correct and judgmental and some conservatives wistfully return to our flawed past rather than our present and future, our country will have issues. And that's fine, as long as we're working on them. Culture wars aren't helpful because one view will never win. Me feeling ashamed because my ancestors were White and benefited from racist land grabs does not help the present or future. Me withholding a tough message of accountability to a colleague or client because I know they face prejudice is not helpful to them. Acknowledge and get on with the work. Dwelling on my feelings makes it about me. No one wants to be at a party with college Brett when he's in a mood.

Financial incentives are bipartisan. I've spoken to conservative and liberal clients alike about how to use tax breaks and government subsidies. Any solution must acknowledge the power of self-interest. If our current system brought us here, perhaps an updated system can take us where we want to go. Democrats and Republicans alike accept Medicaid and food share if they qualify, so money must be bipartisan.

Does money always make everything better? No, but our spending reflects values. If we increase spending on social services, then we can decrease spending on law enforcement. Aboriginal people in Australia received reparations. I won't make a policy statement on reparations here, but African Americans and Indigenous peoples were robbed. When the thief is caught, don't we compensate the victim? Drive across the Great Plains, and you see miles of ranchland, separated from the freeway by a few strings of barbed wire. These groups didn't have a fair shot at ownership of that land; it was stolen before they had rights in our legal system. Every square mile is growing in value. More people equals more demand, but the supply stays the same.

In accounting, the land will keep its value, without any work on the owner's part, while real and personal property depreciates. You can write off the depreciation on your truck, but the land value just magically grows. In studying for the CERTIFIED FINANCIAL PLANNER™ exam, I learned a lot about tax law, and fiscal and monetary policy. This knowledge is not secret, but it isn't promoted either. The message that is promoted to the public at large is: "Please work harder so you can make more so you can spend more on things that don't hold value. We want you to walk in and buy. What you leave with will immediately drop in value, or depreciate, whether you use it or not. Your spending boosts our corporation's stock price, and—unlike your stuff—stock is an appreciating asset."

I dedicated this book to James Bell, an African American advisor and friend who chooses to think abundantly despite all this. And I asked our firm's managing partner Steve Holter to write the foreword for the book because he is making diversity and inclusion a deep priority, beyond public lip service. In the twilight of his career, frankly, he doesn't have to do that. He made a powerful choice. He could cruise to retirement, but he took this on wholeheartedly. He embraced a vision of abundance for all.

At the time of writing, my practice remains inclusive and diverse by household income, race, sexual orientation, and age. As a team, our commitment is to give every person the time and emotional space they need to make meaningful progress. Rather than try to change human nature or the past, I'm working on how to create a financial advising model for marginalized Americans. Its advisors will understand financial challenges in the context of social challenges: one without the other, and we fall short of our potential.

chapter fourteen

the "Urban Plunge"

Once I let go of the past and certain bro/douche attachments, I found incredible opportunities at the University of Illinois. Alternative Spring Break attracted a core group of young people committed to social justice, and that group, with some support from the University YMCA, deployed service-learning trips all over the country partnering with local nonprofits working on wide-ranging issues.

I worked on conservation in Kentucky and learned the how local economies shoulder the burden for invasive species management. I built wheelchair ramps in Nashville, learning just how expensive having a disability is, and just because Supplemental Security Income (SSI) might keep you off the street, it does not "set you up." I learned about migrant labor rights in the Rio Grande Valley and how fear equals leverage. I went to the Cheyenne River Reservation in South Dakota and felt … it's hard to say … These trips were immersive. They included everything I loved: new people, new locations, volunteering, adventure, and mentoring. *And inwardly judging others less enlight-ened than me.*

I love the sensations of a new environment: sights, smells, sounds slightly different than back home. Staying in your comfort zone is certainly easier. Less confusion, less judgment. The aforementioned "core group" included some people I'm still friends with today, people who I felt captured the spirit of social justice and service as well as bright-eyed college kids could. On the periphery were one-time attendees who weren't always sensitive to the environments we found ourselves in. This raised a question. When it comes to inequality, which in our world is measured in Haves and Have-nots, is a botched attempt to reconcile better than no attempt at all?

If an idealistic 20-year-old goes to engage with a marginalized group, and says something insensitive, would both parties be better off if they never went? If yes, what should they do instead? Never interact in any way? Give $50 online and be done with it?

The most emotionally charged service trip I went on was to Washington, D.C. It was organized and hosted by the National Coalition for the Homeless. The peak experience of the trip, preceded and followed by a few days of traditional volunteer experiences and workshops, was dubbed the "Urban Plunge," a 48-hour experience in which we were paired with another student, dressed in clothing that could pass for something worn by a person living on the street, and we … role-played being homeless, without money or phones. It sounds coarse, but the NCH is largely staffed by people who were or are living on the street. They preferred the term "street people" because it defined what they had, not what they lacked. Now it's unhoused. New language, same problem.

The first night outside, it dropped into the 30s. We slept over a hot air vent right along the wall of some federal building. It was cold. Anyone who's worked or spent long periods of time outside knows that it's not easy to warm up once you get cold. We spent each day in pairs, and each night as a whole group with our guide. He woke us up at 5:00 am, because the security guards did their first sweep around that time. I learned that our guide had ended up on the street after his schizophrenia symptoms worsened. He told us he'd been an art major, and had made it work in college, but he couldn't keep a job thereafter. He couldn't afford a place to live and afford his medication at the same time. Having one without the other didn't work either. So, he slipped into homelessness, afraid to seek help. Lack of healthcare is a leading cause of homelessness. Laziness is not.

I sat alongside Jimmy, a man of about 70 years old, who was panhandling along Pennsylvania Avenue. He had seen six or seven presidents parade past, all the way back to Gerald Ford. He gave me the Starbucks cup he was collecting change in. His message "just keep filling the cup" was a story of optimism.

Being avoided by other human beings has a psychological effect. It sounds obvious in writing, but pause, close your eyes, and imagine: you spend a day watching hundreds of people pass by and the only ones who make direct eye contact with you are hostile. My partner and I would sit on the sidewalk, with a hat out in front of us, and people who looked just like our peers, our parents, us …would act like we didn't exist. Again, the takeaway from this experience was to acknowledge, even if only through eye contact and a nod. I almost always say no when I get hit up for money, but human interaction …well, that I can give.

It seemed, especially in a frenetic city like our capital, that it wasn't so much our physical appearance, but the lack of a clear objective or destination that set us apart. We had nowhere to go. We found ourselves in parks a lot getting a breather from the hum of the sidewalks. In the middle of the day, parks in D.C. are filled with the homeless.

On our second day, we got talking to a man about 30 years old. It was one-sided. He talked about "The Man" and the system and so on. He got more and more heated, gesturing wildly, screaming, angry. My partner and I were sitting on a park bench, him standing in front of us, in the middle of a park covering a city block. Not a conversation to ditch easily. I was scared, my heart racing. Later, I wondered if he was messing with us. Then again, I often see homeless people talking to themselves.

An aging Vietnam veteran on the street is to be expected, but we were not. A couple times each day, we were engaged by passersby that hoped to understand exactly what happened to us. How could *we* sink to this low? (Only once did a guy ask us slyly if we were really homeless; he'd heard about this program from another guy on the street associated with the Coalition.)

Okay, so there it is. I paid money to pretend to be homeless. What a prick. I get that it sounds strange, but I did learn from it. Offensive? To some, I am sure it was and is. Worthwhile? It was for me and thousands of others who have done it with the endorsement of the National Coalition for the Homeless. Basically, you are treated like garbage, and it's physically and emotionally difficult. One way to cope with trauma is by developing a callousness and cynicism to survive, but that mindset makes it harder to thrive sometimes after the threat is removed.

When I shared with my wife how meaningful this experience was, she ridiculed me. We were driving in the car, and she made me feel like such a sucker. *Who is she to tell me that I can't find meaning in a personal experience? I could have chosen Daytona Beach instead.* She had a point, though. When we have an experience that moves us, it pushes us beyond the mundane realm of our own worries and wants, but who was I to play pretend poverty when I knew people living it? We were both wrong. We were both right. So it goes with meaning behind money.

Those living on the margins of income are affected most by government policy. Those in poverty and the 1% have the most to gain or lose by changes. I don't have the answer to homelessness. If it were easy to solve, it would have been by now. I just know it isn't a choice. Maybe sleeping outside alone is safer than some shelters, but homelessness itself is not a first choice. If mental or physical health challenges, including addiction, keep people from working, can we make a collective choice to treat disease? Cancer can always rally funding because cancer affects us all, often very suddenly and close to home. Are we all affected by homelessness? Or is it "their problem?" The estranged brother living on the street out west slipped away slowly, by degrees. He pushed you away. His fate is easier to rationalize when we tell ourselves "he made his choices."

Universal basic income is closer to the American spirit of free will and free markets than siloed government services are. The idea is that all people get a stipend that matches living at poverty level in that area, without a means test. Currently, whether your family helps you or the government does or both, there's a means test, which comes with judgment. All citizens get it. The idea of universal basic income is gaining some traction, for a few reasons. One is that governments, schools, and parents are not doing a great job making children ready for the types of jobs that are available, and the total future jobs could be declining drastically from automation and AI. Should the child be punished when the job just isn't there upon graduation? Basic income could be funded all or in part by taxes on big tech. If that sounds too socialist, consider how powerful these monopolies are, given how they organize and harvest data. Another is that $1,000 a month will mean more to a lower-income household, impacting their quality of life and injecting money into the economy by consumer spending. For higher-income earners, it will not represent enough of their total income to disincentivize work, except maybe to allow for decent family leave. For middle-bracket earners, it may be just enough to invest in themselves after putting it off. Another reason is that a simpler system reduces the motive to game the system because it's harder. Those more willing to manipulate the system won't get more than those playing fair. (*Yes, liberal elite, people are gaming the system. Gasp!*)

I don't blame people for doing so either. It's human nature and the rules are designed with that in mind. Even the most socialist client will want to minimize taxes. Navigating government services takes some doing. A phone, uninterrupted blocks of time and some persistence are required. Personally, I like that the individual is given choice when the means test is removed. Save on rent, then get a car. Skip the car, then don't need a roommate. Live with your mother and share the stipend. Choice is a freedom, perhaps the most empowering gift of all. That's what lifts people up.

By design, something universal moves us from a calculating market dollar value and back to inherent human value. All people fortunate enough to live in our country could receive this. A means-tested system forces the individual to prove their human value to receive assistance. *Or do they prove a lack of value?* They get a yes or no answer. All-or-nothing thinking, in food stamps and in politics, is not realistic or healthy, and it further restricts choice. Any system will have drawbacks. I'm just pointing out that we can afford to be kinder as a nation.

I've heard it said that what we really want is the ability to live life on our own terms. Much of success hinges on our ability to separate what we can control from what we cannot. Locus of control, hierarchy of needs, and other psychological frameworks can very thoroughly explain how being homeless is difficult. Why would someone choose this?

When I hear people say homeless people are lazy, not even working, I'd like to remind them that being outside all the time isn't easy, not having any space truly your own isn't easy, and becoming emotionally vulnerable in exchange for money isn't easy. Getting a $5 bill after being ignored by 100 people isn't empowering. I needed to feel that before I could *really* understand it.

Personal growth is hard. Voluntary discomfort is always a risk. And why even try to leave my comfort zone when I will inevitably offend someone? Rebeca and I admitted we both had valid ideas, both caught in a messy reality not of our making. For a while, there was a tent city under the Marquette Interchange, a gateway to downtown Milwaukee from the freeway and train station. This was a visible reminder of human struggle on the way to dinner or a concert. If a person like me could be "canceled" for pretending to be homeless and seeking perspective, then I guess I should just drive past, not ask questions, not risk it. Which is what I did when I drove past 15 years after the Urban Plunge.

Then the following year, the tent community under the freeway was gone, replaced with bulldozers and job site fences. Problem solved.

"dang, look at those shoes"

During my summers in college, I worked at a place called Lake Valley Camp (LVC). I loved absolutely everything about it. As the weather started to warm my first spring semester in college, my mom mentioned that K-Mart was hiring for the summer, so I immediately panicked and started researching a better alternative. Working at LVC introduced me to best friends, the beautiful Driftless Area of Wisconsin, romantic relationships that helped me grow up, and an experiential education side of the youth work that I came to love.

LVC provided summer programming for young people in Milwaukee who qualified for free/reduced lunch program and were recommended by their teacher for the experience. Therefore, they generally came from low-income families, and did not have diagnosed, severe emotional-behavioral challenges.

The middle-school boys in my cabin would often clean their shoes during the after-lunch "rest and reading" period. As in, walk up to the bathroom, and, with spools of paper towels, water, and often hand soap, gently revive their Jordans back to mint condition. *I just don't get it.* First, they were made for hooping in, right? Second, we are at a summer camp in the middle of nowhere. Why did they bring them at all? And if they wanted to show off their new kicks at the dance, which I could relate to, then why not bring another pair of old crappy shoes? The space under my bed and the trunk of my car were filled with a 50/50 split of pretty nice shoes designed for some specific type of sport (soccer, basketball, trail running) and the most beat-up pairs of footwear that I just couldn't part with because of our long history together, like the Birkenstock sandals with my left heel worn through to the ground.

Sometimes a scuff or smudge was too hard to remove, which was a tough blow for the young man in question. For the uninitiated, a pair of entry-level Jordans for basketball could be $150, the Jordan low for streetwear somewhere around $80. Not cheap for any kid outgrowing shoes every year. When I asked why they cared so much about them, they told me it was the whoopin' waiting next week for a pair of scuffed, muddy shoes that left the house brand new. Was that the motivator for free time shoe cleaning? Or just typical 13-year-old posturing for girls? I didn't get it. *Why would they have nicer shoes than me? Not only that, why did they rib my beat-up shoes so much? At least I have options. And at least I have shoes I can afford.*

That same simple and unexpressed thought surfaces thousands of times each day in America. *They spend so much on that? They get a scholarship, but they still want to do that?* I keep in touch with many of them to this day. I came to know and care for these guys. They were intelligent and caring, creative and daring. *He's up in the bathroom cleaning those shoes but he dropped his fresh drawers out on the muddy back steps … what is the deal. It's not attention to detail in all things.*

At age 19 I had much to learn about the ways of the world, yet I had the certainty of a teenager. My first summer at LVC was my first expe-rience living with people who were categorized as "low-income." That is all the participants, and probably about a third of the staff as well, who were full-time college students with financial aid. It's easy to spend three hours in a home, a neighborhood, a city, and have no idea what it's like to live there. Living together goes much further. Our psyche is a product of a 24/7 sensory cycle, and environments. That's why travel broadens the mind. Watching a show, reading a book, having a conversation with someone who was there … not the same. The senses are borrowed, not experienced.

And it's worth saying, for most of the kids in my cabin those summers, it was their first time living with someone like me too. It was equally ludicrous to them that I would be seen in public wearing my crappy Asics or Chacos or Sambas. But it's easier to be unfashionable when you believe in your soul that one day you'll have a future, with your own house, a job that you like, a vacation once or twice a year. If you don't think that life is possible, if you expect a dead-end job, if you feel that college acceptance is possible, but graduation is not, if you wonder if you will be evicted next week, well then … at least you have some fly kicks.

The American Dream is the bigger house and the nicer car. It's easier to have the shoes of your dreams than the car of your dreams, and a luxury car is easier than a luxury house. And if you could seemingly never have the house, or the car, who wouldn't take the shoes? Gotta start somewhere. *And besides, if a gunshot woke you up in the night, then you had to take two city buses to get to school, where you couldn't learn the math lesson because some other kids were harassing the teacher because they didn't eat breakfast, and their uncle has been staying over and he's an alco-holic, and then you find needles in the park by your house, and your mom comes home pissed off because her supervisor yelled at her after he changed her hours without notice, and then you can't fall asleep because the sirens keep going till late* …If that was a typical day for your child, and one thing you could do to make them smile was buying some nice Jordans, wouldn't it be worth it?

And let's say you accepted that shoes weren't going to improve your kid's quality of life, and you wanted to save up to move somewhere else. So, you saved $200 a month for a year, enough for a security deposit in a nice neighborhood and a little buffer for rent. And then you're laid off, because, well, your position is replaceable, and you weren't accepting as many shifts lately because you were making a concerted effort to spend more time with your child after they get home from school (so they're not at the park with the needles). And one month without any money coming in wiped out those savings in a few weeks. So, what was the point in the first place? Maybe you should've just bought some Jordans, made your kid happy and avoided the disappointment for you and them. Maybe it's better to spend for today when tomorrow is built on quicksand.

To be a good investor, they say that you must be optimistic about the future. Because on some level if you're going to give your hard-earned money to own a tiny fraction of some random companies, in the hopes that they'll do something productive with it and you'll get more back 30 years from now when you retire, that requires a lot of optimism. What have those CEOs done for you lately? And why would a young person of color feel optimistic that a large corporate institution would have their best interests at heart when they witness how their parent is treated every day at work?

The math of poverty has to do with income. The psychology of poverty has to do with time horizon. Nothing builds confidence like money in the bank, a car in the garage. Or at least, some Jordans. And if your summer camp counselor seems like a nice guy born with a little money in the bank and still doesn't realize how lucky he is, well …maybe you could cope by ribbing his crappy shoes.

The world sees us in these concentric circles of material possessions. To an extent, we can choose how much we let people see. Finances are the inner circle, glimpsed by a select few. Our home is just beyond that, the car outside that, clothing outside that. Like Russian nesting dolls, not everyone gets to the home. We can avoid our car being seen (trust me, I'm an expert), but clothing is always out there, ready for judgment.

And when the inner layers are in shambles, we need a win on the outer layers that much more. Driving around metro Milwaukee, it's not uncommon to see a five-year-old Prius parked at a Lake Drive mansion and a new Escalade parked in front of a shitty apartment building by the freeway. These layers of exposure to the world affect our decision-making as much as math does. Perception is reality. In the moment, appearing well-off is just as good as being well-off. *I'd rather be an imposter than openly poor. I'm no different.* That psychological reality is why we see headlines about how many households can't cover an emergency expense and yet we all seem to be buying … stuff … constantly.

In hundreds of personal interviews with existing and prospective clients, I have found little to no correlation between current earned income and sustainable financial health for households above the poverty line. By which I mean: the ability to absorb unexpected costs without taking on high-interest debt and using that ability to create wealth by spending less than you earn. If you're better at spending than earning, you're slowly getting pulled by the undertow. Almost imperceptibly now, but a debt riptide soon if you aren't careful.

But in America, spending buys belonging. It's hard to put a price tag on that.

Fashion is ground zero for how we present ourselves to the world. Ah fashion, how I love and hate it. What frustrates me is how it's always changing. First impressions on your shirt are unavoidable. First impressions are determined in part by what's fashionable that year, which goes in cycles. I mean, their Jordans—and so much else—*is* cool. Where does it end? There is always something better. *More, more, new, new.*

Most clothes—especially well-made ones—last a long time. Cars, clothes, shoes will last. The things we buy often last longer than our interest. Maybe that's only because the seller has convinced us we need something newer. Plastic takes something like 400 years to decompose, right? That means my baby toys and Lincoln Logs that my mom kept can spark the imagination of her grandkids now.

The balance I settled on early in my finance career was one $500 navy suit, because I wear it every week, it makes a good impression, and it's timeless. *Just like their Jordans.* On the other hand, I won't spend more than $30 on a casual button-down shirt because it will be drooled on and clawed at until a button breaks, and I don't feel like learning how to sew or getting it stitched for the sake of a shirt that would go at a garage sale for $3. Ah, modern times. I got a winter coat at Old Navy when I was 16. It's going strong today, used only for winter yard work and cigar smoking. My mom still wears a windbreaker she got for my sister in middle school. Our house is filled with furniture older than us and toys older than our kids, all these items fulfilling their purpose just fine. Their resale value, like clothes and cars, will slowly dwindle to an amount we can call "better than nothing" unless we keep them until antique status.

And antique status requires a looong time horizon. The key point on investing for the future is time horizon. How confident are you that you will make it to a future point in time with financial security and dreams intact? *Can the evicted family afford to move grandmother's dresser? Milwaukeeans know it's left on the curb, unwanted after the first rain.*

My investments textbook from the American College of Financial Services plainly stated that "indifference curves are based on one's marginal utility for wealth, which will vary dramatically between investors."

Such a boring sentence to most, but it is a fundamental link between sociology and finance. Translation: how well a person can tolerate every possible outcome is influenced by how well their essential needs and desired lifestyle are already met.

When a person asks me about investing, I ask questions to measure their risk tolerance. You can't legally open an account with a professional without answering them. In my experience, investors who have less income are typically less optimistic about their long-term prospects, which means they are willing to take fewer risks, even risks that have a far better than 75% chance of paying off. Over time, therefore, they gain less ground than someone who does take the risk.

Let's say a teenage parent earning minimum wage with no support system and a professional parent making a six-figure income are each given a wager: put in $100 for a 75% chance of getting $200 back, a gain of $100 for no work; that means a 25% of losing the $100. The teen parent must ask: "What would I have to give up? Should I wait to buy diapers?" Straight away, the opportunity is gone, whereas the higher-income parent won't keenly feel the loss of $100 and will typically take the risk. More often than not, they will make money from it. Psychological studies on decision-making suggest that people are more loss-averse than we realize. We all hate making mistakes, but losses are far more severe for some. A CEO's company stock may lose millions in a week, but they'll still have millions left over.

Fear of the worst-case scenario perpetuates poverty. The working poor have no cushion for taking calculated risks. Lower income? Shorter-term thinking out of necessity. Future? The present is hard enough. And the young parent, frustrated by their fear and circumstance, will buy their baby a cute new outfit instead of settling for Goodwill. Another $20 spent in exchange for temporary respite. *I can tolerate spending the money, and I know my child will enjoy this.*

The irony of being a financial planner is that while we use strategy and analysis, investments and insurance, our existence is built on the present spending of time and money. And that is about feelings, not numbers. The heart of planning lies in the client's perception of their own potential and their hope for the future. Without hope, no one would invest in anything, ever. Hope is water for the seeds of potential. The short-term profit for the financial planner is finding an apple tree bearing fruit, so we can advise how much to eat now, how much to preserve for winter, and how much to give away to neighbors. The long-term profit for humankind is watering seeds. And sometimes growing a plant means encouraging it with a nice pair of Jordans.

chapter sixteen

"I don't have a ride"

In my first full-time job at 22, I developed a teen program for Lake Valley Camp that brought together a select group of teenagers from all over the city. This design made the program unique; they were united by a shared experience through summer camp and wilderness trips, not by neighborhood or school. A program bringing together kids from the north and south expanses of an extremely segregated city was needed.

Still, I'd see a student light up in October and be a no-show in November. I would text the kids from my ancient flip phone: *rrr uu ccc ooo m iii nn g*. I'd call the parents. I would send emails. Even with all this, it was still hard. I knew the kids wanted to come, so what was up? I mapped out where everyone lived in the city and hung it on my office wall. I shared phone numbers of teens that lived within a mile of each other. I asked for feedback from the kids at meetings.

They qualified for free or reduced lunch at the time they were accepted into the program. The majority were still living in poverty.

Mine was a free program. It was *free*. Except for known conflicts, why wasn't every last one of them coming? The attendance policy was an enormous stressor for me. How to discourage poor attendance without any leverage beyond guilt and taking the summer program away … *Who's accountable? The teen or the caregiver? And who's punished?*

The problem worsened along with the weather. My first winter in Milwaukee was … gloomy. I lived with a co-worker in the northwestern corner of the Riverwest neighborhood. This area was not poor, nor was it wealthy, but kind of a transitional border. One snowy morning early that winter, we both walked out to broken car windows, along with several other cars parked on our block. Nothing stolen, not even his GPS unit. I took a personal half-day to get that resolved.

The first big snow, I left for work at 11:00 am and the street still hadn't been plowed. This stood out to me. In Palatine, once the probability of snow surpassed the "let's cover our asses" forecast of 60%, an army of trucks was dispatched immediately, and your morning commute was too salty, not too snowy. If my part of the city was unplowed, what about parts of the city a few miles away, some of the poorest places per capita in the country? Probably worse, certainly not better.

The after-school and weekend programming required transportation: parent, public, friend, or me. It was hard to get kids there otherwise. In the end, the barrier to attending a single program wasn't cultural distance. It was physical distance. The teens in my program were dropped off in all kinds of cars. Some of them were super nice, most of them were old. The thing about old cars is they don't start easily in the cold. They also tend to break down more often. I know my parents wanted to make sure I was changing the oil in my car, so I didn't have trouble driving two hours down to Champaign. I started to connect the dots.

What if your family car was in worse shape than mine? What if you also had little kids, and the street wasn't plowed, and you were broke?

Maybe I wouldn't drop my kids off either. The potential downside was more severe than the potential reward. Driving 20 minutes each way, for a two-hour program on a weeknight was a big ask for some. And if the car didn't start back up at 9:00 pm across town on a 10-degree Wednesday night in January…

When I asked about non-attendance, the answer I heard more than any other was: "I don't have a ride." I began to see the parents' perspective. *My car is a piece of shit. It's freezing. I've got little kids with me. I have to drive through dangerous neighborhoods at night and I don't want to be stranded after dark.*

Most parents didn't want their kids taking the bus after dark or at all. I don't blame them. A reliable car creates a barrier between your loved ones and dangers. I would wait by the door to make eye contact with caregivers as their teen walked over. They didn't want any ambiguity or doubt as to where their baby was or who was responsible for them. Taking the bus would leave much up to chance. Public transportation is more important in neighborhoods where car ownership is difficult, because of space or economics. Taking the bus in a sketchy neighborhood is hard because we give up control. We still have to wait at the bus stop or walk a few blocks to our destination.

During our first teen meeting during the school year, I decided to wear my "classroom teacher" outfit of khakis and tie. I was so nervous, about my lesson and about making an impression in a new environment. I reserved a conference room at a public library. I went to order pizza before we started and was informed "we don't deliver in that zip code." It seemed the parents weren't alone in their concern. And we were hungry that night, another micro-aggression for them that I felt too.

On top of that, none of my kids had their own car (like my friends and I did at their age). They had to ask family to drive them. More of their parents worked second or third shift jobs and were unavailable after school though, so the kids had to bum rides off less reliable siblings, cousins, etc.

Meanwhile, I had to wait for these siblings and cousins until 9:00 or 9:30 at night. *Is it so hard to be on time?* With the guys, sometimes I just drove them home, because it was easier. Whatever the reason, valid or not, I was waiting. I was 22 years old with nowhere to be really. It was fine. But good people leave youth work once they have to decide between another person's 15-year-old and their own 1-year-old waiting at home. They say, "Man, I love these kids but I'm missing my own family right now."

For a class in college, I'd read *Nickel & Dimed* by Barbara Ehrenreich. The gist of it is that it's hard to be in the "working poor." A full-time minimum-wage job is not enough to get out of poverty, not even close. Because the margin of budgeting error is so slim for working families, barriers are compounded. Emergencies like ER visits and car trouble are so much harder to overcome. For some, an unexpected $1,000 car repair is a nuisance. For one girl's family, it meant they didn't have a car for three months. It was enough time for her to miss a lot of programming, lose connection to her peers, be "on probation" according to my ad hoc attendance policy. I'm not sure what she's doing now, but I never saw her again, and it had nothing to do with her character, ability, or desire. It had everything to do with money. Or did it? At what point does personal responsibility dig in its heels? *I can't care more than they do. But if they stick around, given the chance, they'll begin to care.*

The problem of rides was hard for LVC's board to grasp at the time. The idea that we needed to pay for transportation seemed like we were enabling somehow. Transportation is a working poor challenge? Or is it an urban challenge? Whose challenge is it? Why can't/won't/aren't the parents prioritizing this? Education for girls in countries without is not only good for girls; it is good for local economies. Why wouldn't subsidizing transportation in our country be good for local economies?

I went to a workforce development seminar and learned that southeastern Wisconsin manufacturers were struggling to find qualified employees at the time. Years later, it happened again during COVID. But qualified people couldn't find a way to get out there. A factory built in the suburbs doesn't have regular bus routes from the door of the plant at all hours. For a family of five with one car, what is their priority going to be on a weekday at 5:00 pm? Going to the store for more diapers? Picking up dinner? Or coming to our teen program? They don't know when dad will get back from the plant with the only car, because that depends on traffic. So, they wait. All decisions are built on basic needs first.

On the other end, I was waiting for them to show up, wondering why they didn't. My brain knows that maybe their ride fell through. As a person, I was still stood up. Not every kid wanted to come. I knew there were other worthwhile things to do. But I never knew the reason they weren't attending.

While difficult personally, I had to remove teens from our program if they were not meeting expectations. At some point, measurable results are all that matter, not intentions. I can't make anyone do anything. There is a difference between demanding equitable access and accepting less from a person because they haven't had a fair shot in the past. The latter is charity, which may help short term and hurt long term. *The gift of high expectations goes so far at summer camp, but now I just don't know what I can ask in these circumstances. I can work with them on behavior, teamwork, communication once they're here. That's what I do. But I cannot demand accountability now when they don't have the tools to own the outcome.* I too often found myself as another White man passing biased judgment in an unjust world.

Maslow's hierarchy defines basic needs as food, water, shelter, and rest first. That's what we need to stay alive. Second level basic needs are safety and security. Attending my youth program requires basic needs first, so that belonging, accomplishment and self-actualization could follow. We need all of that to thrive in our modern economy. If the bus stop is unsafe and the internet is slow, how can you possibly thrive?

Government is the economy's referee. Consider an infrastructure project funded with taxpayer dollars. As wealth increases, each dollar spent has less of an effect on the earner. The wealthy do pay more in taxes, but how much do their assets and businesses depend on tax revenue to fund public utilities? Amazon needs roads. Major League Baseball fields need sewers. Entertainers and executives alike depend on lower paid employees to make their performances or services possible. We are all connected.

As for me, I have a reliable car and can afford $70 a month for internet already, so why would I want to fund public transportation that is efficient and clean and safe? A true level playing field of opportunity is possible, and a critical goal. I didn't expect every kid to love Lake Valley Camp as much as I did, but I wanted to make it excellent for those who cared most. I couldn't isolate accountability without everyone having a ride.

Why does the wealthiest nation on Earth have worse public transit than other nations? *Because the Haves won't willingly pay for the Have-nots.* Capital organizes. Supply and demand connect us in astonishing ways. I can order groceries grown thousands of miles away and it arrives at my door in hours. It's no accident, however. Much of our government's foreign policy, overt and covert, has been to protect and expand free trade. In other words, for centuries we've prioritized acquiring access to natural resources around the world in our national interest. That focus has made us rich. Capital, like a goldfish, needs a bigger bowl to grow. We've spent considerable taxpayer money to promote "free markets" around the world—free for corporations to mine resources and cheap labor, while often leaving behind civil unrest and pollution. And yet those jobs created pay more than what the local economy was providing, lifting some out of poverty. Supply and demand require freedom to respond. *But in a post-colonial world, what does free really mean? Is a dangerous job for little money still a choice if the alternative is no job and no money?*

Business needs structure and stability in the external environment to innovate, focus, and thrive internally. So do people. When I spent a weekend in London at age 20, I was astounded by the London Underground. This network went everywhere. I truly wouldn't need a car. It was so good that even those who could afford a car still used it.

Civilization is the art of living collectively. Urban dwellers understand taxes because we use services all the time. If we pay steep Milwaukee County taxes, I'm taking the kids to the museums and the lakefront to get my money's worth. Taxes buy civilization. If I lived in a cabin an hour from any town larger than 10,000 people, I would hate taxes too, with good reason: I'm not using much other than forest fire protection and roads. There aren't as many jobs in rural areas. If there were, more people would live there. Land is cheaper and life is more peaceful. So, why do we cram together in cities?

In cities, people, organizations, ideas, art, and entrepreneurship all intersect and fuel each other. Power, amazement, creativity, disgust, insight…all of these human experiences interact to create a vibration of life that is at once overwhelming and inspiring. New York City has such an energy that living among those vibrations makes paying a fortune for a studio apartment worth it. Meanwhile, I had kids in Milwaukee who hadn't seen Lake Michigan five miles away. *Listening to waves is good for stress, seeing an empty horizon…I need that from time to time. How must they feel without it?*

If every young person has enough access to transportation and high-speed internet to have the freedom to choose their extracurriculars, to prioritize their mental health, to explore their passions, to practice their skills … well, ingenuity is infinite. We will all be better off. Yet, because many are stuck at home in dangerous neighborhoods, they're in front of screens. Kids' shows, games, and social media are collecting data. And more Americans become a consumer before they can define the word. E-commerce requires an amalgamation of people, organized and interconnected, to deliver a package to your door a day after you click a button on your phone. To function, it requires reliable internet and reliable transportation. Humans need that too. Again, corporations use broadband and public roads. We subsidize their ability to do business and thrive. Why don't we subsidize personal and professional development of our people?

Teen A has access to a car to go to a job interview. Teen B wakes up earlier and has to walk in the rain to the bus stop. Windblown hair erodes their confidence ever so slightly. The bus is late, so they stress about not arriving on time, distracting them mentally. With reliable broadband in every corner of the country, Teen C can skip transportation altogether and interview online. Reliable and safe transportation is an equalizer. Internet, too. If they're not equal now, it's because organized capital doesn't want them equal.

My brother-in-law Ben taught himself to code and spent years teaching it to inner-city teens and young adults. The free market has spoken; Ben is creating a contract jobs pipeline for urban youth. He's meeting them where they already are: tech. They are in tech because it's cheap to start, and you don't need to leave home to do it. Every dollar counts more when you're starting out. Can a 24-year-old buy a Chromebook and teach themselves skills online and get hired by a tech startup in California? They can if they don't need to save up for college tuition and Bay Area rent, away from their support system. Teenagers are on their phones all the time. Their imaginations find an outlet online. Technology is the link between information, services, and jobs; it has a vibration of its own. When an idea is born, it needs to be nourished. That goldfish needs room. Technology is expanding our access, as it did with the telegraph and the steam engine, and always has.

And ... there are still things, when human emotions and creativity become infinite, that you just have to experience in person. That concert, that speech where one statement changed my mind forever. When a child didn't make it to our overnight camp, it was heartbreaking for me. We spent so much time and effort getting ready. Our country has enough money to make sure our clothing gets safely from the factory in Bangladesh to the retail store down the street. If only every hopeful child could get a ride.

what am I worth?

When I was 23, I asked for a raise. It was terrifying. In hindsight, I should have asked for more. Theoretically, the worst that could have happened was hearing "no" and going back to the status quo, which was perfectly acceptable to me at the time. So, why did the stakes feel so much higher?

After increasing enrollment during my first school year full-time, I built on an existing framework and managed a summer team of four incredible staff to a breakout year for the summer program. I covered for my supervisor, the executive director, during his 48-hour periods of time off, being the de-facto camp director in his absence. After a tornado warning, where it was likely to touch down a few miles from the property, and navigating the lack of urgency of young counselors and control issues of the camp nurse 20 years my senior, I held it down but was depleted emotionally. I broke down crying in my room in the afternoon, just out of … stress? I'm not sure.

At any rate, after the 2009 summer program, I felt that I deserved a raise of 10%, from \$30,000 to \$33,000 per year. After crafting my argument in a two-page document, I invited my supervisor, the executive director, to County Clare, an exceptional Irish pub in Milwaukee, and a place that I felt was cozy and non-confrontational. I had seen the organization's operating budget, and I knew that three grand wouldn't break the bank. I genuinely believed that I deserved it. Like other 23-year-olds, then and now, I felt I was worth it but didn't have the experience to demonstrate why. The liability and pressure of covering for him was a central piece of the ask, and he wasn't even there to see that! I could have been making it up, for all he knew.

Rejection is difficult. Some of us experience it more often than others. I have been fortunate and privileged enough to experience very little of it involuntarily. (I voluntarily create opportunities for rejection now, but more on that later.) We run the risk that our girlfriends will dump us, our bosses will fire us, the bank will reject our mortgage application, the commercial will tell us no one likes us unless our teeth are straight, and our waist is small. Why volunteer for this?

I had just completed my fifth summer at Lake Valley Camp and had made best friends there. I had girlfriends come and go there. I had grown alongside many of the high school kids there. In 2009, some of them were high school graduates and now junior counselors, with campers of their own. My boss, Jim, sitting next to me at the bar, knew me better than many of my friends, had spent more hours around me than my own parents since I was 18. If he said no, it would mean …

…that I wasn't as valuable as I thought. The relationships, the effort, the long hours were not as important as I thought. I wasn't worth as much as I thought.

I made my pitch. He listened attentively, then told me he would think it over and get back to me shortly. I believed he needed board approval to give raises anyway, so I walked out of County Clare feeling a sense of accomplishment. No doubt he observed how nervous I was. I recall speaking for a while without taking a breath, then gulping down air all at once, along with sweating profusely, my nervous tic. *I f**king did it.* Regardless of what happened next, I felt alive.

High stakes are exhilarating. Ever see a photo of a rock climber in Yosemite without a rope? Statistics show that climbers without fall protection are less likely to fall. Were they badass already? Well, yes, but beyond that, the senses are heightened. The rejection makes the acceptance that much more beautiful. All the most worthwhile accomplishments in life involve a risk of rejection. Food and television cannot reject us, which is why they consume so much of our time and energy.

I got the raise. It was immensely validating. The risk of rejection paid off. In investing, there's a term *rate of return*, or ROR. Everyone wants to feel that they'll get more back than what they contribute, that a sacrifice today will create a gain tomorrow. Generally speaking, the higher the potential rate of return, the greater the potential for a loss. Investing is a spectrum. We can loan our money and ask the borrower to pay us back with interest (a bond). We could buy stock in an established company, or an up-and-comer, or one that everyone thinks is too far-fetched but just might be the next big thing. By investing, we enter a relationship in which we don't have full control. We might get burned. Nonetheless, we express our optimism in these companies. Why not also in ourselves?

There is a rate of return on "risk of rejection" too. In relationships and in business, the greater the risk, the greater the potential reward. I'd be lying if I said that $3,000 a year drastically changed my quality of life. I do think that it flexed my ROR muscles though. A few months after that, I bought a ring, and proposed. In my dating life to this point, I'd never taken any risks. I'd only asked girls out after I knew they liked me. You know, like a seventh grader. I surprised her. I bought the ring with no assurance that she would say yes, which made the ask all the more ... everything. Big, unfiltered feelings.

Now it seems most couples go ring shopping together. *Ick.* The risk of rejection or the chance of failure is what activates our soul. Apps allow us to pre-screen every element of shopping and dating until we forget what an unpredictable live encounter with another human is like. Now we don't even leave the house without confirming the other person will be there, too. Gradually, the phrase "being stood up" will disappear from our language, not to mention "blind date."

We cannot test limits in a bubble. Commitment is always inconvenient. Commitment shows the world that you are serious. And once you act, seriously, without proof of success, you run the risk of rejection. Life without ROR is slow spiritual numbing. Like in a story that Jim Carrey tells about his father, "I learned you can fail at what you don't want, so you may as well go for what you do want."

But many of us think that money just arrives. In Ken Leinbach's book *Urban Ecology*, he recalls that early in his teaching career, he thought of earning money like turning on a faucet. You don't think too much about where the water comes from as long as it comes.

Nonprofit professionals and educators tend to think like I did, at least before they get to higher levels of fundraising or executive decision-making. We learned how to teach children, not run a complex organization. Many promotions are sink or swim: we get a job we aren't trained for because we were good at the previous job. When will people become administrators with a logistics or personnel focus without paying their dues as classroom teachers? When will excellent teachers earn more than their mediocre counterparts?

Yet, nonprofits, schools, and governments make our communities more livable. Isn't that worth paying a lot of money to the people who make our communities better? Doesn't that have value? Maybe it's cheaper to underfund public education and services, and privatize for the financial elite.

The late speaker Jim Rohn talked about "value to the marketplace." It is a hard concept to internalize—that a person could have high value to their family and community, and little to no value to the marketplace. It's a hard truth to swallow—that the education of *all* children is not valued in the marketplace. *If everyone is the boss who's left on the assembly line?* The role of government is to intervene on behalf of the human, common good when the marketplace doesn't.

I didn't feel worthy of a raise of more than a few thousand. Some nonprofit professionals and teachers who come my way as prospective clients are skeptical about meeting with me. I don't blame them. I wish I could find a way to tell them that taking them as clients will be nonprofit work for me. When I started when I started in finance, a veteran advisor shared very matter-of-factly, "Teachers are not good clients. They think the government will save them." Another time at an office party, I said to one of the top investment advisors in the city, "Some people don't feel they should earn more than they need; that's part of why I'm writing this book." He was floored, like the notion never even occurred to him. But there are millions of people uncomfortable with that idea, I talk to them all the time.

I had a scarcity mindset when I asked for a raise. I could not shake the feeling that if I earned more, I would be taking from someone: a future co-worker's salary, program supplies, the foundation's cash reserve. Human value is infinite. Market value can be infinite. And the two grow in concert as often as in competition. Deep down, I still felt taking more meant others got less.

In hindsight, I was underpaid. I had a strong work ethic, deep rapport and could perform under pressure. It was hard to quantify my value, and I resisted doing so on stubborn principle. *I'm not doing 10% more work,*

I'm not 10% more effective. It was a classic example of external rewards (income) snuffing out my intrinsic motivation (our mission). My brain knew I was worth way more than I asked, so why was I so conflicted? *What is wrong with you?*

Three years later, I asked for a raise again. To his credit, Jim went out of his way to develop measurable goals with me that were relevant and achievable so I could earn a raise. He likely needed some specifics to rationalize my pay increase to the directors, but I just couldn't get on board. I could have shifted my priorities to hit the new goals that were set, but only at the expense of current work. *I want how much I do now to be seen and appreciated. No one gets how much I pour into this. I need to demonstrate value above and beyond the current job description. But what about the quality and complexity of the job now? The intensity I bring compared to what's reasonable? If I leave, they'll spend more money for two people to replace me. Isn't that worth a raise right there?* In the end, I struggled to communicate and quantify my value, which is Salary Negotiation 101. And I left it on the table, bitter and frustrated by my own actions.

One of the top TED Talks of all time is from Dan Pallotta: "The Way We Think About Charity Is Dead Wrong." In it, he describes how nonprofit salaries and advertising are "overhead expenses," which donors don't like to see. They want their dollars to go to direct service. However, overhead expenses grow the overall size of the pot. Corporations spend money all the time in pursuit of growing revenue. Innovation is encouraged, and mistakes are made. Mistakes in the pursuit of revenue, like ad campaigns that flop, are still "worth it." In nonprofit work, we have a shorter leash. It is such a double standard. Maybe self-esteem is as important to income as supply and demand.

I had coffee once with an older and wiser expat from nonprofit work. He validated my desire to bring financial empowerment to the nonprofit sector. He too saw the need for nonprofit professionals to better communicate their value to their boards, and their reluctance to do so. Once the low salary became too much of a sacrifice, he left, and we both knew lots of talented people who had done the same. People want freedom and security. You can get that as long as you have enough to pay your bills and something extra. People leave nonprofit work once their salary is no more than basic bills plus job stress. They lose the security, unless the spouse makes big money. It usually isn't a sudden awakening to the corporate world. It comes from an inability to live life on their own terms. And that ultimately becomes more important than the work they're doing.

To all those serving others, I am rooting for you, and may the public teacher's pension remain well-funded. For those with more flexible compensation, everything is negotiable if you can stomach hearing no. You'll either get it, or you will fail forward. If it has never occurred to you, that's a sign that it is time. We tell our students and children to reach for greatness in spite of adversity, right? Why not us, too? Your gain is not their loss. You create gain for others by becoming your best. As I read in the book *Creating Money: Keys to Abundance*, the greatest gift you can give others is the example of your own life working. Young people want a role model, not a co-ruminator.

"we're in a bi–SES relationship"

I met Rebeca just after my 23rd birthday, when the winter was dragging on and I was struggling with teen attendance at work. That Tuesday around 6:00 pm, my buddy persuaded to me to change out of my hoodie and pajama pants, and turn off the movie I was settling in to watch alone. I met him halfway by keeping the hoodie and changing into dad jeans. Then we hustled down the block to one of our favorite neighborhood bars to meet a friend of his from the teaching program.

She looked good. White blouse, expressive eyes, dark hair. I cringed at my clothing choice. Nonetheless, we had a stimulating conversation that night, and were a novelty to each other for many months of dating. Apart from my glorious two weeks with DeCiona in seventh grade, I'd never been in a biracial relationship. I learned that Latinos like to eat and chill all weekend long. That was an adjustment. She learned that White people like to go out in the woods and deliberately take very few things with them. That was an adjustment. We'd each made commitments socially and professionally to social justice. Sure, we had our shortcomings: I could be naive in the suburbanite tradition; she could talk mad trash in the hood tradition. In our first month of dating, she did give me an actual "critical White ally quiz." I passed. Crisis averted.

On a deeper, ongoing level, the real merger of our relationship played out in the different socioeconomic scripts we grew up with around money. Ours was a "bi-SES" relationship, and this is where the real work happened. As in most relationships, getting accustomed to the other's parents in "real time" led to a slew of questions right after leaving their house. *Have they always been like that? When you were little, what was it like?*

Rebeca spent years living in a Compton neighborhood where she could hear the shootings from her home. It was hard for me to stomach, and harder to accept, that this girl I was falling in love with had to deal with that. Plus, her first-grade teacher abusing her, the apartment that was infested with cockroaches that would scurry away when you turned the light on, her brother's dealing, her uncle's dogfighting …My feelings toward her childhood approached …pity.

Pity cannot exist between two equals. But I self-identified as an advocate, dammit. The feeling of pity toward her alarmed me. And it was straight-up confusing. It was different than a desire to protect and provide. I felt bad for her … She was also more capable than me in so many ways: bilingual, more fashionable, amazing dancer, better grades, etc. Her family was more capable than mine in many ways: better mechanics, better cooks, better hosts. So, how could this family live with roaches in the kitchen?

Rebeca must have seen it on my face at times. Now when we're out in mixed company and she drops into conversation about her uncle breeding Rottweilers to fight, I see a flash of astonishment on people's faces. *Dogfighting? But that's only for bad people.* I must have had that fleeting look early on. I had never been so close to someone with a past like that.

She struggled with my privilege. There were things I just didn't have to worry about. I would tell stories about our annual summer vacations to Colorado, or Maine, or Florida, and that could get awkward sometimes. My parents still lived in the house they bought before I was born. I played travel soccer, was given a car. My friends all went to good colleges. She was with me for a reason. She felt that I "got it" and supported her. But now and then, my pity's ugly counterweight would surface: her resentment.

Nothing is neutral. Every encounter and every dollar has energy. Beginning to spend money together on new shared memories is joyful. We went out to eat all the time. Weekends at wineries, concerts, movies. *Courtship is expensive, damn.* Sharing money is usually stressful for couples. All our values, priorities, and traditions are built in. Our first date, we stopped into a 24/7 diner to end the night. We got some coffee and something light to eat, for around $15. I didn't offer to pay, deciding to play the part of "enlightened feminist." I later found out she was like, "Oh hell no. Is he that cheap? The guy pays. Always."

My parents always told me, "Don't spend money you don't have." And so, I didn't. I just spent every dime I made. I had $5,000 or thereabouts that my parents gave me as a graduation present. I put it in my savings account as if I had "saved" it. I didn't touch that, but otherwise with no car or student loan payment, I was out and about, traveling, drinking, etc.

Everything is relative, but I know that I don't like cheap things. Some people look for deals; I look for what I want, because I'm the type who will never throw things away. I have used the REI lifetime guarantee on my North Face backpack twice over 13 years. I still have it, and will need to go back again. When I look at it or use it, I think about all the places it has gone with me, where it's been rained on, that time I almost lost it. These things hold my memories. (This is a great Radiolab episode. I'm on Robert Krulwich's side.) I had camping, biking, and rock-climbing gear that I barely used within a year. Ten years later, it's still in my basement in great shape. Rebeca thought this was total nonsense, of course. Not only do you want to go out in the middle of nowhere, but you need to have all this stuff to do it? You'll use it, like, four times a year? In her defense, who would want a nice raincoat when your lifelong answer to rain has been to, uh, stay inside when it's raining?

I spent next to nothing on food, clothes, and technology. I've been simple like my parents in this way. The food part changed when I met Rebeca. This girl loves food. Every time we would go out and drop $50 or $60, I would think of what outdoor gear I could buy at REI for that price. Food just didn't speak to me. *That tiny plate of calamari is $9 … Aren't you poor? Am I a sugar daddy?* It seemed so fleeting, like that was too much for something I "used" just once.

The first time Rebeca and I did a budget, we spent something like $700–800 a month on food and drink. One month, I spent more in bars than I did on my rent ($425). It took a long time for me to see that this was her adventure, her way of building relationships and exploring the world. I was a cave man in this genre, but that's okay. We fell in love over dinner.

When we were 24, Rebeca had $2,000 in student loans outstanding, and I had the money sitting idle. She drew up a loan agreement—which was as official as Word 2007 can be—and we both signed it. I remember feeling very satisfied with myself, like we were going about it the right way, even though I doubt I would've asked for it if we'd broken up (see: White guilt). I was impressed with her. I could see the strain in her face when she brought the contract to me. Guilt that she hadn't been more frugal in the past, fear that she was relying on a man, annoyed she had to make it official, frustration that I couldn't relate to how she felt, that we were two parties to the contract, not teammates. And still, we both signed it.

A rudimentary means of understanding is comparison. People love to compare things so that they know where they stand. Comparison, compromise, compatibility. A new relationship creates a shared future, full of possibilities. While I love the benefits of the sharing economy, research shows that moving in with your significant other before a commitment doesn't work so well. Dr. Meg Jay's book *The Defining Decade* is a must-read for those in their twenties and thirties still trying to "figure it out." She says relationships where the couple is engaged or married before living together have a way better chance of lasting. Sharing money before publicly committing to sharing your lives is sometimes nothing more than convenient cuddles and cutting rent in half. And to be fair, how tempting is that?

One of the most difficult client calls I've ever had came from a former Lake Valley Camp student, one of my favorites. She had been involved in the program from a young age, and I worked with her year-round throughout high school. She was hard-working and kind, but timid and lacking self-confidence. I remember the first time she spoke up in a group setting, making a statement that was important, wise, and unpopular. It was a turning point, a moment that makes being a teacher worthwhile.

She became a client of mine in my first year as a financial advisor. By that point, she had finished college and had a solid job as a teacher herself. We began saving systematically, while also navigating some HR mishaps at her school that affected her retirement, and a personal trainer contract that she couldn't cancel. She needed an advocate. She had been too trusting of other people's intentions to follow through. She was soft-spoken when speaking up would help, it seemed.

After a few years checking in and talking about her unfolding plans, she requested a phone call to talk about making changes, reducing this, and moving that. *She sounds timid.* The request was fine, as life isn't linear, and I was with her through thick and thin. What followed was chilling. After about ten minutes on the phone, where she updated me and helped me understand her rationale and so on, her boyfriend started talking. He had been listening the whole time. Turns out, it was his influence in her voice. When she wavered, he grabbed the phone, as manipulators do, and gave me directions for her life. *That's what's really going on.* Never mind that they were serious but not engaged, I was planning for her future, not his, and not theirs yet. He came from money, and she didn't. The strategies would be different.

Don't start taking advice from your partner just because they have or make more money. In most cases, they have more because they had a head start. Who knows how they would have handled your adversity? Put a ring on it first. Rebeca and I treated each other as equals. The fact that our financials were not equal was inconvenient, but it was something we could detach from and explain. *This prick thinks his parents' money makes him a genius.* My student, like Rebeca, had a "privilege-adjusted" return far better than her man's.

There are two sides to a relationship: supporting with encouragement and delivering tough truths. Anyone will accept encouragement, but it takes a lot of trust to deliver truth. Even more so when you come from a different place. It takes a strong relationship for me to call Rebeca ghetto when she's being ghetto. And for her to allow me to use that word. All we can do in a bi-SES relationship is focus on our shared future with optimism and acknowledge progress in each other. Only we will notice all the little things we do for each other and our children. Otherwise, it devolves into social comparison. How much of our circumstance is a product of our family? Our health? Society? How will we ever know?

And with money, we both had thousands of money thoughts and decisions made internally over our lives until we met. When a relationship reaches the sharing-money stage, all of sudden we are witness to choices that make no sense in our world, but are completely normal to the other person. Can we say something without being condescending or self-righteous? *Should I just wander into the kitchen and ask what that Amazon package was? Can I be nonchalant enough?* Rebeca and I may know how we arrived here, but even now we are unpacking our habits with money. It's so hard to self-diagnose and harder to regulate each other without starting a fight. *She's getting another massage? Well, I did get my motorcycle running again ... Who am I to judge?*

We all spend out of habit, but when feeling overwhelmed or worried, we tend to be more judgmental. Sometimes we transfer stress to those closest to us. Many couples are looking for financial advice because they are getting married or are in some stage of merging finances. And it is difficult. And many of my meetings do feel like marriage counseling. The words "guilt," "shame" and "stress" come up a lot. All financial choices are cultural. There is a culture of repressive wealth-building norms; there is a culture of live in the now. Comparing spending in a bi-SES relationship is like comparing stress: it's not helpful because it's connected to a thousand other factors, dynamic and shifting. Saying "we can't afford it" is often code for "I don't think it's worth it." Our quest to manage spending and stress is a lifelong one. The last thing a person wants from their spouse or financial planner is judgment.

I've met with a couple in their early fifties who just couldn't take any action because of a serious disagreement on savings philosophy. I've met with divorcees in their twenties, and money is big reason why. Marriage is probably the biggest financial decision you'll make. Although we aren't talking about bloodlines and alliances like *Game of Thrones*, the merging of houses is no small thing. The "commoner" might say "live well today since we aren't promised tomorrow." The "lord" might be immersed in work, beholden to preserving family legacy. They can both be right. All financial choices are cultural and contextual. Is spending the tax refund the same week at Red Lobster, or working 100-hour weeks to make partner at the law firm, really any different from the plotlines we see on screen?

For the bi-SES household, an unnamed category to date, I recommend a guilt-free money bucket. The "savings account" used to require a trip to the bank to request money. Now it's two clicks on a mobile app to get it back. So, despite the name, let's be real. Most people aren't "saving." Divert your paycheck into "deferred spending" categories: vacation, new car, Christmas gifts, flight home twice a year, and so on. This will create boundaries.

One of these auto-transfers from your joint checking should be *your* fun money, also known as your solo-identity bucket. I emphasize "your" because this bucket is a judgment-free zone. You each get an allowance of $10, $100 or $1,000 a month. The amount doesn't matter; the boundary does. Whether it's saving for a motorcycle or a daily latte habit, if it comes from your solo account, then your joint ventures are intact. If it comes from the joint account, in hard times, your spouse will review the transactions. Resentment over the little things, anger over the big choices, the last thing we want is for your dollars to bring your identity into question. All financial advice is a means to arrive at "earn or have more than you spend." This is a simple truth. Why we can or cannot manage to do that is where the hard work begins.

Like most worthwhile things, it's simple but not easy. If you are unable or unready to speak with a professional who can hear your money story objectively and problem-solve, then find another couple and counsel each other. An outside perspective is critical. It's easy for me to deliver the message because that's what I do. After the meeting, I say goodbye, not ask what we should do for dinner. I'll tell clients where they are similar to their peers and where they deviate from the norm, for better or worse. All they had prior was their childhood observations of adults, their douche cousin bragging about real estate, and each other. Not a representative sample.

Things become routine over time. Something exceptional to one becomes mundane to another. I recall being a year into my time in Seattle, and just starting to take the mountains for granted, no longer staring in wonder as I drove east on I-94. Sensory experiences make us come alive: food for Rebeca, extreme adventure for me, travel for both of us. Setting financial boundaries can be the difference between experiencing these as a means of distraction from a floundering relationship or pursuing joy together.

chapter nineteen

entitlements

The next chapter in our life together was a year of AmeriCorps service in Seattle. AmeriCorps is sort of like the domestic version of the Peace Corps. You register and apply through the national portal and then indicate areas of interest, past background or skills, and geographic preferences. She went to City Year, and I went to Habitat for Humanity, and we joined hundreds of other Millennials that moved there for AmeriCorps.

With the recession in full swing, it was competitive, landing me my first rejected job application ever. Yet I held out for my first choice: Habitat for Humanity, an international organization that builds houses, partnering with future homeowners and volunteers to do so. I got to be outside a lot, I hosted volunteers, and I made sure people were safe and having fun. *No, don't wave that around. Please pay attention to the exposed nails. Maybe I am a worrier like my mom.* Above all, I got to live out a sort of blue-collar daydream. Only an established nonprofit like

Habitat provides the opportunity to do "real" construction without "real" deadlines. Some days, I drove an enormous truck to the city dump, or dug ditches, or built walls. The kind of thing that was great for a year, knowing I'd go back to youth work soon.

As AmeriCorps members, Rebeca and I received a stipend that, by design, gave us an income below the poverty line. We decided to move somewhere out of the Midwest in December 2009, were engaged February 2010, settled on AmeriCorps somewhere in the Western US by spring, and moved that summer. At City Year, a youth program that supports teachers in struggling schools with tutoring, after-school programs and positivity, Rebeca and every other corps member made $700 each month. I was at Habitat for Humanity as a construction volunteer lead, meaning I was the guy who took orders from the staff who actually knew how to build houses, and then made sure volunteers stayed safe and didn't screw things up too badly. My peers and I made $1,100. Rebeca and I both qualified for food stamps, with a monthly benefit of $200 per month each. So, our pre-tax monthly income was about $2,200, after tax like $1,900 or something. We were able to get back on our parents' health insurance (the first wave of Obamacare implementation was the 26-year-old extension in 2010) and that saved us some money.

We built beautiful homes in beautiful areas at Habitat. The majority of the local daily volunteers, mostly retirees and corporate day-trippers, were very well-off. At AmeriCorps, we were full-time, 10-month-long volunteers, and came to expect certain things from the Habitat site staff and volunteers, because we had a group identity and were an essential part of executing the mission. We carpooled in a large 15-passenger van, for example, and they even let us take it camping in the mountains for a weekend.

Yet we all had different past lives. Our group included a Peace Corps alumna, a recovering addict, and an unemployed architect. We hailed from all regions of the country and all socioeconomic backgrounds. Under this program, we were equal, so in small ways we reconciled our past with our present. Who did what last year, why they joined, where they lived, etc. There were differences, but we were treated equally at work: all temporary cheap labor.

The stipend is enough to have a place to live but little enough to qualify for food assistance (aka food stamps or food share). The federal program wants members to ostensibly focus on their service and experience on some level the challenges faced by others. Our group hung out together a lot because we all made the same amount of money. So, there weren't any awkward exchanges: "Let's go here for dinner? Oh wait, can you afford that?" We found community that way, especially in an expensive city like Seattle.

Food is a great leveler around the world. Humans will do anything to get it, and everybody needs it. Many have too much, many have too little. As AmeriCorps, we were given a $200 monthly government allowance as food share. Now food could mean ramen noodles, organic pizza, Good Humor strawberry shortcake ice cream bars, anything you could buy at a grocery store. If you've been to Aldi and Whole Foods, you know that food prices vary considerably. Foods produced cheaply are generally less healthy (more preservatives, wider distribution, low-quality ingredients, etc.), so people on fixed low-incomes eat worse on average. But it's the system, not the person, making the choice.

My first time going to the grocery store and using the food assistance card was awkward for me. You know the experience of doing something for the first time, something that others do all the time, and must be simple, and therefore people expect you to know how to do it already? Especially in line at the grocery store around 5:00 pm, a high-activity place where we are least likely to tolerate delays. As I moved into the on-deck position, I realized I didn't even know how to use the thing. *Was the benefit set up yet? What if it was declined? Stop sweating.* Paying for the groceries out of pocket would be tough.

The card itself wasn't ugly, but it didn't look anything like a credit or debit card. *C'mon, there's no reason for that.* Like, obviously, it wouldn't have the VISA logo, but it could be discreet. Pulling it out and swiping it, I felt eyes watching me. I don't know if they were or not, but I felt exposed. I felt the urge to say to the cashier and next in line, "I'm in AmeriCorps. Ever heard of it? We do a year of service ...on a stipend ... we get this ...I am working full-time ...just started ..." trailing off slowly. *I'm making a choice, so why I do feel defensive?*

I don't think anyone thought anything of it that first time. On other trips, I did experience some micro-aggressions. One time, I locked eyes with a woman who clearly thought I should make real money and stop living off her taxes. Even though I paid taxes on my poverty-level income. Other times, I remember that fed into a feeling of shame. Once I was behind a mother alone with two small kids, also on government assistance. As the last few items crossed the scanner, her eyes fixed on the display. She was over; it cost more than what was left on her card. So, she had to decide which items to put back. I won't presume to know how she felt. It probably wasn't the first time. But you know how check-out lines work. Everybody's there, now we're waiting longer. Her daughter started whining because one of the desserts had to go back, drawing more attention to the situation. When my total appeared on screen. I was over too, but I just put the rest on my debit card. I was on a poverty field trip, after all.

When you pay with food stamps, you get disapproving looks every now and then. As an able-bodied, educated White male, this was totally new to me. I may have been projecting, but I felt the next person in line was thinking, *"What happened? This guy isn't supposed to be struggling."* Some people felt the $200 disappear quickly, like we did at the time, and others felt it was enough for a month. I suspect that had much to do with the lifestyle of our past lives and how many baseline calories we needed. Our 18 months of dating leading up to this was *very* focused on food and drink. That was our entertainment. Mine went fast for both reasons.

At first, the $200 a month felt like free money. *How cool is this? How amazing to be a US citizen!* Then we began to realize just how little money we earned, and the novelty of the so-called "entitlement" wore off, and eventually I felt I "earned" that money by sacrificing a higher income for the greater good. Some of you no doubt read this and felt that I was, in fact, an entitled asshole. And you may be right. After all, I wasn't drafted into AmeriCorps.

This pressure made me reliant on work-sponsored lunches, which either came from a corporate volunteer group or an organizational training. Throughout the year, we hosted volunteers on Wednesday, Friday, and Saturday. There were a handful of regulars who volunteered solo, but most volunteers came as part of group volunteer day. So, Boeing or Bank of America or Wells Fargo or whoever would bring 20 people. They were happy to not be working in the office, but their interest in volunteering varied, as did their aptitude for the task at hand. Many of them weren't used to being outside, and their mind, like ours, drifted to lunch.

They brought enough Chipotle for their 20 volunteers and the six AmeriCorps on site. After burrito number one, my friends and I loitered near the table for a shot at snagging a second, which was eaten then and there or stashed away for dinner at home. Anything extra was stored in our work trailer for lunch the next day. Anything tastes good when you're numb and damp in the Seattle winter. On Friday, Wells Fargo came, and they didn't bring lunch. I was frustrated. Not by either banks' role in the subprime mortgage crisis, but by lack of lunch. Without the basics covered, principles seemed irrelevant.

Humans have a hierarchy of needs. And you guessed it, lunch at work comes before career satisfaction. This, too, evolved over the year, and I felt our group gradually come to expect and negotiate for food and work hours. This reflection feels very negative as I write this. I have fond memories of breaking bread with bankers, retirees, future Habitat homeowners, staff, and individual volunteers. I used the program's grant for my master's degree. I learned a lot about home construction. But by the end, I allowed a feeling of entitlement to impact my attitude in subtle ways.

The thing about being in AmeriCorps is that you are looking for favors. I was absolutely looking for "handouts" in any form. Everyone knew we were at the bottom of the food chain. Over time, I noticed that the way my co-workers and I spoke about the volunteer groups was linked to what they could give us: an easier workday by being pleasant, a connection to a job opportunity for next year, and the grandest offering of them all, the type and quantity of free lunch they would bring. We received a weak lunch or off-site lunch with outright indignation. "WTF? They went to KFC by themselves? All I brought was this PB&J and nothing else!" Over mumbled exchanges in line, "Looks like there won't be extras, those cheap bastards…" *When did you get so whiny?* Habitat sponsored a chili cook off, and I ate chili—and leftover chili— for lunch for two weeks straight. Money makes people do unhealthy things. Even at internal Habitat fundraisers, we arrived on the scene like hyenas from the wild, reveling in our build-site attire and scanning for free food without pausing to exchange pleasantries.

The reality was work or volunteer provided lunch was like 10–15% of my total compensation. Scavenging paid off. A free burrito at lunch and one to go was 1% of my monthly income. I was hospitable to my team of Microsoft engineers in the morning, but when it came time to line up for lunch, I knew they earned at least ten times more than me. *I'll appreciate seconds more than him.* When humans become accustomed to receiving something, they are angry when it is taken away. Regardless of whether it was deserved in the first place. And I was no exception. *I chose to volunteer; I'm entitled to a full lunch.*

By nature, we feel entitled to certain things. Entitlement programs in the United States include Medicare, Medicaid, Social Security, unemployment insurance, and food assistance programs… These are not givens in much of the world. In building a culture, as a nation or a summer camp or an AmeriCorps group, it's critical to start strict and then loosen up as the year goes on, as appropriate. It is virtually impossible to reverse the direction, because once we have something, we don't want it taken away. Getting a 10% raise doesn't remove the subsequent sting of a 5% pay cut. Clients call concerned about their account value falling 10%, but they didn't give it much thought when it rose 15% the year before. Someone may not "need" an entitlement program until they know someone else in their same circumstances gets one.

I met a lot of great volunteers and found my work useful, meaningful, and enjoyable most days. But I would have internal flare-ups of animosity toward volunteers at times. If a volunteer on my crew would go to his car during an afternoon downpour, my first reaction would often be "what a little bitch" (translation—*I wish I could do that*) and secondly "of course he has a BMW." I think the BMW stung more, because it was just another thing I didn't have. I could go to the grimy trailer, not my luxury car. Hating on volunteers with nice things was one way I got through it. He could walk away. Our AmeriCorps group developed an unhealthy us-versus-them narrative.

Some of my peers even transferred that frustration toward Habitat office staff. *Why do we need to do this stupid training? Why can't we change the volunteer schedule? Why are we all on one site?* A lot of complaints without solutions were offered. It was as if we were entitled to as much convenience, swag, and perks as humanly possible, simply because we were in this low-income, volunteer grunt category, not because we deserved it. That's a key distinction; entitlements given made us wonder what else we could be entitled to.

We had valuable skills, experience, and education. But like others on a fixed income before us, we spent too much time scheming about how to qualify and find more entitlements. I should have talked about my career intentions with all these volunteers. I could have managed up to my supervisors better. Or researched job market trends. On a fixed income, the short-term profit motive wins out. We were a group surrounded by opulence, and willing to leverage pity to our advantage.

But sustainable progress depends on long-term planning and profit motive. I've always been proud of my work ethic, but there were days I was running out the clock. Why not? I was a volunteer with no hope of promotion. I was, by design, easily replaced. And if I were promoted to an entry-level position at Habitat for Humanity (posted at $34,000 annual salary, same as I just left in Milwaukee), I may earn just enough to lose our food stamps.

As it stood, my $1,100/month, after taxes of around 12%, rent $425 and car insurance $150, left me about $100/week for all spending, plus $200/month for food share benefit. Let's say my income doubled in 2010. That would mean I'd pay 15% income tax on the increase, my healthcare from my parents would expire adding $250/month. I'd lose food share of $200. I'd likely need to buy a second car ($300/payment) since my transportation would be gone. I'd lose pity points at work (resulting in $150 less in handouts). For many, there was also a student loan payment. And wait, this was Seattle. Boom, your rent doubled too.

So, it's sort of a wash. I'd almost rather keep this job with no responsibility, a member of the "ostensibly low-income" instead of the overlooked working poor. I'd get more respect for working a lot harder earning $34,000 a year, but the cash flow margin of error is about the same.

No one likes an entitled kid, except maybe their pushover parents. But it would still be nice to be entitled … *Being White is your de-facto entitlement program.* The xenophobic voter hates welfare but wants their social security in retirement. They're both entitlement programs.

Entitlements, while a critical safety net, can be a psychological burden. They reinforce a poverty mindset, making it harder and harder to break free. I know I wouldn't have interviewed well for a job right after being shamed in the grocery check-out line.

Contributing to American progress and prosperity does entitle us to privileges, right? The pursuit of happiness may be an inalienable right, but entitlement programs are a human construct. All humans have value, yet we insist on making some assign dollar value to others. It's no surprise the social security office is veiled in a cloud of frustration. Trauma can block gratitude. And gratitude is good for mental health.

Americans don't want government assistance; they want to earn enough to attain a feeling of independence.

A handout from a smug elitist doesn't elicit gratitude, especially when you debase yourself to qualify for some system the elites devised to "help" you. A system of entitlements makes the applicant prove they deserve the benefit; they prove it by demonstrating they can't do on it their own, reinforcing low self-esteem. Talk about mixed messages.

If a young person qualifies for entitlement program assistance, those born with entitlement often judge them. All people have inherent value, yet here taxes on the entitled fund entitlement programs. Entitlement fund recipients have their human value questioned using a dollar value argument. It's as if they need to prove financially that they're worth someone's dollars in taxes. Of course, they can't.

Which is why policy ideas like universal basic income make more sense: there is no means testing to throw worthiness into question. Everyone gets the same amount regardless of income, so it's fair and not a secret. It also returns more choice to the individual to save, spend or give. (Rebeca and I both got $200 food share, but I consumed $300 of it.) It addresses relative impact of support. It's a fact: that extra burrito did mean more to me financially than the volunteer earning ten times as much.

If we don't understand how financial winners and losers are created, we are left with a fixed mindset. We think we are entitled, or being punished, for our circumstance. A feeling made all the more difficult by the daily reminders of those on the other end. The homeless under the overpass. The Ferrari driver at the fundraiser. Evidence of inequality is clickbait. Your dollar value does not define you. Once you believe it, your dollar value will increase.

I was talking with a client once, a Peace Corps alumna. She worked in Zambia. She said that in spite of overwhelming poverty by global standards—a subsistence farming community—there were almost no reported cases of mental health disorders, far fewer than in the US. Acknowledging other contributing factors, she suspected the primary variable was the relative lack of social inequality. Everyone went with less, so you may be worn out, but so is your neighbor. When on our own, we in AmeriCorps were different: we had comradery, empathy, and income equality. The inequality beyond led to resentment. And the American brand of capitalism, in an effort to keep us all hustling, sure has a way of making you feel like shit if you aren't keeping up.

Let's remove the chances to judge each other. Begging and resentment is bad for self-esteem. And low self-esteem makes us less employable. I went from being a fully activated and engaged leader at Lake Valley Camp to a passive freeloader in months. I would be embarrassed if that community saw my behavior, a casualty of low expectations. Perhaps comparison is as toxic to the mind as poverty is to the body.

the Let's Build a House Party

When I was 24 and doing AmeriCorps for Habitat for Humanity, I volunteered to pick up extra hours one night helping staff a swanky fundraiser. My co-worker Andrew and I wore our freshly printed Let's Build a House Party t-shirts and headed over to the hosts' house, which was on the eastern shore of Lake Washington. I don't remember who the owners were, but one of them was in management with Microsoft through the 80s and 90s, so …Hard work meets good luck. *Right place, right time, I guess.* In any event, Andrew and I were in for a free (and expensive!) meal, a nice warm night loitering outside in a beautiful neighborhood, and about three hours toward our requirement of 1700 service hours for the year. Not a bad deal.

Upon arrival, we learned we were coordinating parking. After about five minutes of excitement over getting behind the wheel of Mercedes and Porsches, we realized there was no way we volunteers were the valets. Bummer. Our role was to make sure none of these folks took up too much room parking on the narrow cul-de-sac cut into the hill-side. I felt it was kind of foolish at the time. I know now that you don't take chances with inconvenience when serious money is on the line. Someone prepared to write a check for ten grand might turn around if they couldn't find a spot.

So, we directed people. Most saw our shirts and politely asked us where to go. There were some badass cars there: I had to bend 90 degrees at the waist to make eye contact with a Lamborghini driver. The guests we spoke to were cordial, but most had a hint of paternalism. One couple was very friendly, as in "thank you so much for your service," because this wasn't their first go round. Others didn't even acknowledge us. I mean nothing, not even eye contact. As a college-educated and somewhat likable guy, this was my first encounter with being ignored as a part of the service environment. Andrew and I shrugged it off, like "he was a dick" once the front door closed. But it stung a little bit. *This is what thousands of people experience every day. And sometimes you're the dick.* And this was a soft, pleasant job! Do you thank the person cleaning the public restroom? Most of us don't. Maybe we don't acknowledge them because it's awkward. I'm still guilty of that sometimes. Maybe you don't think about it because you don't have to. Many people in this world work to make life more convenient for others.

People tend to focus on how money can buy things and experiences. But money also buys convenience, and convenience saves time. People with more time might be more able to: (a) figure out how to earn or save more money, and (b) relax, work out, sleep, do yoga, lounge on their boat, play with their kids, or whatever they want to restore their spirit. Those who cannot buy convenience cannot find balance in the same way.

When some other AmeriCorps and I went to the executive direc-tor's house for our welcome party, we had to figure out where to park, try to find the address number, be embarrassed about the car we were driving, identify the front door, wonder if we were first, decide to leave shoes on or take them off, etc. That was a mental drain, even though we were actually guests! In this public service context, our income was visible. As micro-aggressions wear on the person of color, inconvenience wears on the low-income. Maybe wealth had less to do with having stuff, which never motivated me that much, and more to do with the tailwind of convenience. That "dick" saw us in branded t-shirts, so he knew he was in the right place, had us identify a parking spot, was greeted at the door, had food prepared, and then was treated warmly and respectfully because he had discretionary income to donate. Probably not the only reason for that treatment, but that reason alone was enough.

I'm not saying he was a bad guy. There are good and bad in every conceivable category. But extrapolate this experience to every single experience of every single night of every single life. And most evenings he was consistently getting the subconscious message that he was successful, respected, and appreciated. People smiled at him when he left for the day. His nice car reinforced his value, and his nice children greeted him when he arrived home for dinner. Others get a message from cleaning up human waste and trash each night. They don't see their children after school because cleanup happens when the guy with the nice car goes home, so that everything is clean when he comes back. How does that affect a parent? *Rebeca's mom.* The exhaustion of such daily circumstances compounds. The inconvenience adds time, and time away from family drains the spirit.

It is hard to be born poor and become very wealthy. But it is also hard to be born very wealthy and become poor. The confidence, connections, and capital are instilled from birth. I'll tell you; it is hard to identify with either extreme when you've lived only in the middle. Wealth has a culture and poverty has a culture. Most people hang out with their own not because of prejudice. It's just all we know how to do. As we looked at the house from the street, I tried to imagine what living there would be like. And then we were invited inside.

We came straight from the work site and were wearing our work boots and pants. *We are props in the pageant.* Andrew and I stuck together at first. I had never been to a fundraising dinner before nor a house like this one, the kind of place that had original artwork and panoramic windows. At an event like this, everyone has an agenda of sorts. Who to meet for the first time, who to catch up with, how much time to spend with this person or that one, and who gets polite pleasantries only. I had three types of conversations with three different tones. The first was with people who had done some kind of service or blue-collar work in the past and wanted to relive a chapter from the old days. The second was the obligatory "thank you for your service" type, more of a checkbox conversation and brief. The third was service inquiries, either "when does the program start?" or "how many sites in construction right now?" which allowed them to be more efficient in other conversations. Based on my position and stature in the organization, there was little social capital to be gained chatting with me.

Even the "dick" was nice to everyone else. *Who am I to say it was insincere? Who am I to complain when I'm technically working and getting a free dinner?*

I left that evening thinking about how confident and generous I would be if I were wealthy. The attendees were, by and large, giving, courteous, and kind. *I can act like that, but how to get wealthy is a total mystery.* I'd seen things on TV, but this give me a vivid, detailed glimpse of what being wealthy might be like. It wasn't the luxury car out front. What I observed then and since is that being competent and disciplined, kind and approachable, well…increases the chances that good financial opportunities will find you. And it's harder to be those things when you're scraping by. It was the emotional buoyancy of being valued, respected, and thanked, compounding day after day.

I still didn't want to do what I perceived to be necessary to become wealthy. *You'll become a dick too.* But it was important that I saw it.

Writing this a decade later, I still hope that I won't become a dick. And the fear that I might still holds me back.

What I have learned since that night is people generally don't respond to logic. Logic only reinforces their response, which is emotional. We act out our feelings, our identity, our impulses. We buy experiences. I know now that those donors needed an experience because they were being recruited to donate to other things too.

At any level, fundraisers are pretty formulaic: and that formula is to play on emotions. Food, drink, public praise, mission appeal, fun prizes. This is more of a science than you might think, honed by decades of trial and error. The silent auction, the free drinks and hors d'oeuvres; all of these wear down our inhibitions and inflate our ego. And apparently, I'm all for it. At one event, I texted to donate while the event was happening, and I got to see my "Brett Heaton Juarez $100" on a donations banner behind the speaker for the next half hour. Immediate feedback. The person I was talking to wasn't on there, I noted smugly. (Thankfully, it didn't show "charged to AMEX credit card, current balance: $10,956.")

Without a meal, busy and successful people might not go unless they were already connected to the mission. Most high-capacity donors— typically decision-makers that are hiring/promoting/collaborating—also benefit from some publicity, even if they aren't seeking it. And the tax breaks! Charitable giving is an intricate system. One of my clients— bless his heart—thought that his $20/month gift to NPR would earn him a tax break. Sorry, buddy. But the tax code does reward giving in a big way. And gifts can be made in a variety of ways, some with more benefits than others if you know all the rules.

A charitable gift, up to a percentage of the donor's income, is fully tax-deductible. The difference in type of asset given and the timing can amount to significant savings to the donor with little to no effect on the receiver. Integration of the donor's financial team and the development team are important. Big donors want deductions. For a high earner in the 37% marginal tax bracket, giving $10,000 means they will avoid $3,700 in income tax. That is straightforward. If the $10,000 is donated, the charity keeps the full $10,000. And if you can give it publicly, by standing up in front of crowd of people you're trying to impress? Even better! So, it's not just about the holiday spirit, these people are calculating their end of year tax liability.

Donors, individual or corporate, pay for nonprofits after all. They profit from our consumption, and then they give to causes that make our lives better directly or indirectly.

Presumably, the tax code wants to incentivize giving, in part because it reduces the need for government spending on services. It also facilitates social cohesion: the wealthy are generous; the poor are deserving. See? It all works out. Or does it?

Now, the skeptical historian in me can go on and on (see previous chapters) but I need to remember to be optimistic (see previous chapters). This is a system: one that works…sort of. A system funnels causes and effects into predictable patterns. Giving, in a human context, brings us closer, like cooking a meal for a grieving friend.

Giving in a systems context can push us apart. The donor gets a self-esteem boost, a tax deduction and recognition, like those at the Let's Build a House Party. Considering they could have created an off-shore shell account, that's pretty great. Even I got a meal and a t-shirt.

Since then, I've attended a fundraiser where the "props in the pageant" were children, performing the mission in a way that made me feel… uncomfortable. The recipient can be demeaned instead of empowered.

One group has the money, and therefore more influence over the rules. Dollar value does not confer human value. Dollar value is measured by the marketplace. Human value is measured by the community. Both can increase exponentially.

Here I was, miffed that a guy I didn't know didn't say hello or thanks. Maybe he'd had a terrible day. I'd hate to be judged for my worse day. I felt defined by my circumstances at the time.

That evening overlooking Lake Washington, my ego was put in check. I saw a one-time pledge that amounted to what Andrew and I earned through AmeriCorps for the year. Combined. On the other hand, these people said "um," hid yawns, and did other things regular people do. Because dollar value doesn't reflect human value.

I was given an example of what was possible. I just had to believe it was possible for me. The power of that belief, even when inconvenienced, ignored, and taken for granted, is what changes our dollar value. It's not just money that compounds over time. Belief does too.

it was not a loan

What better way to kick off a year *living by the mountains* than with $1,000 of new gear I bought for $500?! As I left Lake Valley Camp, I took advantage of the pro deal (an outfitter bulk discount) I set up to replace worn out camping gear, and headed west on I-90, trailer full and madly in love. *My lifelong dream is happening.* Rebeca had moved out ahead of me when her last job ended and was absorbing our new home while I was back at LVC, preparing to say goodbye and close a chapter of my life.

We moved there with no money and no debt. My parents helped out by giving me my grandpa's car, which looked like a car a grandpa would drive, but was well-maintained and had been sitting idle since he passed away two years earlier. I had to admit it would be more practical than the Black Pearl, now approaching 300,000 miles. Rebeca's parents took on her car payment that year, since we would be making less than $2,000 a month combined with about half of that going to rent and electricity.

In the fall of 2010, we embraced exploring our new home with new friends. We continued on the path we were on: not taking on debt, not saving a dime, and not having a plan for any real kind of emergency or expense. Not uncommon for 24 year-olds.

But after the New Year, the wedding plans started to feel more real. I loved the venue we had chosen as much as she did, and thought it was so cool that all my friends would be in one place at one time. I wanted a wedding that was reasonable. Neither of us were particularly materialistic or over the top about "the party of the century, bro" or "if the fabric isn't this color, I'm going to cry." We were mature, I would say. We cut costs using family connections for things like the cake, and Rebeca's friends pitched in, set up, and helped in so many ways. With me and others as delegates, Rebeca was planning a wedding from 2,000 miles away while in City Year, a work culture that didn't allow breaks or flex time the way an office job would.

Altogether, it was hard to say how much the tab was. I would guess something like $7,000–9,000. Her friends and family probably chipped in about $2,000–2,500. They also did so many favors and things on top of that. We maybe paid about $2,000–3,000 over the course of the year, between deposits, services, and all the other little things mandated by the wedding-industrial complex. We had, according to Google and anecdotal friend opinions after the fact, a modest and tasteful wedding that reflected us as people.

Where did the other $4,000–5,000 come from? A year earlier, Rebeca's dad had announced that he would contribute $5,000 toward the wedding. He was so excited, maybe because Rebeca was his first child to do things in the "traditional Christian" order. We were thrilled and grateful and left it at that.

(Deep breath …)

A few weeks before the wedding, my soon-to-be father-in-law and I were both in Oregon to help my future brother-in-law, Ben, move out of his apartment. They would be driving straight back to Milwaukee, and I would take his cat for a week. He pulled me aside, put his hand on my shoulder, and told me he didn't have the money…He apologized and just looked at me, waiting for a reaction. This was like a week before the wedding. Rebeca was already back in Milwaukee. *Um, what? I don't have the money, and the balance is due for the venue next week.* "I don't know, maybe your parents could help out?" *What?!* I was shocked. I have no idea what I muttered back, if anything.

Not till I got back to Seattle, alone in our apartment with Ben's irritating cat, did it feel real. The weight of it was heavy. At that time, the only option that came to mind was to ask my own parents to provide $5,000 for the time being "just to make sure all the checks clear." I knew they could do it and thought they would since they were able to and didn't want anything to go wrong. I called and asked if they could transfer money to my account so I could pay the last round of expenses, saying Rebeca's dad was driving back from Oregon and unable to get the money until he returned. And they did, as I expected. That lie bought me some time. *I'll figure it out after. We need a solution now.*

I needed checks to clear, but as it stood, those checks wouldn't "clear" for months, until we started our next jobs. We didn't have the money right now, and I was on my way to the wedding in a few days. I had to push it out of my mind, even when my parents met Rebeca's for the first time as planned, while expecting some resolution on this that never came. I knew it would be a mess, but I just thought I would deal with it in a month. I didn't know what else to do.

I enjoyed every minute of our wedding, went back to work for a few weeks, then went on a five-day honeymoon to the San Juan Islands, camping one day, bed and breakfast three more. It was great, not extravagant for a honeymoon, but in hindsight really nice for not having any money beyond cash wedding gifts. *For the first time, you have less than no money.*

Then, I had to tell my parents. The call came. "When can we expect you to transfer the money back?" The dread mounted in me. The kind of dread you feel as a child when you know you'll get in serious trouble, but you don't know exactly when it will happen or how bad it will be.

I don't remember a thing about the actual phone call when I told them. I know I told them the truth: that Rebeca's dad had promised to pay that amount, then hadn't. Couldn't or wouldn't, we will never know for sure. With money, it's always some of both anyway. All financial choices are relative. That's why financial choices involving your relatives are messy.

I felt the silence and tension from 2,000 miles away. Two weeks later, my dad flew out to Seattle to help me move back to Milwaukee. The drive back east on the I-90 felt different again. As she'd done before, Rebeca had moved back early, so my dad and I had planned to go to North Cascades National Park. He called that off. We didn't process what happened at all on the drive. That wasn't our style. I was so eager to minimize the time spent with him that my buddies Sean and Nick helped me pack the trailer beforehand, and I picked him up right from the airport, ready to head east. The dread continued, but in a less intense, more drawn-out way. I sensed this wasn't over.

I dropped off almost all our things in a storage unit in Milwaukee. We would be living with her parents until we found a good place to rent. Rebeca met me there. After a continuous 40-hour drive (about 60 mph with that car/trailer combo) and feeling suffocated by the waves of unspoken disappointment of my father two feet away from me, Rebeca brought me a cold Mountain Dew (perfect) and then pointed out how messily the trailer was packed (really bad timing on her part). I yelled at her, and told her to "just leave," which she did. Something had changed in my core. She didn't really know my parents. This was worse than she realized.

The dread I was feeling didn't translate into action. Looking back, it is inexplicable to me. I can't remember what I was thinking, but the action was avoidance. I know I was afraid of my dad's anger, and people don't think rationally when they're afraid. Time passed. We hadn't made progress on returning the $5,000 I "asked" for "temporarily." Five months later, visiting at Christmas, my dad blew up. "It was not a loan!" he shouted and stormed out of the house without waiting for a response. My mom, Rebeca and I were frozen in our living room chairs. My mother in sadness, Rebeca in shock, and me in shame.

My dad felt that Rebeca's dad had taken advantage of us. "Who says they'll pay and then doesn't?" He maintained it had been the plan the whole time to stick the cost on him and my mother because they could afford it. I knew he didn't trust easily. Some venomous thoughts surfaced once or twice.

We took out a personal loan for $6,000, paid my parents back in full, and made payments to the credit union. And you know, this was easier than I ever could have imagined. *You idiot! You could have done this in Seattle.* My credit score wasn't great because I had never used credit before, but I got the benefit of the doubt. *How can you be so in sync with the physical world and so naïve about the financial world?*

Even after we returned my parents' money, it seemed to infuriate my dad that Rebeca and I weren't more visibly affected. He didn't want us to take a loan, he wanted the wrong to be righted. It was an all-round shit situation. That's the nature of money: it's not a problem until it is. Money is a blank canvas, and individuals place different meanings and interpretations onto it. I knew my dad's dad had made some costly money mistakes over-trusting others. Of course, that would influence his worldview. I found out later that Rebeca's dad had loaned money to siblings in El Salvador, and never got it back. Rebeca was like, "It sucks but that's life." In her past of financial poverty, people just got through the day and had to keep moving.

In my head, I screamed, day after day, "Dad, this has never happened before. You didn't give me any advice in this area." *Sorry I was young and foolish. I learned your values of responsibility and fairness by observation, but I couldn't observe this one. I've never been into numbers…You know I hated math.* But I was too proud to apologize. I was angry, too.

Like many people, my dad represses feelings until a tipping point or trigger comes along. But when it surfaces, it is powerful. We didn't talk at all for about 18 months after that holiday season in 2011. I met my mom here and there at a diner halfway between our houses. She wouldn't ask him to leave his own house so that she could have me around. She told me he was fine with us visiting, but implied some family ties are conditional.

Rebeca, like my father, holds grudges. She was done with my dad, and resigned to accept her own father's flaws. My wounds healed with time. I had started budgeting and getting our house in order around the time we took out a loan. With Rebeca's support, I told her father—heart pounding—I wanted him to pay me what he had originally promised. *It was not a loan.* Slowly but surely, he did.

I hated how my dad handled it. I hated how small he made me feel, how he couldn't give me practical advice, just anger. I wished there could have been this "live and learn" movie moment where we had grown closer. I hated how he couldn't express what he was feeling when he was feeling it. Easier said than done, I know. I was too intimidated to "stick up for myself" like Rebeca wanted. I did raise my voice in response to him a few times, but it was out of character, and he escalated even further. This didn't help. His scorn brought me to tears, even at age 25.

And maybe he knew that his anger was the only thing that would reach me. Maybe he didn't hold back for a reason. In the time he didn't speak to me, we paid off $6,000 of debt and saved another $10,000, a rate of about $1,000 a month, while paying rent and traveling too. Amazing what a little redirected pain can do. I was shaken. I'd been rationalizing everyone else's choices instead of taking responsibility for my own.

I swallowed my pride, composed myself, and called him one day, on his cell phone. I knew he wouldn't answer, and I left a sincere voicemail to the effect: "I learned a lot from this. Thank you for demanding better from me. I'm sorry I didn't have a plan B. I will in the future. I hope we can talk soon." My feeling of utter incompetence, after a life filled with things going right, may have been the catalyst for the career I embarked on, this book, and my purpose.

Around this time, we learned Rebeca was pregnant, and shared the news with my mom. My dad would become a grandfather. Shortly after that, my mom called and asked, "Can we come visit sometime?"

"Who's we?"

"Dad, too."

Without a word on what had passed, things got better.

Knowing what I know now, I would have borrowed money from an institution. I could have. Even in a week, I could have looked at the bills, searched "how to get $5,000 in a week," and made it happen. I could have gone to a payday loan store; anything would have been better than getting family involved. I just had no idea there were options. I mean, my brain knew, but nothing occurred to me. In fact, what I asked for from my parents was a 0% payday loan. I desperately needed money to pay bills until more money came in, and I was willing to deal with the fallout in two weeks. In my case, a safety net meant I paid 0% interest instead of 400%. But the fallout cost me far more.

In the years since, it's a lot easier to go into debt than I thought. There's a whole industry standing by to help you pay them interest, in fact. The debt industry is designed to lend you money, charge you interest, and not be a catalyst for change. Credit offers in the mail imply that you "deserve the best" and just haven't caught a break. That's why you need "platinum," "prestige," "cash back," and so on.

Yes, I could have borrowed money, but I wouldn't have changed. At least not until the next emergency. I learned in grad school about life span theories of development. Research shows it is hard to change our attitudes and habits unless we have a dramatic life event. Our diet will change after a heart attack. We spend more time with family after an unexpected death. We course-correct.

It was the shame that forced my change. Shame and the feeling of incompetence in front of my parents and my wife. I wasn't accustomed to making mistakes. Fear that other mistakes were lurking on the horizon. Fear that mistakes would derail my success. *You're not as smart as you thought.*

It was not a loan. It was a buffer, I guess, a safety net. When we went to the bank, that was my first time borrowing money. Before that point, I really didn't get it. I didn't pay for college. I didn't pay for a car. I earned, and spent, and gave. Borrowing was a first. I was still insulated from the number $0. It was a new feeling, applying for it, and making the payments. It sharpened my senses, brought me into a new realm of adulthood. The best and worst thing about my "relationship" with the bank was how transactional it was. They wouldn't be proud or disappointed. It was good, as long as I paid on time. With family, it's never that simple.

I've always been good at relationships, which is why almost losing one with my dad was so memorable. My dad's anger was triggered by an intense feeling. His starry-eyed son being taken advantage of. *I'd be mad too.* His anger taught me a lesson about money after all. The greater the risk, the greater the potential reward. He took a risk because I could have turned my back on him forever. He held out until I repented and admitted I had made a mistake by lying about the situation I was in, asking for money under false pretenses. What if I had never done that?

By taking that risk with our relationship, he created a new money consciousness for his son. We could've settled for a numb truce where we make small talk. When nothing is risked, we cannot grow. Because I never claimed to be good with money or have a healthy relationship with money. In hindsight, the naivete of no back up plan, no details asked from her dad, was young and foolish of me. My best qualities had carried me this far, but suddenly I'd miscalculated. An over-reliance on my strength had become a weakness.

Over the years, the value of services performed by her dad has added to his repayment. He has helped us move three times now, let me borrow power tools, picked out and installed a new water heater, fridge, and washer since we moved in, all on short notice. He's always willing to help. He helped me put up 100 feet of fence around our yard, and has done frequent repairs. Rebeca's mom has watched the kids for free on countless days. These things, family or not, add up to tens of thousands of dollars of services we would pay for if we still lived in Seattle. Something for couples to consider when starting a family but dreading the idea of moving back home. Many of my clients have childcare bills equal to their mortgage payments. When clients lean heavily on their parents financially, I always advise paying the parents back first no matter what they say, or to define "help" in writing as a gift or loan with very specific terms. I may as well have a "trauma disclaimer" in my recommendations.

We will never add it up. And we will never ask what happened to the promised $5,000 when it came due on the wedding day. Keeping tabs is impossible and unhealthy, and we can't change the past … My parents paid for sports teams, books, vacations, college, things they love and believe in, because it's a reflection of their values. So, they aren't into weddings. That's their choice. The lender defines the terms. And whatever the hell this was, it wasn't a loan. It was a Band-Aid. In the end, my relationships with money, with my parents, and with my in-laws have emerged better for it. I continue to be a risk-taker. But if I'm borrowing to leverage a growth opportunity, I use an impersonal institution where all the fine print is spelled out.

chapter twenty-two
intro to self-help

Other than losing my wedding ring, the wedding went splendidly. (We found the ring the next day. The best man's thumb ring worked for the ceremony, but I did get a little nervous when the wedding party started stalling coming down the aisle.) Wedding gifts are great too. The shortfall covered by my parents was weighing on me, so cash was even better. We received a number of personalized gifts as well as standard wedding-registry things. My favorite gift was, of course, a book.

The gift itself, received the next day along with all the others, changed my energy immediately. Useful? Yes. Complimentary? Hard to say. Fun? Most would say no. Not a book I would ever buy. But a relief…

Dave Ramsey's bestselling personal finance book, *Total Money Makeover*. Ramsey's face is absolutely ginormous on the cover, so much so that I would keep the book facedown so I could have privacy. I didn't want him "looking" at me. *The lack of subtlety I'd expect from a self-help book. Ick.* Ramsey is a public figure that makes news beyond his financial advice. From a distance, he seems to attribute all income and asset gaps to differences in personal grit and ability, dismissing the continuing role of racism and public policy inequity. *Easy for a child of real estate developers to say.* Wikipedia says he identifies as an evangelical Christian and conservative fiscally and culturally. I do not. And yet, I found his advice life-changing in 2011. I want to give credit where credit is due. It is possible for us all, as imperfect people, to create value in some ways, and offend in others. *He is right, blaming doesn't pay the bills, even if it's valid.*

Our gift giver and officiant said they were introduced to the book through their church. The Bible instructs Christians to be good stewards of financial resources. Don't lose the sheep. Don't buy more goats just to show off to your neighbor, etc. I was skeptical, but I knew that this would be important in marriage, and I knew couples fought over money a lot. This was so not me, in every possible way. What did I have to lose? I like to read, even if it's a financial version of a *Goosebumps* book. I'd just made a colossal money blunder, after all. *It was not a loan.*

I started reading it right after I got back to Milwaukee. I knew I needed to get my shit together right away. It's not that I was worried that things wouldn't get better. That year, Rebeca's income went up about 30% (still in AmeriCorps) and mine 300% to about $60,000 combined. I was still rattled though. All my life things had gone pretty well until now. I was perceived—and self-identified—as a successful person. I maintained friendships and made new ones, managed to get married, got promoted at work, kept up with the news …you know, I was "on it." So, my inability to anticipate this wedding fiasco, and utter dependence on others, really caught me off guard. *I am successful …right?*

I. Tore. Through. The. Book.

Although I judged it by its cover, the page-turning, eye-catching style was combined with critical information about the financial system in the United States. I learned sooooo much. *New car depreciation?! Compound interest?! Oh my!* Some of the numbers blew my mind. Things so obvious to some had never been explained to me. The closest I'd come was Intro to Microeconomics as a college freshman. Perhaps it was assumed I knew. Perhaps it was a rite of passage. Apparently, there was more to learn than "don't spend money you don't have." That was a powerful lesson that I could observe in my parents, and one that I followed 100% until my fresh failure. But the structure of financial systems in America can't be observed through the senses.

And there were steps. Like a 12-Step Program, the actions were clear, concise, and achievable, as in you knew when you had finished the step. You could answer directly, yes or no. While the steps to financial freedom were sequential, they still accounted for backward progress: roadblock on step 3, go back to step 2. I knew from behavioral psychology, in class and hands-on with kids, that people, even me, needed quick wins to stay motivated. Attainable benchmarks, like setting aside $1,000, gave me a win.

Once properly motivated, we were paying off debt, and then saving, at about $1,000 a month, or about a quarter of our take-home pay that first year back in Milwaukee. The "makeover" was formulaic, but it acknowledged the messy nature of the human soul. Without that, it would have been another dry, bland math problem of the sort I despised growing up. This book was written for people in need of a change: a sustained effort to pay off debt. If we were thinking logically, we wouldn't be in this situation. And mission accomplished: I read it, dog-eared it, wrote notes in the margin. I applied it.

The book seemed pretty simplistic sometimes, but it was entertaining. It played to my ego while bruising it at the same time. "Dumb math and stupid tax" was a common tagline he used, which tactfully allowed me the reader to exclaim, "OMG! People are so dumb for playing the lottery" or "Oh no, I was almost that dumb person who financed a brand-new car I can't afford." I found community in the anecdotal experiences of others.

Much of the mass market finance self-help assumes the reader is motivated already by money. Making millions day-trading stocks is not a viable starting point. Neither is real estate, nor entrepreneurship. These are absolutely possible, but most people don't want that or don't have the support system to try. These paths may lead to wealth, but they are incredibly stressful even without credit cards piling up.

Specificity was crucial for me because I wasn't motivated to do this naturally. Tell me what to do, so I can feel I'm making progress, then let me go back to what I care about. This gave me a framework to decide whether to pay extra on loans or grow an emergency fund. His sequential baby steps model of saving $1,000 in cash, then paying off debt other than mortgage, then saving up three to six months of expenses …It was so frustrating to not know this earlier!!! Every online article spoke to a specific scenario, like index funds or bankruptcy. Now I had a system. The book also talked about credit, cash, insurance, and retirement investments. Since most other resources were siloed, focusing on only one in depth, getting these pieces integrated into a sequential blueprint was immensely helpful.

I was astounded at the personal testimonials in the book: couples with six figures of credit card debt, two home equity loans, payday loans. So many people were in such worse shape than I realized. I thought about all the new cars in Palatine when I was growing up there and wondered how many car payments were sparking arguments in the kitchen once the kids went to bed. I naively thought my parents' way was the common way.

I thought of them and the other parents I knew while reading, because this guy Dave basically said what my parents had role-modeled all my life but never told me: live below your means and you'll have more financial security. Until now, the system for doing so had remained a mystery.

The system was fluid, too, with products and opportunities shifting. I'd never had any employee benefits other than health insurance. My dad had worked for the federal government my entire childhood: with a wonderful menu of automatic and voluntary options for health, life and disability insurance, a pension and 401k. Without any of that, the makeover book was my introduction.

There is no doubt in my mind I would have signed up for a retirement account, if I'd ever been offered through work. Then I'd have forgotten about it, and spent whatever money hit my bank account. Rebeca and I did stay with my in-laws for three months when we moved back after the wedding. If we had put the money we kept not paying rent ($850 × 3 = $2,550) in a mutual or index stock fund growing at an annual average of 8% compound interest, we would have $61,897 at age 65. Without any more contributions. Once again, I remembered Einstein saying compound interest was the ninth wonder of the world.

The irony was that I deliberately ignored it because forging my own identity was more important than admitting my parents might be right in their caution. I didn't want to hear it from them (or this looming face on the book cover), because I "didn't identify with them." I needed their message from another source.

I thought again of my parents: my dad's poker face at the car dealership, my mom having the audacity to challenge and refuse the orthodontist's recommendations. "That's ridiculous," she would say. I would get embarrassed by the social interaction. As I kid, I didn't consider that they were prioritizing, that a mistake in a major purchase could affect my college fund.

This had such an impact that I shared the book at "Team Time," a monthly lunch in my office, where the other directors and I would take turns either bringing a guest speaker or sharing a subject we were passionate about. The intent was personal development, not at all work-related. I brought the book in, badly chewed up by our new dog, filled with Post-its and hand-scribbled notes. I remember people said it was helpful, but it was a tepid response compared to my feverish "awakening." It's hard to receive a message like this before you're ready. *You didn't think you needed help either. Look at you now.* I just hoped something would happen to lead them to seek more understanding. *Instead of a f**k-up like yours.* The best time to review finances is before you have to. The most common time to do it is after a big change.

Vulnerable people are targeted for more mistakes. When we're desperate, we want so badly to believe ... *Yes, you're right, Hollywood celebrity, cryptocurrency will fix this.* What Ramsey's book does not explicitly acknowledge is that some people are targeted by these deceptive offers more than others. It does not acknowledge that debt becomes necessary when real barriers to earning and saving exist. I know that "dumb math and stupid tax" is embedded in our culture, and deliberately perpetuated via advertising and discrimination. Still, I got quality financial advice from a problematic person. Which is more effective than problematic financial advice from the most quality person I know. Which a lot of people do.

My accountant doesn't have to be cool. They have to be qualified. Identity politics is counterproductive, but it persists for a reason. People just gravitate toward in-group versus out-group thinking. When a client refers their friend, colleague, or family to me, and that person declines to have a non-committal first conversation with me, it's not because they doubt my credentials. They are grappling with elements of identity. "Can I trust a professional who doesn't know me yet?" "I'm self-reliant. I don't want to pay for help." "I don't care about money, so what would we talk about?" "I spend all I earn, so what would we talk about?" "I'm all set with money, so what would we talk about?"

I am well-qualified to advise on growing assets, mitigating risks, and managing exposure. A financial planner is best suited for taking a financial situation that is generally positive and optimizing it. On the other hand, the book outlines a plan that will get the target audience, in debt and acknowledging a problem, to a better place. Simplistic, of course, but debt reduction, while simple, is not easy. The book's audience needed a makeover, not a financial planner. In fact, I've given clients the book after getting minimal life and disability insurance in place for them. The book does the "makeover" better than I can, and I don't have the time to read it to them. The beauty is in the simplicity.

Personal finance experts can debate the validity of certain points in *Total Money Makeover*. For example, he promoted the debt "snowball" approach, which says pay off the smallest balances first. Another nod to the psychological importance of visible progress sooner. By contrast, a finance "robot" would promote the debt "avalanche" approach, which prioritizes paying off highest interest debt first, regardless of the balance. As a financial planner now, I say: whatever keeps the momentum going. What I have learned through thousands of conversations is that the goal is progress, not perfection. The biggest barrier is often analysis paralysis, and the first action step is always the hardest.

Life is too short to argue over which way is best. Now, there are things I read in *Total Money Makeover* that are misleading. I understand why: when you are writing a self-help book, "it depends" doesn't move copies. Nothing sells like clarity; just ask a politician. On the campaign trail, clarity and strength sell. Once in office, effective governance is about due diligence, judgment, and compromise made in context. As a CERTIFIED FINANCIAL PLANNER™ practitioner, I have a code of ethics that requires me to work through the details, and the advice is almost always "it depends."

I don't hold a grudge because this book got my ass in gear. I'm not in Ramsey's target audience anymore anyway. He has an excellent mass market message, and the need for financial guidance is so great that bickering is a distraction. Confusion doesn't inspire action. A former colleague at Lake Valley Camp told me years later that my newfound passion at Team Time in 2013–2014 sparked a conversation with him and his wife, and they started to save more. Sharing that book was a catalyst for them. *And he's a Buddhist, so identity isn't everything.*

I found core identity alignment with the author in the final step of *Total Money Makeover* on giving. Yes, giving money away freely because you have enough for yourself. This was a novel idea. I instinctively associated wealth with greed, not generosity. Now even I was motivated. At the time, being a millionaire sounded great, but not if I had to work and sacrifice to do it. I started to think bigger now, realizing that my prosperity could lift others up: it wasn't me or them.

This gift enriched our lives. That's thoughtful giving—how often do we just get a gift card? Why not think about the person, and say, "Please read this. I could be wrong, but I thought of you, and I think this will make your life better." You run the risk of offending them, yes, but all lasting relationships offend at some point. You just might turn their life around. When a client refers someone new to me, and we meet and talk, they often say, "I feel so much better." That's worth more than a gift card.

chapter twenty-three

doing doors

"Where's Ben?"

"He's still doing doors."

The year Rebeca and I lived in Seattle, my brother-in-law Ben was also in the Pacific Northwest, which brought a sense of home in a faraway land that year. He was getting his master's in public policy at Oregon State in Corvallis. Ben is very cerebral guy, the kind of guy people might say "has his head in the clouds," but once you talk to him, you appreciate how deeply connected he is to people and places. He's a guy I relate to because he's an idealist overcoming an execution problem like me.

We moved back to Milwaukee in the same year, and with some early encouragement from a cadre of close friends and budding political junkies, Ben decided to run for alderman in the neighborhood he and Rebeca grew up in and where we all still lived. It made sense. The incumbent alderman was a crusty old guy who had been maintaining the status quo for a few decades under the banner of "law and order." Ben was the young guy full of optimism, and, well, "policy."

Local politics is important. We tend to flock to national presidential politics for the same reason we follow celebrity: the stakes are higher, more people are talking about the same thing, and it's more … gossipy. Local politics is gritty without glamour, legislation without reporters. Elections are won door to door, block by block. A nitty gritty grind.

I thought this was super cool, and I wanted to help Ben not just because he was my brother now and was the real deal, but because I wanted to learn how this sphere of our civilization worked. I was part of Ben's "Kitchen Cabinet" as we called it. A group of nine or ten people, half personal supporters as close friends or family, the other half people with a political background, excited about him specifically entering politics. By the end of the campaign, we all fit in both categories.

Local elections are won or lost by tens or hundreds of votes, not thousands or millions. I learned quickly that success hinged on name recognition as much as anything else. Be honest. You've made some random guesses voting for circuit court judge after proudly checking your presidential and senate candidates. And without some kind of super PAC (political action committee), the door-knocking strategy was essential. There were two primary aspects of supporting his campaign: (a) counseling on strategy, key relationships/endorsements, and putting on fundraising events, and (b) putting in the hours to hit the doors, and deliver flyers and yard signs, so people would remember his name on the ballot.

First on the fundraising and promotion side. Money and power are intertwined. Everyone willing to talk to him liked Ben, but not everyone gave him money. Many friends were supportive, but this just wasn't as shareable as other ways to donate. Donations are public record, so some were worried about alienating more powerful players in Milwaukee politics. "I would support you, but you are still unknown and unproven, so let's wait and see." Incumbents have access to power, today, unless the challenger has enough money to erode that power. People are risk-averse, and a young guy with a beard and graduate degree talking about business improvement districts was a little over the top for some. Money tends to maintain the status quo, because the money was usually acquired under the status quo.

And money and age often correlate. Ben was living between his girlfriend's and parents' place, and was doing this full-time. He was broke. His family and friends, also mid-to-late twenties, were broke. A challenger in another local race that year owned several income properties. The budget to print campaign literature was chump change to him. He was in his forties. Most incumbents on the Common Council were in their fifties. *I sure hope we will have more money to donate in our fifties.*

Older folks tend to have more assets as well. The 8th alder-manic district is very densely populated for the city. There are a lot of working-class families with children, but they often didn't show up on our list of registered voters. Homeowners did. They care about property taxes and home values. They have some skin in the game in the way that renters don't. Rebeca and Ben's parents lived a block away from a busy intersection with quite a few vacant storefronts. If Ben could turn that into a thriving scene, their home would grow in value. This district is where he grew up; he wanted that for everyone. He understood that he could grow the pot for everyone by making the neighborhood more desirable to homeowners and business owners, which increases tax revenue, which makes room for reinvestment in local projects and infrastructure.

Money and faith are intertwined as well. The thing about donat-ing to a political campaign, especially a major underdog like he was, is that you don't see a return in any tangible way unless he wins. He got a lot of donations from friends and family who were supporting him. A gift to a long-shot challenger felt more like charity for some. I don't think they thought of it as "making an investment," which is what earning points with the incumbent can feel like. His opponent maintained some key relationships, providing service in exchange for support. To the Tavern League and business owners in the neighborhood, writing him a check felt like an investment because he was in a position to deliver. He seemed to effectively tap into one of Milwaukee's best qualities: loyalty. People stuck by each other; shared history is valued in Milwaukee. *"You went to _______ High School? My sister went there!"*

This kind of connection goes further than you would think. *What about results? What about competence? Can't a newcomer deliver too?* I couldn't figure out why this wasn't a bigger issue. The 8th district was not thriving. Ben pointed out multiple missed opportunities to attract large businesses and community efforts that could revitalize streets and keep kids busy. So, why was the incumbent still around after 12 years? He wasn't too popular city-wide either.

The answer came at the doors.

Every person would benefit from some time spent in teaching, the service industry, or sales. Disrespect, bad tips, door slams: routine rejection is the common thread. Going door to door for Ben was my first "sales" experience: the world of skepticism, first impressions, and forced friendliness. It was fascinating, joining the long line of door-knocking political hopefuls before us. I thought of how I felt when we got a door knock at our house. "Jehovah's Witnesses or Mormons?" Rebeca calls from the kitchen. "I don't know … Oh, I see the clipboard now, yeah politics or community organizer." And now I was that guy. There were some rude responses and some terrifying dogs at the fence, but for the most part people were cordial. Especially in winter when they just felt sorry for us slogging two hours in 10-degree weather.

We usually handed out a lit piece, like a two-sided 5x7 flyer, and the clipboard with a printout mapping all the addresses to hit with our route. Voter turnout is so low in these elections that we just go to houses of registered voters, which was probably only one house in five. Of those, usually one in four was a person who was knowledgeable about the neighborhood and city, civically engaged beyond voting. Many of those liked the incumbent, and of that group, almost all were White homeowners. What did they like about him? Our neighbors across the street, who we liked personally, said that he responds right away. Streetlight out? Fixed next day. Graffiti on your garage? Removed that weekend. They loved the responsiveness. They couldn't care less about policy, and we got the impression they felt that was for the mayor's office or the state.

Ben's supporters lived in a neighborhood that became more Black and Brown, and saw household incomes drop in the past 30 years. They wanted an advocate. They wanted … customer service. One guy told us a story about a city crew that was going to cut down two beautiful trees in front of his house, apparently for some curb extension. They were unloading the chainsaws, so the guy called the alderman, and five minutes later the crew drove away. Ben, with his regression analysis and bilingual charm, was a risk. And social change moves at the speed of trust. And because voting in this country is treated as a privilege instead of a right, people who aren't as established (who were more likely to vote for Ben) are less likely to vote.

Most residents had never heard of their own alderman by name, though. They may have had their property tagged, and streetlights and potholes, but … they didn't ask for help, and they probably didn't vote for him, if at all. It was a two-way street. The alderman knew his core voter base and spent his energy keeping them happy. After all, a family of four earning $40,000 a year may have $100 to donate if they felt heard. An empty-nester couple earning $120,000 may have $1,000. So, naturally the incumbent spent ten times the energy on them. Sales at work in democracy. Double down on what works.

Widening the tent is tough. I remember rounding the corner doing doors, clipboard and pen clutched in fingers numbed by Wisconsin winter, scanning the next address. *F**k me, they've got a yard sign for the other guy. You can skip it. No one will know. Just mark them not home…* I slowed down. Sigh. Knock knock.

The greater the risk, the greater the (potential) reward. While I was more likely to get rejected by a known supporter of the other candidate, persuading this person to reconsider would be the greatest reward. And if I swung and missed, who cares? It's not personal. But it sure felt personal. And that's why selling anything requires conviction.

The informed voters who didn't like the incumbent were mostly turned off by his show-of-force press conferences and lack of solutions beyond more police. Even those with beautiful homes probably never experienced his top-notch customer service because they didn't pledge their support. Those without the clout, who still believed in America's promise of democracy, seemed to be left out. We had some great conversations, and wanted to execute, but life got in the way. There were many elderly neighbors who needed a ride to the polls, so we drove some but not all. Parents with four kids couldn't make time to vote. Roofers and carpenters were carpooling to work at 5:30 am before polls opened, and were exhausted when they got dropped off at 4:00 pm. Work and family comes first. If the regular voters turned out to protect their interests, the least our country could do is make election days national holidays, so going to vote didn't mean a smaller paycheck.

If it takes 30 minutes out of your already stressful day, and you vote for reasons you don't really understand, for an office that hasn't represented you before, and that nice young man you met the other day might not even win? Well, maybe you won't. Going to vote is a matter of principle. In the hierarchy of needs, principle comes after many necessities the voter wasn't getting.

Ben won the primary, and six weeks later on Election Day, I was at one of the polling precincts ready to send in the tally to be added by the team in advance of hearing the results. He got 400-something out of just over 1,000 votes. Forty percent was heralded as a big success for a newcomer like him. His dedication to doors served him well. But money in the bank would have helped.

You've no doubt heard it said that successful people do what unsuccessful people are unwilling to do. Doors are one of those things some people will never subject themselves to. Campaigning and doors are likes sales jobs: it's easy to get started but sticking through to the finish is much harder. *Don't look at that text. It's Rebeca asking when you'll be home. You'll just get sad. You said you'd finish this turf.* I remember the grueling effect on Ben. He lost too much weight, bags under his eyes. He was routinely ignored or rejected, but every encounter was a fresh opportunity to win someone over, hear a story, earn a vote, keep a promise. Strangers finding common ground in the midst of differences is messy but worth it. It's democratic.

Ask and you shall receive. You won't always get what you asked for, but put the work in and it will come back to you. He didn't win, but by entering the arena, he flexed his focus muscles. In politics and sport alike, competition provides focus. You win or lose. If we don't like politicians, we need to vote them out. By focusing on winning a campaign, he had to define and share his vision. He had to be passionate about it, or it wouldn't be compelling. And every day he faced the possibility of outright rejection and opposition. Face-to-face and online. Learning to focus during rejection made him stronger.

Lasting power is built from the ground up, one relationship at a time. With people and money, the investment always happens before the results are proven.

Although Ben had great policy ideas, he may have been too inexperienced to execute or gain support in an old boys' club system back then. He could now, but timing is everything. His natural network knew other people who were young and just starting out. He needed to get out there to grow the network. Relationships that become partnerships allow people to be in two places at once, double their resources, double their network. You can't build a new relationship without risking rejection. He didn't earn anything campaigning for District 8 Alderperson. But his value—and in turn his earnings—as a future employee, partner and citizen was multiplied.

Ben has since gone on to a prolific career: salaried political staffer to a US senator, nonprofit coding instructor, now a tech entrepreneur and co-founder of two startups. He knocked consistently, and doors of all kinds have opened since. Everybody knows Ben. It is a testament to hard work, and focus.

As for me, I too gained some experience facing rejection head-on. Doing doors was a form of exposure therapy, which is a method of treatment for anxiety. I hated doing it every time, but I believed in the mission, and rejection got easier. I thought it was funny eventually. Everyone should have a door slammed in their face a few times. You work through those reactions: *I'm out here hustling, helping my bro help others, and they won't even talk to me? He cares so much, and they say, "I don't vote?"* Once you learn how to process and can move forward, conviction and enthusiasm intact, you are ready to knock on any door before you. Now it's just a part of my life, more than I ever would have guessed.

hey roomie!

We were blazing through our debt reduction. *It was not a loan.* The 2011–2012 school year, I was making $45,000, and Rebeca had finished her second AmeriCorps year as a Team Leader where she was earning slightly more. We now earned three times more than we did in Seattle.

With all of us in the same boat in Seattle, there had been an unspoken social contract to do things on a shoestring budget. It certainly had downsides, because money is money, but it was an important lesson in communal living. Being engaged, we lived in our own place, but just about everyone we hung out with lived in either the "Ameri-house," a gross 14-ish-bedroom building City Year corps members occupied, probably for like $200–300 apiece, or the grungy "Habitat house," a slightly better arrangement with 6–7 bedrooms. Our shared experience was a financial reality that made more luxurious quarters unattainable, and after a while, less desirable. I learned that community is a more substantive source of happiness than I thought.

Back in Milwaukee, we were a freshly minted married couple, dual income with no kids (or "DINKs" as we say in the biz). And most folks in that category spend like crazy. Social outings now carried a higher price tag, as we settled into an almost imperceptible "keeping up with the Joneses" pace. We saved—and spent—more than ever before. Because we could. All of sudden we "needed" things we could do without months ago. *Need is strong word.*

Our rent for a two-bedroom lower unit in a stand-alone duplex was $850 a month. We had about 1,000 square feet, a small yard with privacy, lots of basement storage, and were a block away from the Milwaukee River greenway in a beautiful corner of the Riverwest neighborhood, one of the only rental properties on the block. We paid that same amount for a one-bedroom in Seattle half the size with no outdoor space at all. Location, location, location. Our upstairs neighbors were a married couple, too. They were pretty chill, sociable. They had a roommate, who was an architecture grad student and friend of theirs. As far as we could tell, this worked out just fine. The roommate was on campus a lot in his studio, and the couple had varying hours, so a lot of the time there were only one or two people there anyway.

With the same floor plan downstairs, our tiny second bedroom was pretty much empty. *Philosophy question. Can a room in a house be left empty? Can we suppress this nesting instinct?* We had put a desk in there for some sort of study/office because that's what people do, but we never went in there. It had a nice private view toward the backyard, good natural light from the other window, and ample closet space. *Why don't we get a roommate?*

The more we talked about it, the old-school impropriety of a married couple living under the same roof as another didn't feel like a problem for us. And having another $200–300 a month for absolutely no work meant more vacation, more date nights. I began to see the opportunities.

Of course, we'd have to find the right roommate. Rebeca and I were both pretty picky, and we didn't "need" to do this. What we were looking for we found within a few months: a friend we knew and liked, but not an extremely close friend. Someone clean, reserved, not a known party animal. Our first roommate just wanted a little space from her parents. Free usually has some strings attached after all. She would be saving some money, because most comparable arrangements in Milwaukee would be $400–500. Someone who was comfortable in an impermanent arrangement with flexibility to leave. I wish I could report that having a roommate was awkward because of all our loud, wall-pounding marital sex, but alas, that was never the case. We wrote up a Word doc contract and signed, giving each other two months' notice to end the rental agreement.

A potential downside was getting on each other's nerves, which was no different than any other living arrangement. I got on Rebeca's nerves already. The informal contract was low risk, because we were able to cover all the rent anyway. Doing this in a rental property was risky, because although our landlady liked us, we did not disclose that she was living there. But she was from Milwaukee, and her parents lived a few miles away, so she used their house for a mailing address. If she had ruined something, I suppose we would have been liable.

The upsides? We got paid for better utilizing a space we were already paying for. *Buy only what you'll use, use often what you buy.* We occasionally cooked together. She helped clean here and there, and always after herself. She benefited from me taking out the trash and helping her move stuff. We benefited from having someone around when we were out of town, to handoff keys or other little things. And we got to have her kind presence in our house. In short, it was awesome. "Hey roomie!" we'd say in greeting, sort of tongue-in-cheek, like we discovered a secret life hack. About a year later, she moved on to live with her boyfriend. Happy ending and happy beginning; we were able to fill a gap for another friend with a lease that was up three or four months before her Peace Corps deployment.

About a year later, six months into our new house, our good friend's brother moved into the spare bedroom after a sudden break-up. The understanding from the start was it would be for a few months. He was living out of a hotel and paying dearly for it. We never became more than acquaintances, but his brother vouched for him. He was a medical resident, so we never saw him. *How is this amount of work legal? He doesn't have time to sleep, let alone find an apartment. I guess you get a doctor salary at the end.*

Everybody needs a place to live, even people who travel all the time for work, keep strange hours, or spend nearly all their time at their girl-friend's place. Some need an art studio. For whatever reason, we all need that occasional retreat to a room of our own.

Our final roommate checked all the boxes too. Rebeca had supervised him at City Year in the past and vouched for his character. He was a total homebody, but was very polite and respectful of space. He and Rebeca meal-planned together, trading off nights cooking for all of us. Yet another plus to pooling resources and living in community. Again, he paid less than he had before for a larger, cleaner, more hospitable home. (His last roommate was not ideal, it seemed.) It was $350 a month of passive income for us, and $350 a month on his part all-in: no utilities, water, internet, no roll of quarters for the laundry. We kept grocery receipts, and a quarter of the grocery total was added to his monthly rent. That way we could shop and share, but still account for it somehow. After a prior toxic roommate experience, he found some pleasant company.

In our three-bedroom house, he could always close the door and watch TV. Don't need much room for that right? His mom ran an in-home daycare growing up, and he had the patience for kids. Important, as he was our first roommate as parents. He never was asked to watch our son, but having another pair of adult eyes to say "don't touch that" was nice. Being very clear about these boundaries up front was key.

Living with Roque from age three to four, he always obliged a constant barrage of Thomas the Tank Engine questions. "What about Edward?"

"What about him?"

"He's here."

"No, that's Gordon. He's blue, too."

"WHO'S GORDON?!"

"Gordon thunders down the line."

The world is filling up. I'm so glad we found the humility to invite people in. I'm so glad our four roommates humbled themselves enough to live with a married couple and kid. Maybe it's time to share more, so we can be useful. The main use in having an immaculate spare bedroom that's empty is filling an ego-driven narrative that you can afford a bigger place than you need.

Our deliberate choice to have a roommate required me to change the narrative. From "can't afford our place" to "passive income," and from "we need to do what married couples do" to "living in community enriches our quality of life." Every financial transaction can benefit both parties. In true free market theory, it's the only kind. Our first roommate wanted an affordable step to moving out of her parents' place. Our second wanted a temporary set up without the cost/commitment of her own place. Our third needed a cheap place to sleep with minimum hassle, since all he did was work. Our fourth wanted to … well, I don't know. He doesn't elaborate, but it worked out great. I had to frame the narrative of a transaction from "we might be friends, but we will charge you to stay in our house" to "we're happy to give you an option, and we enjoy having you around." We can be useful to each other.

We can lower our fixed expenses, lower our flexible spending, or increase our income. Some people think constantly about this equation and its long-term ripple effects. Some people think about it almost never because the status quo is fine in their view. A subtle tweak on the American Dream: have a little less space that is exclusively yours, and be able to have more experiences as a result. In our case, we earned $4,200 a year. If we did that for 10 years, it would be $42,000! If that were reinvested along the way, it could fully fund a few kids' college tuition by itself. Or we could take an incredible vacation. Or donate to our favorite nonprofit. $4,200 into a growth fund IRA and forgotten about it, we could have another $75,000 or thereabouts at 60. Likely $150,000 at age 70.

You can be a slumlord or a landlord. You always have a choice. The former leverages the tenant to exploit. The latter leverages the asset to earn. If the tenant and consumer have a voice that is protected (a big if), they influence the market in profound ways. The explosion of organic food, fair trade textiles, and eco-tourism is evidence of that. The buyer and seller are useful to each other. Even if they're both hippies, that's still good old-fashioned capitalism. *Get in the game. You're an athlete. Figure this out. Stop feeling guilty.*

Many cultures share space because it makes financial sense and social sense. Living with others is healthy because we all need a support system. Reasonable privacy and ongoing isolation are different. Extended family helping in subtle ways and living in close proximity has been the story for most people for most of history. It works because different family members, in different life stages, have unique rhythms and gifts to share. The teen driving the adolescent to school. The cousin giving wisdom after an argument. Grandfather makes dinner and has it waiting when others get home. Grandmother rocks baby to sleep. These encounters happen in most families, but they happen more when living together.

The need to make sure everyone knows that this space is totally *mine*, that I *own* it, and I'll *host* but I won't *share* … it's a very Western, colonizer mindset.

Our dominant financial narrative in America is "move out and make your own way in the world." I don't think these are always mutually exclusive or sequential. The parents' basement can be framed as a crushing blow to the self-esteem, or an opportunity to save a year's rent of $10,000–20,000. But accurate framing is crucial. Moving away while single or cooking enough for two, even though there isn't a second person around, those aren't the most efficient ways to do things. Every transaction has some startup costs. Cooking a meal for one is still cooking. Listing your place on Airbnb once is a hassle. On an ongoing basis, it could be lucrative.

Urban planners and the public are moving toward more intentional co-housing and developments with shared spaces. Back in college, I had a long phone call with my buddy, now a real estate developer in Detroit, about how cool it would be to pool the skills of our friend group to create a co-housing utopia. A lawyer, a civil engineer, a teacher (me), an urban planner, all we needed was a health czar. The talk energized me so much, as it extended ownership from property-only to ownership of lifestyle choices. *I remember the grove of trees by Lincoln Ave Residence Hall, so vivid was the talk. Essentially, it's taking the rationale for cities and neighborhoods, and pushing it into the most intimate zone: communal sharing of expertise and resources in one home, just like the extended family.*

If we can strategically share more, and do it kindly, we can have more flexibility in our lifestyle instead of less. As the gig economy grows, I think we're missing an opportunity with roommates. It's easier than ever to book a room, or a car, or a snowblower, so why is homeownership out of reach? More and more, residences are purchased in cash as-is by large companies, to be rented out later at maximum profit. Also, many municipalities limit sharing space, for example renting a cottage house (an accessory dwelling unit). And you need an LLC to buy property with more than two owners. Ever wonder why you can't get five friends together and buy a dope house with 20% each? That very well may be a bad idea, but … that's how business ownership works. Partner drama, people buying each other out, and building equity all the while. It's all defined by contracts, so that feelings can't take over.

Healthy relationships are built on boundaries. Most bathrooms have a door, after all. So, don't share bills or money without talking through if-then scenarios. You can't control the feelings after being triggered. But you can refer back to the contract.

The slumlords of today don't want the landlords of tomorrow catching on. Assets appreciate. If I can buy fractional shares of Bitcoin, there's gotta be a way to buy a percentage of a home.

Be informed, not fearful. Boundaries are coming down in the 21st century, and financial and human resources will have to stay relevant. Tech is making a sharing economy possible; contract law just needs to keep up. We can reduce our expenses, and, more importantly, our carbon footprint. I'm not saying suffer a bad roommate if you don't have to; financial freedom is living life on your own terms. I'm saying there just might be a perfect match out there who can add some fresh energy to your home. Another person to chat with over morning coffee, or to stop at the store on the way home because you forgot. Like intergenerational families, a roommate living another chapter of life can remind of you of lessons and joys forgotten, or be a window to observe a future path.

I'd like to use a home we've made to teach and host young people to follow in our footsteps. We have a yard, a garden, and an unfinished basement. We could charge rent and incentivize stewardship projects— like shoveling, sealing windows, and gardening—to offset it. Efforts to grow food or save energy costs are inherently good teachable moments.

Victory Garden Initiative, the nonprofit that set up our raised beds, has a slogan "move grass, grow food." And we did for a few years, a lot of it. Eating your harvest is exciting, as I witnessed in our gardening program at Lake Valley Camp. Edible food coming from the ground, not the store. Our home has a large dining and living room, ideal for hosting large parties. How much unused utility? If we have a thing, let's use it as frequently and as fully as possible: that's the maximum return on investment. Even a rarely used third chair in the living room: get people enjoying it! Otherwise, it's no better than a dusty treadmill in the basement: a reminder of good intentions. Our fenced-in yard could be all production garden or be a full-time toddler playground. Our unfinished basement could be an up-and-comer's art studio. We could move on and use the space for events. We could host a Thanksgiving meal and invite anyone who can't afford a flight home. Let's get creative with cash flow.

Homeownership is a pillar of financial security for many American families because it offers stability. Owning a home allows families to welcome kids and siblings who need a place to stay. What about people who would prefer a room in our home if we just asked? Because it's closer to work, it's away from a toxic relationship, it's in a quiet neighborhood, whatever the reason.

Control is not the goal. Stability gives us more room to breathe, but efforts to control have a diminishing return. Relationships, like assets, tend to appreciate. Let's redefine the perceived benefits, norms and roles of renter and landlord. The best transactions are a win for all of us ... You never know who might choose a room in your home instead of an apartment alone.

expecting

I'd never been to LA, but I expected to hate it. Glitz, glamour, and hot weather are not really my things. I love Rebeca's family there, however, so I was excited. We had a fantastic time. LA is made for entertainment. Living in LA is probably a lot like living in any city: you have your hangout spots, your favorite restaurants, you go to work, you come home, etc. As a tourist, though, there is so much food to try, so many sights to see, people to watch: lots of good old-fashioned, "OMG did you see that guy!?" I did my first public karaoke there, impulsively picked a song that has a lot of sentimental value to me, but also demands significant range that I didn't have. (It was Elton John's "Your Song.") On top of that I was preceded and followed by aspiring performers, so it was embarrassing. Over the week, I became much closer with Rebeca's family over a blur of food, drink, and scenery. All of it at a pace you can't maintain with a newborn.

Deciding to try to have kids is unlike most other decisions in life.

I'm guessing Rebeca and I were like most couples in that we asked questions like, "Are we emotionally ready for that?" and "Should we wait a few more years and enjoy our freedom?" then "But a lot of couples can't have children. What if we can't either? We want a kid or two eventually, right?" From there, it usually morphed into some iteration of her biological clock, and my coaching the soccer team daydream. At any rate, right before we went to LA, now 27 years old, we agreed to give it a shot, and see what would happen.

A few weeks after LA, we were at home, and Rebeca said she didn't feel like herself, so I dutifully went to Walgreens and picked out a pregnancy test. I stared at the three options for a while, and wondered: *Is a pregnancy test a product that one would buy cheaply? Is another $4 worth a lower margin of error? This is important, right?* I got the middle option.

So, I was in the kitchen, and I heard Rebeca not shout or exclaim, but very calmly say, "I'm pregnant." I rushed in and joined her on the bed. I looked at the stick. (Very typical guy reaction: "Why don't I take a look at that to check?") Then I looked at her in shock for about five seconds. *Really?* And what do you guess was my next coherent thought? Joy? Me as future soccer coach?

Can we afford to raise a child?

The question that did not cross my mind in the decision phase flashed to the forefront now. I don't know if Rebeca noticed or even knew, but it was the first visceral reaction. Joy came shortly after.

Evolutionary psychology would tell us that males have an instinct to provide. Christianity and, I would assume, most other faiths tell us this too. Up to this precise moment, I had rejected that notion. I suppose men are on average physically stronger and faster than women, so hunting large prey to feed the clan made sense. Beyond that, I really didn't buy it. Now I deeply believe that most men have the subconscious desire to be providers. This doesn't mean a *Leave It to Beaver* role, but it does mean providing resources that make family life possible.

Moreover, men often struggle with ambiguity, but do well with clearly defined outcomes. Left unchecked, this will cause marriages to suffer. Anyone working 85 hours a week to maintain their income is likely "worth" less to their family than if they took a pay cut and worked 40–60 hours a week. After the question of affording a child, my answer surfaced: I will need to make sure of it. Not "we", but "I." I'm not proud of that, but truthfully, I saw it as my sole responsibility. And frankly, if Rebeca was going to give birth, breastfeed, etc., it was the least I could do.

In the eight years that had passed since joining Lake Valley Camp, I'd attempted to define manhood somehow for the adolescents and teens in our leadership training program. I heard young men share examples they observed at home and in the media, searching for an elusive alchemy of confidence, freedom, and love. The best I could come up with: the essence of being a good man is assuming responsibility for your choices, your words, your actions, and your results. You don't have to be a great father, but assuming responsibility means you'll do your best. Finish what you start.

I poured everything into LVC, and the kids grew from age 13 to 21 as I went from 19 to 27. I was a more consistent presence than fathers for some. But I wasn't working all those hours to make partner at the law firm. It was just time away.

My experience of becoming a father emotionally drove that home. As a father who is privileged in every way, I have fewer barriers when I try assuming responsibility. Millions of others have a much higher hurdle. Bringing a child into the world is the ultimate responsibility. Success or failure in this regard will define much of your life. The thing about love is the more you care and provide for someone, the more you love them. Love, like all emotions, compounds when fed daily. When

I ask clients what they learned growing up about life and money, the amount of money isn't correlated with parents' love in their eyes.

Expecting … That's an interesting term. We know it's a baby, but what are we *expecting*? It's such a radical life change. Rebeca and I would recommend the book *You Are Your Child's First Teacher* for parenting advice, but on page 7, the author, Rahima Baldwin Dancy, makes a connection between two seemingly disparate demographic trends. She writes: "Today's economic situation often requires income from both parents to pay for high mortgages and to maintain the lifestyles to which people have become accustomed, and not many people want to sacrifice financial comfort for their children." This was background for primary topics of the book, but I paused to let that sink in. In the years since, I've never heard a client articulate their plan for welcoming a child was to downsize their house and downgrade their car. *More, more. New, new.*

People are waiting longer to have children, often until their mid-to-late thirties to "be ready," whatever that means. Nothing gets you thinking about your financial situation like having children. But after a decade or more of weekend getaways in Chicago or two date nights a week, it is hard to break those habits. People grow into a more lavish lifestyle, and they grow in their career, and the DINK household has the most flexibility of all. Parkinson's law, which states that "work expands to fill the time available for its completion," can be applied to spending. Money that is unassigned purpose will be spent until it is gone. Dollars, like people, need purpose to reach their full potential. Kids provide purpose, that's for sure.

People are also saving less for retirement than ever. For the American-born Baby Boomers (and often immigrant couples) that had children in their late-teens to mid-twenties, adulthood and parenting are synonymous. Is it any surprise they want to spend big in retirement? I know I do. When I hang out with a best friend of mine, we always have so much to talk about, even though he doesn't have kids, and has no plans to have any. *He goes home from work and can do whatever the f**k he wants. Every. Damn. Day. Bastard. Stop bitching. You're at least as happy. You chose this life.* He's all-in on cycling: he trains daily, and as an amateur, he also pays his own way to races around the country. I can remember a life before parenthood, but I sure didn't have his mid-30s salary back then. Maybe that's not "purpose" in the way raising kids is for me, but it's certainly where much of his time and money goes.

I don't judge him at all. *You judge yourself for feeling jealous.* I do not think everyone should have children, nor should want to have them. I hear they're expensive. But … if you don't have children, find another purpose and act on it. Purpose makes us happy. If you worry about climate change and overpopulation, then nurture and advocate for that cause as you would a child. The irony is that DINKs often have the capacity to become very wealthy and very influential, but they don't in the absence of their own kids to motivate them to a legacy.

Two expecting DINKs sit in my office, nervous and excited. They've sent me their current monthly spending and bills in advance, with the intention to "prepare" for baby financially. They have $1,800 extra to spend on whatever: travel, hobbies, TBD. With a few clicks, I add $1,900 daycare cost to the budget, and … silence. I cut the dining out spending in half. I add a new line item for diapers, wipes, and so on. Like plants growing in fast forward on BBC's *Planet Earth*, you can see the worry lines of responsibility form on their face. Even so, not many people want to tighten up the budget once baby comes.

Love is manifested in spending and giving, and there's nothing wrong with that. *In moderation. Roque got three remote control cars this Christmas.* Take the idea of the nursery, for example. It is considered sort of bizarre in much of the world. A baby who can't crawl has their own room. Why? Baby cries when alone unless they're asleep. The nursery is a manifestation of preparedness and control. Whenever I worry about our kids, I remind myself that (a) much of the world lives on $2 a day or less, and (b) baby's brain grows when we hold him and play with him, not by his sleeping next to five stuffed animals in his own adorable room.

A new baby…no other experience is so commonplace, yet so expensive. (And more so for my LGBTQ clients, who must plan for $40,000 toward IVF or adoption.) No other experience is so desirable but so scary, so motivating but so…optional. When nightmares came in the past, they were work-related, like a participant at summer camp gets lost or critically injured. My responsibility. Now my own kid's misfortune is in the dream. My responsibility.

My first experience in fatherhood of "not providing" was when we put Roque in the aftercare at his school. It was very cheap at $60 a week. It was essentially a minimal effort holding space designed to prevent physical injuries and not much else. At $60 a week, the staff could not have been well paid. One staff person in particular spoke to Roque and others in a very harsh tone, one he wasn't accustomed to in his K-3/K-4 classroom or at home. At age three, he began to speak and act with anxiety. After a few months, we put him in an off-site daycare, which cost four times as much. We couldn't really afford it, but I'd say we couldn't afford to have an anxious and fearful child either. We had the option because our income was trending up over time. Others with limited job prospects will have their kids there for years. As parents, our role is to focus on keeping a loving household free from fear. Spend on that, and the rest doesn't matter so much. Sadly, when parents can't or won't, trauma, like compound interest, accumulates across generations.

For Millennials waiting another 10–15 years to have children, some of your retirement fun is happening now. Your travel and hobbies, your fine dining and home projects are a luxury not enjoyed by past generations. If you have children, you will almost certainly need to adjust to less freedom and less spending money. You'll never be ready. It can be hard to shift an identity, to automatically always be less of a priority, to put something ahead of yourself. Rebeca sometimes feels like a bad caregiver for working as much as she does. I sometimes feel like a bad provider for not working more.

Adulthood without kids is great, so live it up. I had a ton of hobbies and four glorious years of it. But the paradox of choice is real, and the decisions you make won't get easier with age. Now years into my parenting journey, my takeaway here is that parenting does provide goal clarity. My kids come first, which doesn't mean I buy them lots of stuff. I don't want to be high earner but an absent father.

Our basement, where the bar for cleanliness and rules drops a few notches, is filled with toys. The most popular toy after the iPad? The timeless cardboard box. "My kids come first" means that I have a responsibility as a father to be present and available, with the energy to play and the will to correct them, instead of distracting them with a screen. Creating a game with the cardboard box is free and rejuvenating. I need to get away from my career and get off the screen myself. That gets harder when I'm worried about bills, so money is important. Working harder to buy more stuff doesn't make me a better parent. *Working on myself as a person does.*

Every year, I try to get a little older and a little wiser. I get a little better handle on accounts and relationships. Given how long I spend considering which car to buy, I'm glad we became parents before we were "ready," so if you're considering "expecting," search your heart even more than your accounts. Love is infinite. You'll find a way.

house hunting

Get married. Get pregnant. Get a house. The most exciting and vexing sequence of emerging adulthood perhaps. More and more people are only doing one or two of these, but many still go for the trifecta.

The exciting part of each is obvious, I think. The vexation comes from (a) the order—which makes the most sense to do first?—and (b) the way—how are we supposed to do it? We think about what the proper order is, what our friends are doing, and the most nagging for some, how we compare to our parents. "They seem to be doing fine now, so whatever they did must make sense, I guess." I love watching HGTV, but living it gets complicated. In your own life, you have to live the deleted scenes, too. *Besides, I don't have an alternative plan for the next life event, so …*

For me, buying a house became an obsession. Zillow and Trulia multiple times a day. Even in our modest price range, it would be the biggest thing we'd ever bought. So, I should get it right. *It was not a loan … I've* always made big decisions slowly, but tended to make pretty good ones. The higher the stakes, the more I would feel it out. My Myers-Briggs personality type is INFP (Introverted-Intuitive-Feeling-Prospecting), so my decision-making relied heavily on considering of all the possibilities, and then imagining how I would *feel* in each one of them. In other words, it took a while.

Where, when, how, how much, and why?

When to buy? Well, being in my late twenties, it seemed like a good enough time, frankly. Some people my age had already done it, and I self-identified as "mature," so dammit, it was time. I can't even remember the timing much with Rebeca. I know I got hooked on looking long before I got her approval to start actually looking to buy. I seem to recall a recurring scene: me sitting in our living room in Riverwest, hunched over the screen, her asking me something, and me muttering a response indicating about 20% attention. Then she asks, "What are you doing?" And I reply, very low, almost inaudibly, "Looking at houses." She rolls her eyes and walks away.

I'd never bought a house before, nor even a car for that matter. All my knowledge came from Zillow case studies. I would scan incessantly, noting price per square foot, which features were highlighted, and how quickly certain homes were purchased. One thing that made a strong impression early on was that, when a place seemed like a really good deal, it went quickly. Houses that were listed for anything less than $100,000 went fast if they were in a neighborhood that seemed like it could maybe possibly gentrify in the next century. Especially duplexes. So, I got the impression that people with lots of money were buying houses they didn't necessarily live in.

During that time, whenever we would drive anywhere in our favorite spots, we would scan the For Sale signs. "Oh, look at that one," we'd say, like when my family went cruising around looking at Christmas lights as a kid. So often, the good ones would go right away. The sign would be gone five days later. *Wait, didn't buying a house take time? Like, with a realtor, and a bank, and inspector, and all that?*

In the spring of 2013, the matter of when was decided for us with a pregnancy test. It admittedly was hard to shop when we knew we wanted to start a family, but hadn't done it. A baby or two changes what you're looking for. Real estate is relatively cheap in the Milwaukee area, and I did know that I wanted to buy a house we could keep for a long time, something we could grow into. The place we rented was a two-bedroom lower unit in a stand-alone duplex on a quiet street. We had ample basement storage, a small covered front porch, the built-in wooden cabinetry seen in Milwaukee homes, and the stairwell inside connected to the basement and our neighbors upstairs, who had an identical floor plan. In other words, it was perfect for Rebeca and me now, and it could be perfect for Rebeca and me with two kids.

I started focusing on duplexes only that year. Before we found out she was expecting, I had a brief period looking into a tiny condo in this older development up the street. Rebeca was not impressed, and the realtor was not impressed with us, a mid-twenties couple with a naive husband, annoyed wife, and a $40,000 asking price.

Where to buy was a tough question. That unimpressive condo was in a nearly perfect location. Milwaukee is often called the most segregated city in the nation. I didn't know if that was actually true, but it was bad. For Milwaukeeans, though, it was sort of normal. When things have always been the same, you don't realize what you've never had. I went to a well-funded, neighborhood public school in a Chicago suburb that was pretty diverse, racially and socioeconomically. That combination was seemingly impossible to find in Milwaukee, and Rebeca didn't think we could either. This was a real bummer. Should our home address make a social statement? Or just be a nice home? How would each feel?

So, the thing about all those Zillow comparisons was that seemingly identical properties varied wildly by neighborhood. I mean a lot. The same house a mile west could drop in value by half. As in: going for $200,000 here, but $100,000 there. Why? As one moves from the east side of Milwaukee bordering the lake toward the central city, the color of the neighborhoods changes pretty rapidly.

I already knew that real estate was a last bastion of racism. Issues of race and poverty are often diagnosed separately, but they are very hard to separate. White rural poverty and Black urban poverty have more in common than we think, and a divide-and-conquer culture war from ideologues keeps it that way. Our feelings about our home are very visceral. Mix feelings about home and our kids together, and that risk-aversion is through the roof.

I knew I wanted to live in a multicultural neighborhood, but I didn't want to feel unsafe every day. "Feel" was the operative word. Most crime in cities is between people who know each other, domestic or gang-related. That being said, I didn't want to draw negative attention to our family by standing out. Having married a Latina helped in this regard. If we lived in a diverse neighborhood, and people knew that Rebeca married me, then I couldn't be *that* bad. It was a small vote of confidence that I was alright.

Her parents, sister and younger brother lived on the south side of Milwaukee in the Silver City neighborhood. And what Seattle showed me was that having family far away can be very inconvenient. The idea of immediate family a few blocks away sounded better and better. We currently lived about 15 minutes away if there wasn't freeway traffic, but in Milwaukee that feels like a lot. Looking in our current neighborhood meant we'd still be on the "other side of town." I started to think about the time saved going to their house and back. 10 minutes each way × 2 times a week × 5 years = 10,400 minutes, or 173 hours, or 7 *days* of time. Not to mention the perks of going there, like free dinner. It was also centrally located, period. Close to the freeway, close to downtown, close to everything. The effect of small things, compounded daily, weekly, monthly, yearly, adds up. I considered what it would feel like getting ready to bring baby over for an hour when it meant 30 minutes of driving, versus 5 minutes if we lived nearby.

Some other factors for the neighborhood helped. One was that there was a large retail strip close by: Target, grocery stores, etc. Another was that it was a racially diverse neighborhood. Another factor important to me was housing choices themselves. Beautiful woodwork, original floors, unique bungalows, and duplexes in different styles. I remembered from Ben's aldermanic campaign that many homes dilapidated on the outside were immaculate and ornate on the inside. We could afford to buy a beautiful house if we were fine with some trash in the street and graffiti tags on the playground.

This neighborhood's zip code was listed as "moderate" income, the second-lowest income tier of four in the US Census. From that campaign, I also knew that a high percentage of people owned homes rather than renting. This promotes stability and safety, because even on a lower income, those homeowners are invested in their house and their block, and will look after them. As far as neighborhoods go, there is a big difference between the working families making ends meet with $45,000–50,000 for four people, and those families unable to find a work or childcare arrangements more beneficial than accepting government welfare and watching their own kids. Work keeps people busy and out of trouble. Anyone who's worked with or raised kids knows that boredom leads only to bad things. And I knew that there were a lot of kids in the neighborhood outside, which also discouraged naughty behavior.

Just to be sure, I would drive around the area we were considering late at night to try to get a sense of how it really was. What I found from that was the occasional prostitute sauntering or addict hustling down the street. Oh, and lots of loud cars with loud music. I knew that Rebeca grew up with all that. Part of me wanted to "give her the world," but I also knew she wouldn't be entirely comfortable in some cushy, quiet suburb. *Too much of a 180. She may not feel welcome.* Having a big enough dog with a bark loud enough to intimidate was going to be a must. Dogs were domesticated in large part to prevent people from getting snuck up on, not just for costumes on Instagram.

How much to spend? Well, part of this question hinged on what goes into the mortgage. Through researching property taxes, I knew that they tended to be higher in cities, supporting not just schools but transit, museums, parks, and all the pillars of public life. For a while, I was looking at estimated mortgages on Zillow, and getting excited, but then I somehow figured out that this number did not include property taxes or insurance. Oops! That added something like $400 per month to the total.

If you want to be a homeowner, I learned that you're going to start funding municipal services whether you want to or not. If you want to do everything yourself, buy in the country. The person committed to using metro area green space, the park district, public transit, publicly funded arts and so on should pay property taxes. Estimated Milwaukee County taxes on this starter home will be around $30,000 a decade. "We're going to the park, and then the museum, boys, whether you want to or not." "Why Dada?" "Because our property taxes went up this year! Now get in the car."

We got pre-approved for more than we expected, which I suppose made sense. The banks would want as much mortgage interest as possible, as long as they felt we wouldn't default. I read online somewhere that housing costs should not be more than a third of income, so I went with that. I think my parents' example of a modest home coupled with lots of experiences for us guided me there.

Why own a house? I never even paused to ask myself that. The notion of being a homeowner was so deeply embedded in me that…I don't know. It was an idea I couldn't trace, like in the movie *Inception*. It was just a subconscious feeling from childhood, one reinforced by many layers of good old-fashioned American grit, self-reliance, and competitiveness. *It's what people do.* Everyone I personally knew a generation ahead of me owned a house. It was the American Dream, right? *Take your covered wagon out to the frontier and set up the homestead.*

Ever since manufacturing jobs left the city, Milwaukee has not had a thriving middle class of color. Zip codes matter here. White code for subtle racism in real estate is: "Are you sure you'll want to deal with the noise?" Those effects are inflated by fearmongering. Before you talk about violence over there, check your local sex offender registry. Bad things can happen anywhere. It is complex, though, because the truth is noisy neighbors and trash in the street are not what anyone wants. And these things are more likely in lower-income neighborhoods. Rebeca will say the Brown translation, "I'm sick of this hood shit." Remember, things are usually "on sale" for a reason. But in our case, we have profited from prejudice in Milwaukee real estate. Lower demand, lower prices. A mortgage of $500 less a month meant $6,000 less a year. It felt worth some "noise," at least for now.

Our primary residence may build equity, but it is rarely the very best return on investment, because we fall in love with it. Good investing is rational. Good investors buy low and sell high. In the stock market and real estate, this holds true. Those with the means and knowhow gobbled up properties in the early years of the Great Recession.

There is a diminishing return on "ideal" real estate. Demand for it drives up price, making the necessary sacrifices needed for a middle-class couple to live there pretty steep. Hawaii surf doesn't look as good when milk costs $10 a gallon. The truly wealthy don't feel the milk price change, which is why they have multiple homes. If you do feel that, though, why not live below your means in Omaha, and take awesome vacations to Hawaii? All desirable things lose some magic once they are normalized into your everyday life anyway. Seeing Mount Rainier from my daily Seattle commute the first time was jaw-dropping. A few months later it was beautiful, and months after that it was cool. Material things lose their luster even faster. If you approach buying a home as an achievement, the high will fade. Then we're looking for the next fix. Of course, the ability to say "this is mine" and show it off is appealing. From dinner parties to social media, no amount of bragging is in bad taste, it seems. That's often the hidden cost for new homeowners. The list of things they "need" to "finish," and "re-do," and "fix." A beautiful, rented home isn't as satisfying for some reason.

Buying was a mountain to climb, a stamp of approval. We know we'll be judged, so we have to give it all we've got. Ownership is so smugly satisfying. I hate it, and I cannot deny it. It inevitably draws your attention inward, toward what you own, instead of outward, toward community (unless you bring community in).

Without knowing it, the typical homebuyer looks to buy high. A price signals a desirable property and/or area, things that people are willing to pay a premium for. So, the "return on investment" has much more to do with your personal satisfaction of acquiring access to that neighborhood, access to a change in identity. That's not the same thing as improving your quality of life.

The little, frequent actions really add up. *What will it feel like shoveling snow longer on this corner lot? What will it feel like needing to close the blinds after dark every day? What will it feel like having a mortgage payment of $950 instead of $1,450? What will it feel like looking over my shoulder when I take out the trash to the alley? What will it feel like with six adults crowded around this kitchen island?* The things that make an impression on us initially often aren't what add up over time. For example, one of the most popular things to bitch about has always been traffic and commuting. I am happy to report that my thoughts on location were perfect. When I drove the three miles to work, I avoided the freeway every day. When I biked to work, I got great exercise and alone time. The trips to Tita's (Abuela's) house were just as frequent as I thought, and shuffling kids and the lawn mower back and forth became a five-minute trip door to door. The effect of small actions, compounded over time, has a greater effect on our physical, mental, and financial well-being than large actions done infrequently. After all, winning $2,000 sounds better than $50 a month for five years. But it isn't.

When I ask first-time homebuyers what they're looking for, the elements tend to be more general: a "good" school district, a "big" yard or a "nice" kitchen. When I ask empty nesters what they want in a retire-ment home, I get answers like: "An acre-an-a-half lot ought to do it" or "definitely an attached garage" or "within 20 minutes of our kids." They've experienced lifestyle compounding from the best and worst things about where they live, and they've learned from it. The homebody "nester" should buy and gain the ability to make their sanctuary truly their own.

If I were asked back then, at age 27, "Which describes your mindset better: nesting or exploring?" I would have said exploring, no question. Rebeca and I spent every extra dime on date nights out and travel. The baby was coming, but not here yet. I had to imagine what my future self would feel, visualizing it before it happened. Which is key to all financial goals.

Anyone onboarding clients, customers or patients knows confu-sion doesn't sell. When confused people buy, they are more likely to have doubts. For that reason, I generally don't advise clients to buy just because they can. I look for one of two things: they reasonably know where life is taking them in terms of career, location, children, goals and so on; or they could see renting the home out if, for some reason, they weren't living there. Both increase the likely length of ownership, which reduces the closing, moving, and furnishing costs relative to the purchase price, not to mention time.

For the "explorer," renting makes sense because you want to be out and about, not at home. Rent versus buy calculators generally say renting is cheaper if you plan to stay less than three or four years. I'm not saying renting is cheaper. I'm saying you get the freedom to spend a year in Argentina or move in with your girlfriend.

There is no reason we can't rent from ourselves. The property likely appreciates in value, and you'd earn some money—tax-free—when you sell. The mortgage interest is tax-deductible if you itemize. If the interest is $4,000 a year, that could save a middle-income, self-employed earner about $480–880 a year in taxes. Just because we buy doesn't mean we have to nest, or remodel everything, or feel compelled to perfect every aspect of it. The next owner will re-do most of it anyway. If you can't shake the feeling of "throwing your money away on rent," you have choices other than spending your weekends driving back and forth to Home Depot and IKEA. You must have the confidence to tell the world, "I can afford to make this place look nicer, and I choose not to at this time."

If home is where your heart is, just remember it doesn't have to be where the money is. People ended up crammed in our tiny kitchen regardless. Because that's where the food is.

"sign here, here, and here"

In the spring of 2013, we started looking in earnest for a house. We'd already been checking out houses—and by "we," I mean "I"—but only when we found out Rebeca was pregnant did we get serious. Fortunately, once we finished that aggressive loan payment, we shifted toward saving right away instead of spending all of it. We went on two vacations to see family, El Salvador and LA, and then got focused on the house.

My online research added a new subject: how to buy a house, and maybe take advantage of programs along the way. In the post-housing bubble, there were a lot of programs to promote homeownership, especially in Rust Belt cities like ours where a decline in manufacturing had led to a slow exodus well before 2008. Although we wanted to buy in a low-ish-income neighborhood, we weren't low-income anymore. That year, at age 27, our salaries were $50,000 and $34,000. We didn't qualify for anything as a household of two, until I found the American Dream

Loan offered by US Bank. I can't remember whether a person, flyer or Google led me to it, but it had what we wanted: a way to save money on our mortgage.

The American Dream Loan was for first-time homebuyers who were either: (a) below a certain income threshold, or (b) buying in a low or moderate low-income zip code according to US Census data. *Yes!* We were in. Discovering this gave us three immediate advantages. First, my in-laws' neighborhood, Silver City in zip code 53215, qualified, while our current neighborhood, Riverwest in zip code 53212, did not. Riverwest was on a socioeconomic cliff spanning riverfront condos to crack houses, encompassing the full housing spectrum, whereas Silver City was a lot of working-class families. Second, this program let us put down less than 20% for the house, allowing us to buy faster. I knew that 20% was the norm, but it just…seemed like a lot. I was an intentional, serious guy. Why wouldn't they trust me with less of a down payment? We were buying way below what we could technically afford, but getting to 20% pushed us past baby's due date. The third benefit was avoiding private mortgage insurance. PMI is tacked on to your payment each month to protect the lender or bank against you defaulting on your loan. So, it is intended to make sure you're an intentional, serious buyer. *Fewer people could get to 20% down, and the bank wants to get paid, son. Paid, but not burned.*

So, having no connection to US Bank prior, we stopped in to get pre-approved. I don't really remember anything about this process. I know that our personal loan, taken out because we didn't have any money, boosted my credit score, which helped us get approved for more money now. Bizarre. *Because you needed that money, and paid us back, we'll now give you more!*

We were pre-approved $160,000, which was more than we planned to spend, so we were ready to shop! Oh wait, turns out that when you get help, there are strings attached. The American Dream Loan required attendance at a first-time homebuyer class. It made sense, of course, but ... *Ugh! C'mon.*

There were three two-hour sessions. We had to schedule them right away because I was leaving for full-time work at resident camp after Memorial Day. Turns out the only one we could fit into our schedule was in Spanish. So, my house-lust overcame my pride, and I pretended to be fluent in Spanish for six hours. Okay, so I do know *some* Spanish, and more then than now, actually. But this was complex dialogue with lots of nuances. Rebeca couldn't openly translate, or the jig would be up. I love to rewrite rules, but don't naturally break them, so I was initially concerned I'd be outed. Still, most people there were going through the motions or very focused on their own circumstances, so I didn't get much notice. Rebeca, in keeping with tradition, was silent for five minutes and then would translate the one phrase I understood in the last ten. "*Cinco por ciento interes ...*" the lender said. "So she said 5% interest." *Thanks babe, always on it with the obvious cognates.*

The class was good. It turned out there was a lot about buying a home I didn't know. More importantly, there were things that I still wouldn't know had we not taken the class. Those things may have cost us money without us ever being aware. And the one thing I had heard of at all, private mortgage insurance AKA PMI, was more expensive than I'd thought, potentially $12,000 on a $100,000 loan with the 3% down payment we qualified for under this program. We heard from all the people who would typically be involved in the process: realtor, mortgage officer, inspector, appraiser, and property insurance agent. All these people knew a lot about very specific areas.

Milwaukee has a lot of old houses, so the inspector part seemed kind of nerve-wracking. *Is a historical home off the boulevard worth all this? Everything could be good to go, and this guy says there's a crack in the foundation.* Funny how we often resent people who are there to help us, in this case to avoid an ugly situation with the bank's army of lawyers. No one wants to pay more than they should for something, and I learned quite a bit about residential construction in Milwaukee just by trailing Luis through two prospective homes, taking two tours with him. He walked through the prospective house with us, looked for defects and necessary repairs, and explained them to us, then reported back to the bank, represented by the mortgage officer. *Can't we just take care of that later? Oh, he's giving me a disapproving look. Shut up.*

I don't recall much of what the mortgage officer Tabatha did other than quote us an interest rate and write up the mountain of paperwork. But I know she was evaluating us via pay stubs, job history, etc. A quality professional makes it look easy.

We met our mortgage broker, home inspector, and home insurance agent through the HRI class. I have no idea where we met our realtor Kim, but she seemed like a quality professional too. Her office was in Brookfield, and she was about 10–15 years older than us. She was short, high energy, and friendly. The kind of soccer mom that all the other parents like to sit by. The kind of woman that a 1950s chauvinist would call "a real spitfire" or something. In many ways, she fit my stereotype of what a realtor was: deliberate yet impatient, likable yet pushy, which suited us just fine. We entered the summer full steam ahead looking for houses with Kim.

In early June, we found a match. I had seen it on my own in May during a thunderstorm, hosted by Jeremy, the construction director for the Layton Boulevard West Neighbors Association (LBWN). This neighborhood association did great work in a lot of ways. I had my eye on their Turnkey Home Program. LBWN got money from grants, donors, or the city to rehab houses. Then they would sell them for a "nonprofit" price. The rehabbing was done with the original character of the home in mind, so we could get the old charm and the fresh fixes. No inspection problems here! We found a 3-3 duplex through this program. Attic and basement, two-car garage, tiny yard, but lots of porch space, upstairs and down. The bedrooms were small, but it checked all my boxes. Rebeca and her dad liked it too. So, I went back to work at camp in Western Wisconsin, agreeing to make an offer, and daydreaming about this new house.

That week, I got a voicemail from Kim. An issue had come up: we made too much money to qualify for the program. *What?!* I didn't remember seeing any material with that stated on it. I'd met with the staff member running the program, and he hadn't mentioned it. He wasn't the finance guy, but still … I don't know if it was willful ignorance on my part or poor communication from LBWN. It's usually both in these situations. And it was as though they had never had an applicant over the income limit.

If working in the south side market had been Kim's area of expertise, she may have caught it or asked earlier. She had actually drawn up our offer and sent it to LBWN, so she was surprised. Bummer. I had to admit that we weren't the ideal fit for the program. I had great intentions to be a contributing community member, but if the place went to a first-generation immigrant family with kids, I couldn't complain.

This was the first time in my life that I experienced the income crunch of too high for help but not high enough for options. The deals that popped up were gone almost immediately, probably paid for in cash. We were close to qualifying for the program. With a kid, we probably would have. I began to see the paradox of making more money, and how the system could be manipulated. We likely could have figured out a way to get around this, but as it stood, I was in the middle of running a summer camp, and Rebeca was now visibly pregnant, so back to the drawing board.

We found another one. This was a 2-2 duplex just around the corner from the first. It was smaller, but very well-maintained. Beautiful actually. The tender love and care were apparent right away. Inside and out, the home was immaculate. Still with brick with original woodwork, this place had more modern fixtures. Really, it was just … *nice*. It didn't have a front porch, but it did have a finished attic space, with a kitchenette and cool windows on the gable ends. I imagined my man loft. When an offer was made, the inspector walked through it with us, and was impressed. He kept saying, "See how this is that way? That's well done, a nice touch."

This home was owned by a long-time resident of the neighborhood. Apparently, he owned many income properties in the area, and lived upstairs in this one, renting the lower unit. It was clear he had a flair for design and appreciated quality. My kind of guy! We never met him, but apparently, he was looking to withdraw from his property business. Getting older, he wanted to scale back and downsize somewhere, probably somewhere quieter. Kim implied that he was selling his baby here. And that became an issue. The house was appraised at less than the listing price. A new type of challenge. The owner asked for either $149,000 or $159,000. The appraisal came back somewhere around $115,000 *Wait, Kim. What does this mean?*

The role of the appraiser is to determine what the house could reasonably sell for, using the inspector's information, but also market conditions, trends, and demands. They determine for the bank how much to lend. And they did not think this place was worth $149,000 or more. Not even close. So, they wouldn't lend that much. Kim tried to sweeten the deal in some way and negotiated with the seller's agent, but to no avail. The seller wouldn't budge. So, we had to come up with the difference in cash or walk away. I was enjoying a perfect autumn day, going for a run by the Milwaukee River with the dog when I got this news. It was so deflating. And for a while, I actually tried to think of ways to come up with another $35,000. That's what home-lust and the sunk-cost effect will do to an otherwise rational person.

It was a tragedy of over-investment. The owner never sold. I guess he couldn't get an offer deserving of his craftsmanship. Had the home been somewhere else, it would have sold for hundreds of thousands. Every property value is a function of its surroundings. I remember campaigning door to door for Ben on this block. The seller's next-door neighbor told me then he wanted his alderman to "get rid of the hookers on the sidewalk." As long as the neighborhood dynamics were stagnant, he wouldn't get what he wanted. The majority of people willing to live in that area wouldn't or couldn't pay what he was asking for.

A pastor at our church raised his kids down the block in this same neighborhood. They put a lot of work into their house for over 20 years. In the end, they sold at a loss. Not only less than the purchase price, but the next resident was able to enjoy their handiwork. Crime and poverty wore on, and I suppose became less tolerable with age. They left their asset appreciation behind.

Homes in majority White metro areas tend to appreciate in value. Buying a home in any majority non-White neighborhood can be risky financially. Yes, the place may gentrify, and you'd make some bank. But if you sell at a loss like the pastor, you cannot even deduct the loss from your taxes! Again, the tax professor Dorothy Brown pointed that out to me, which I can see has no other explanation than cowardly racism buried in America's fine print. Any other asset loss, like on an investment account or a business, can be deducted.

Kim was bummed by this news. *Uh, Brett, that's her job, dummy.* Well, yeah, but I felt it. She was rooting for us and wanted to get paid. In this final phase, I saw how those two weren't opposing sentiments, but worked in tandem. She was putting in the service, despite our price range being low-end for her.

Third time's a charm, but it still wasn't easy. With cold weather and a baby closer each day, I opened the search to single-family homes. We looked at one that I fell in love with. Lots of windows, a sunroom, covered front porch, decent yard, and big at 2,300 square feet. The bedrooms were large, too, which suited Rebeca's clutter-free, empty space style of decorating. Know thyself is Homebuying 101. We made an offer, slightly below asking price.

The inspector found some issues with this one. The water heater was sucking down its last breaths, there was asbestos coating the exposed pipes in the basement, and some live wires running to the second-floor window were reachable from the balcony and had to be moved. *Okay, whatever, let's just get it done, right?* Well, this owner didn't want to pay the $5,000 to fix these things before we moved. *Really? Your renters and their kids were living with asbestos, and you still don't care?*

Timing is everything. It was November, Rebeca was eight months pregnant, and time was running out. Kim, the seller, and Rebeca and I knew that we weren't moving this year if this one didn't happen. We couldn't hide our hand; she already knew it. We agreed to bundle the required repairs into our mortgage payment. I just needed to get this done. *Mom always said beggars can't be choosers.* I was also getting updates from Tabatha about the interest rates slowly rising, and was feeling that pressure too. Suddenly, I was paying attention to the news about the Federal Reserve like an adult.

Kim worked on commission, and—in cases like ours—I see how that can make all the difference. Persistence, response time, and the little things add up. I appreciated her distilling the big ideas for us, and answering detailed questions. The customer service rep at the 800 number is not earning commission for satisfaction, and it shows.

I see why realtors are useful. *You don't tip in Europe, and the service reflects that.*

On November 13th, we went to the US Bank branch on Howell to finalize everything. We didn't expect any snags, but the owner could've pulled out last minute. We knew we had to have less than $6,000 in the bank the day we closed, another American Dream Loan requirement. *So, we pretend to have less than we do?* I was mentally prepared for bad news. We had a middle-school program running at LVC that day, and I left a room full of middle-school kids doing improv to go buy a house. It was surreal. I met Rebeca there. We signed all the papers that were explained to us, but frankly not fully understood, and were given the keys. Getting excited over the keys is totally cheesy, but that's how we felt. A concrete sign we had done it. We moved in the day after Thanksgiving.

After all that, I would have signed anything to move in. "Sign here, here, and here." "This page has …" *Blah, blah, blah, slide it over.* No one assumed we would read the whole contract. We didn't even get it in advance. In hindsight, the amount of trust I put in every entity involved was mind-blowing. These days with electronic signatures, it's next, next, finish in ten seconds. The software assumes I don't want to scroll through. But when we increase the speed of business, we increase the chance of an accident. Like an impressionable kid buying crypto because a celebrity said so. Sometimes you need some handholding when the decisions and the numbers are bigger. *Or a seatbelt, and airbags.*

I am grateful for consumer protections in this country. As a history major, I knew the power of reading primary source documents. But that's a lot of work. Like everyone else, it was easier to form an opinion, based on what my friend said, after they read an article, based on the author reading part of the document. The whole process was a professional synthesis of complexity … *They could've screwed you over. It was not a loan.* The law follows the signed contract, not what was said in the room.

I read all the documents later. I know, the ideal time. With our insurance and tax escrow included, our mortgage was $860 a month, $10 more than our rent. That felt good. In spite of the *Total Money Makeover* advice, we got a 30-year mortgage. I sincerely believed we could pay it off early, and I did ask Tabatha that before signing. I just wanted to have as much money on hand as I could with our baby boy coming. Our interest rate was 4.625%. Making minimum payments, we would end up paying $109,000 for the house, and almost $93,000 in interest to US Bank over the next 30 years. I knew all these things, but I didn't read anything except purchase price, interest rate, and monthly payment in that 40-page contract before I signed. By avoiding PMI, I slept like a baby knowing that at least we weren't throwing our money away in rent. Then we had a baby, and I didn't sleep much at all, but I was so glad we got this done.

Even when I talk to mortgage brokers/officers now, they report a wide degree of lending scrutiny between professionals and banks. A true professional has a code of ethics, both in their recommendations and in the dignity they show their clients. Tabatha, Kim, and Luis treated us with respect throughout, despite our cumbersome American Dream Loan stipulations and low ceiling price. I know now we were a small commission, a high restriction case, but they saw it through.

That's why I am most often turned down by prospective clients in their twenties: they don't have enough money or responsibility yet to feel pressured to get it right. They're driving slower so they don't "need" a seatbelt. If they screw up, they have time to fix it. The older we get, the more we realize we can't be knowledgeable about everything. The cruel irony is that the biggest opportunity to get better financial outcomes later in life is often the habits we put in place in our twenties.

We bought our home in 2013 for $104,000 and sold it in 2020 for $180,000. That's a decent return, about 8% per year, which is double the historical average for real estate. We used that spread to buy our next home.

But wait. The adjusted rate of return will have to account for the cost of improvements and maintenance, basically everything beyond our mortgage, taxes, and insurance. If we count all that, not to mention the time spent by me and Rebeca's family, and we're back closer to 5%. Better than the historical average rate of return of 3% or so. However, inflation or the cost-of-living increase is also about 3%, based on past trends. So, we really averaged 2%. For comparison, the historical rate of return for a stock market growth fund is twice as high or more. And that return doesn't require any "work" from you to get it. Just commitment.

In hindsight, all of that sweat equity that was well worth it personally. Every time we spent money on our home, I asked: "Is this essential?" (Example: the washing machine broke.) "If not, then will it regularly improve our quality of life or save time?" (Example: the couch in the basement so kids can blow off steam while I chill.) "If not, then do we know it will bring joy, because we keep bringing it up?" (Example: getting more plants). If it doesn't fall here, we don't do it. The addition or project must have a concrete impact right away. Even with those litmus tests, it is undeniably a labor of love. But was it all worth it financially?

Definition of "risk" in investing is getting a return lower than expected. When buying real estate to live in the long term, the return on investment hinges on the neighborhood as much as the home. A beautifully maintained home with custom woodwork and leaded glass in a high crime neighborhood will be undervalued, no matter how great the house is. The plot of land is permanent, the building is not. That's an added risk, unless you have faith in the area improving. Then it's an opportunity. Real estate developers have the cash to will this gentrification into existence, which is no small feat. On the other hand, cheaply made, uninspired homes in affluent neighborhoods are overvalued, because the home can be redone to the buyer's liking. The neighborhood itself is the financial asset.

Once a client of mine decides to buy a house, they are as obsessed as I was. So, I make myself available for questions, but generally leave them alone until they've closed. It is financial goal clarity in action. *The point of no return.* The most aimless "I don't know where all the money goes" young professional will magically buckle down and squirrel away $1,000 a month when it comes to home shopping. Like a man hoping to be invited inside after a date, their one-track-mind will give them focus they never knew existed. And like a man trying to get laid, that focus might narrow to the point of missing important cues and warnings.

The hardest thing to do is to suppress a feeling that got us to the final lap and think, *"We finally got to closing day. Why would I be looking for red flags in these documents?"* Capitalism is a game, with government as the referee. At such a vulnerable time emotionally, I sure hoped Congress passed laws to cut any sketchy shit out of this mortgage contract. The American Dream Loan, and required homebuyer education course, mandated safeguards for us. Emotion makes the decision. Logic reinforces it.

Homeownership still reflects a transition from working-class to middle-class stability. The barrier to ownership is not the mortgage payment, which may equal their rent. It's the down payment. Without a surplus, how do you save? Nonprofits supporting homeownership, like ACTS Housing in Milwaukee, have helped former students of mine own an asset that is appreciating in value, and experience the confidence of homeownership. They will have the flexibility of sheltering family, or leveraging a home equity loan, or renting a room, or selling at a profit. They will appreciate the satisfaction of making a repair instead of waiting months for the slumlord. The stability has value.

What's the difference between the homesteader on the frontier and a sharecropper in the Deep South? Ownership. The reality and the feeling of ownership. The achievement, security, delayed gratification. A sharecropper has the sweat; the homesteader has the sweat equity. Daily chores might not look all that different: backbreaking work, early rise, work till sunset. Work the land versus own the land.

Buildings, cars, and things will all decline in value unless they are kept up, and often not even then. The tax code allows us to deduct depreciation, which is the decline in dollar value of an asset. Land, however, cannot drop in value from the purchase price. Land is emotionally charged for all Americans with a long family history here, whether our ancestors are Indigenous, African, Asian, or European. Manifest Destiny for some at the expense of others. You can't deduct the value of land because it never depreciates no matter where it is. It could, technically, from pollution or misuse, but according to IRS.gov, you cannot depreciate land (say property is losing value) for taxes. This is one of those mathematical truths buried deep in the tax code.

The homesteader was given a plot by his government so he could work the land, taken from peoples already using it, but never "owning" it. Ownership is a feeling, yes, but it's based on a set of rules and legal rights outlined in boring contract and tax law. At the end of the day, the appraiser, inspector, realtor, municipality, federal government, and public all have more say about what my home is worth than I do.

Urban centers today are being redeveloped, rents pushing many out. The teachers, servers, and city workers who keep things running can't afford to buy, and must live near the "land they work"—modern day sharecropping. A working class is required to maintain these insane price bottlenecks. Their homes may be the same. Their way of spending money might be the same. That is … none. But the homesteader owns the results, which imbues them with a sense of optimism denied to the sharecropper. The sharecropper's terms may be changed at any time, keeping him fearful, and living life day by day. The homesteader may go without, but at least they know that their land can't be stolen from under their feet. They know what the "rent" will be next year.

I see that subconscious legacy play out in conversations today. The Black or undocumented client must focus on survival, the future terms always in jeopardy. A mortgage is another promise on a paper trail. That may be worthwhile over 20 years but limits options in 20 days, when the hospital bill goes to collections. The White client earning the same amount as them, and having the same bills in collections, will be so focused on homeownership no matter what as a way to persuade themselves that they are middle class, that they have a castle. The jeopardy of their mounting bills will never extend so far as to threaten their *right* to own. The powers-that-be have always protected them. I believe that if I pay hundreds of thousands of dollars for a piece of land with a house on it (not to mention six figures of interest), it will be worth it decades into the future, because my legal rights are protected, and there will be a market demand for my house. Higher property values, higher taxes, better services, higher home prices.

In Milwaukee, cycles of affluence and disenfranchisement compound in opposite directions mere miles apart. That can be lucrative when a property value goes up, because the tax code allows a married couple to pocket up to $500,000 on the sale of a primary residence, without paying taxes of any kind! If capital gains tax of 15% were charged, the couple pays $75,000 on the sale. Meanwhile, if another couple loses $10,000 when they sell their home because of disinvestment and "White flight," they can't even deduct that from taxable income, which would save them $1,000–3,000 depending on their income. WTF? See why lobbying politicians is big business?

Real estate is a financial construct embedded in culture. Unbiased math is twisted by biased social demand. Expensive realtors for high-end homes spend money to cultivate demand, while foreclosures don't even have an agent listed sometimes, just reinforcing the trend. When we bought our next house, spending five times the money, we got better service. There's a lot of money to be made in real estate, if you can stomach the gap between dollar values and human value. Is owning worth it? A man's home may be his castle, but the value belongs to the market. And the market is nothing more than a mixture of people. I'm glad I found people on our side.

"have you ever met with a financial advisor before?"

While we were in the final stages of closing on that first house on the south side, I was adulting in another way too. I met with a financial advisor. This was uncharted territory. Then again, meeting and interviewing new people was not, so I thought it would be worth it. Moreover, I had met this guy, JB, once or twice before. He had been a McNair Scholar with my broski-in-law at Marquette. Ben had given him my number and told him to call, so that was good enough for me to meet once, and hear him out. I suppose I "checked all the boxes" of steady income, married, expecting a child, buying a house, etc.

I asked to meet at the coffee shop down the street. A mid-morning meeting worked well, as I had several 12:00 pm to 8:00 pm shifts at that time. I chose the location for home court advantage. He no longer had the braids and was wearing a suit. In a more formal setting, I wouldn't have given it another thought. In this neighborhood, he looked very out of place next to the university faculty in sweaters and hipsters in flannel.

We had a memorable conversation. Significant is a better word because I remember the feelings but no facts. I remember he was sincere, and he poked a few holes in my comprehensive "life plan." I learned that not having any employee benefits other than health insurance wasn't as commonplace as I thought. More specifically, he brought up disability insurance. At the time, I was making close to two-thirds of our household income. He simply pointed out that if I were unable to work for some reason, I would get nothing for months. With a pending mortgage, and a baby due, that sunk in more. I did remember reading that this type of insurance was important for young professionals. He also noticed that I didn't have a retirement plan, so … what was my plan?

Agreeing with JB that insuring my income, my life, and starting some type of retirement plan were important, we set it up. Rebeca and I were both healthy, fortunately, so the insurance was cheap. Putting $350 a month into a Roth IRA the first month also wasn't as hard as it sounded. At the time, we were able to save—if properly motivated— about $1,000–$1,500 a month. His recommendations totaled just over $400 a month. This was not a stretch for us.

At the time, Rebeca was so consumed with work while pregnant that I did the two or three meetings with JB. Her complete trust in me gave me confidence, which may have been why she didn't come. Her intuition has always been so good.

The net result of these actions did not feel significant. They were all intangible anyway. Maybe this was the first time I voluntarily paid for something I couldn't experience through the five senses. Even a book can be felt, admired on the shelf. Sitting down to discuss protective and proactive measures did feel significant: an acknowledgment of reality, and a need for strategy that was beyond me just a few years earlier. If I told my teens at work they should assume responsibility, I guess I'd better walk the walk too. In a world of posturing and prayers instead of action, I had done something concrete, and I felt good about it.

I remember only one of the specifics of that meeting with JB. I'd probably sounded a little smug articulating our plans, but then he asked, "So, you two build this life together, and something happens to you. How would you feel if she had to remarry for money?" This stuck in my mind. *That was brave. He really said that?* It was not something people asked every day. Competing parts of my mind said: "You'll live forever, and if you don't, she won't remarry" and "You moron, you know that some people die young, and widows remarry all the time. She would be a young, single mother with no shortage of suitors."

That question hit a nerve deep in my masculine subconscious, something deeper and more permanent than an op-ed, or belief, or worldview. I wanted to take care of her no matter what. I wanted losing me to be made easier by our foresight. I didn't want to create a struggling single-income household because I was hit by a drunk driver one day. And in a primal way, a possessive way, she was my wife. Given our situation, she didn't have a financial safety net I could rely on. Her being with another man out of necessity, however unlikely or irrational, was enough to move me to action. *Take responsibility.*

So, yes, it was bold. I could have said, "You know what? Go f**k yourself, JB." That certainly wasn't in his formal training. But he saw the error of my ways before I did, and had the courage to call me on it, knowing that I could walk away doing nothing, leaving both of us where we started. We recognized the human value in working together long before either of us had any dollar value. There are so many things in life that are always important but never urgent. Like millions of others, I had read a book and an article, and lulled myself into thinking that was enough. Knowledge isn't power. Applied knowledge is. I haven't died yet, but I did control something within my power to control. It was a youthful mistake to think I didn't matter to others financially. It was a philosophical mistake to think I knew everything about my own profession of youth work, *and* financial planning.

This is America, and people are people. We are always buying and selling. The word "sales" sounds icky, natural, or obvious, depending on who you ask. If you think it sounds negative in today's world, ask yourself, "Do I like to buy. Anything? Ever?" Then ask who's on the other end of that.

The sale of ideas, relationships, and services makes the world go round. Sure, the person may be veiled by layers of computer code or advertising, so it doesn't seem like sales. It's easy to explain away a bad result when you buy online, but when JB sat with me and recommended these concrete actions steps, he assumed responsibility. I put his face on the outcomes.

Money comes to those who help others get what they want. It's not win-or-lose when done well. JB sold me on the idea of protecting my family, my income, and starting to save for retirement. That was a noble thing. If he hadn't sought me out, I may have delayed another year or two, maybe more. The following years were rocky financially. The decision wouldn't be getting any easier, the timing no better.

Selling, like spending, is as positive or negative as the item in question. An acquaintance of mine left a large law firm to take over his parents' family law practice. As he put it, "You go to law school, and you get excited about practicing law. You don't realize how much time you'll spend looking for people to practice for." Accountants, dentists, realtors, mortgage brokers, financial planners, family businesses of all kinds: we do business development. Our expertise isn't distasteful. Selling becomes distasteful when it loses focus on you.

The fact I hadn't been contacted by a financial advisor before was a sign that I was stereotyped as a nonprofit "camp guy" spending every spare cent on travel and craft beer. And yeah, that was true, until post-wedding when we started saving. But also, I was a very ambitious young professional with a deep sense of responsibility to my family and community.

Social norms run deep by class. A lower-income person may question a finance professional's motives because they're always getting squeezed or ripped off. Why would I be different? Distrust leads to fear, and fear limits growth. Unfortunately, fear-based selling can be very effective. A higher-income person will typically ignore me initially, or if they do see it as relevant, they'll hear my offer, evaluate it, and compare it to others. Rightly or wrongly, they feel in control and good about themselves because they are pursued, used to getting offers. The middle class will Google and ask, "What are other people doing?" And because Google plays to averages, the middle class gets advice to become … average. We are indoctrinated to be responsible, self-sufficient, and average. *Sesame Street* says dream big, but over time, school and work culture beat the spirit out of most.

Despite challenging the credibility of every teacher I had ever had, I naively accepted my employer's lack of benefits. Taken advantage of … by omission? Do you really think your employer is committed to providing you with the best possible benefits money can buy and guidance in selecting them? Of course not. Most want benefits to be just good enough to attract and retain top talent. And some want them to be as cheap as possible. I've seen the fine print on some group insurance contracts. I learned later that my employer's board felt that employees should pursue the amount and type of benefits they wanted, rather than have a mandatory payroll deduction. So, nobody was taking advantage of me. I signed things. I just didn't know what I didn't know.

If we believe that access to financial planning is a right, then the status quo is de-facto discrimination based on class. My professional duty to a client of mine, under the CERTIFIED FINANCIAL PLANNER™ certification, as a is to give competent and ethical financial advice, and reasonable oversight of accounts we service. I am not responsible for their overall results because I cannot control their employment, their extended family, their decisions, or how much effort it takes to get through the day. Those with the most barriers to success tend to need the most encouragement, but they have the least money. Ideally, I want clients to be motivated already. Which means that some people get better service than others. My clientele is my responsibility; the public is not. I'm for hire, not an elected official. I can say to a prospective client, "You're not an ideal fit for my practice."

On the firm's Diversity and Inclusion Council, we are trying to create systems to develop and retain advisors and clients across lines of difference, and we are getting better, but frankly, it's tough. I've heard it said that relationships move at the speed of trust, and finding common values amidst difference takes longer. Money tends to follow the path of least resistance. People leaning into headwinds often aren't ideal clients because math is still math. My compensation, no matter how I feel about the person, is always correlated somehow to a client's assets and/ or income. In my heart, my ideal client is someone who navigates their way to newfound prosperity in the face of challenges as I guide them. In my wallet, my ideal client is already prosperous, and now they've sought me out for some strategy. Status quo reinforcement, one interaction at a time. I left nonprofit work, but even now, I must ask myself: *"How many "nonprofitable" relationships am I willing to maintain at my family's expense?"* If the qualified financial planners focus on relationships with a profit margin, then we compound income inequality. Attorneys who "make partner" get pestered by financial advisors. Teachers who "make parenthood" get ignored. One group irritated and one overlooked; but both in a transition where quality financial advice would be helpful.

As a country, we seem divided. Is money a game to be discovered, and played of our own free will? Then the best players on the playground become the captains, and they pick teams, passing only to their friends and ignoring the rest. The friends get more playing time. They get better. Alternatively, do we commit to giving every person equal playing time regardless of their ability or interest? Then we mandate a contrived scenario where no one really wins, and we all resent the teacher for influencing the outcome.

JB filled the elements of trust: his ride-or-die character as my family's advocate, and his access to comprehensive solutions with a top tier company. A financial planner and client should be a long-term, quality relationship, and I would argue, comparable to your "skill level" professionally and personally. Now I tell prospective clients, "It doesn't have to be me, but keep searching till you find someone."

I am glad I met with him while closing on our house, because after Roque was born, I had a lot less time. Then I would have been another father who procrastinated. Waiting on investing when you can afford to do it now is a lost opportunity. As the adage goes, time in the market is more important than timing the market.

Waiting on insurance is a high-severity, low-risk bet. Wait a year, but don't die. I was busy, but the ideal time wasn't coming. Insuring your potential has more to do with self-esteem. Do you consider your life valuable? Not everyone does. The first step to grasping your human life value in financial terms is to add up all the bills and expenses you pay for in a week, a month, a year, a decade. Does any other person rely on you paying some or all these bills? Do you buy food and clothes for your kids? It's hard to see how valuable we are as an income-producing machine when most of our cash goes to bills and expenses. But it can be a lot.

Sometimes I hear the joke (only from men, I've noticed), "I'm worth more dead than alive." Ha! If you worked with a person who calculated your human life value like that, well, you allowed it. Your worth dead should equal your worth alive. I interpret that comment as a sign of low self-esteem. It's not leaving *extra* money. It's designed to allow your family to continue the life you planned for, to the extent possible. The longer I'm around, the more I want to spend and give to my friends, family, and community.

In the film *Coco*, a boy Miguel and his deceased great-great-grandfather are racing to delay his final death: the moment the last memory of you is forgotten by the living. I see now why JB, as a Black man in Milwaukee with his family history, was so focused on legacy. I want to leave a legacy of generosity and love, even if my life is taken before my work is finished.

Many people don't realize how valuable they are. I had a first draft financial plan from the self-help book I read two years earlier. It included recommendations that JB also gave me … But I needed a catalyst like JB to actually act. Access to information is democratic, but if we're initiating the research unscientifically (asking friends, clicking on sponsored ads), the research reinforces what we want to hear, known as confirmation bias. Access to professional coaches, attorneys, therapists, planners, accountants, and partners is critical for us to hear what we *need* to hear. As the African proverb says: *If you want to go fast, go alone. If you want to go far, go together.*

JB had one year of finance experience at the time, but decades of character. He challenged me to care, and prompted me to act. He saw my full potential before it was profitable.

helplessness

When our first son Roque was a newborn, he kept getting really high fevers, up to 104, for his first month of life. Eventually, we and the ER felt this recurrence warranted some more investigation. He was admitted to the hospital and subjected to a number of tests to identify what was causing these infections.

Being a first-time parent of a newborn is kind of terrifying under the best of circumstances. As parents, we were untested, unsure. *People are having babies every day under all sorts of circumstances worse than yours. You'll be fine, Brett. You're a pretty observant guy. You're not gonna "lose him" somewhere.*

There were magical moments. In those first winter mornings, we'd go stand in front of the bay window downstairs and look through the glass at the birds chirping in the shrubs. I could see his dark eyes tracking them. Often, he would twitch suddenly like infants do, and the birds would scatter, and his eyes would widen. Caring for a newborn is like life support in many ways, though. A lot of feeding, diapers, repeat. And newborns cannot speak or say where it hurts. More than that, they don't even respond physically to illness or pain in the same way a toddler will. This makes diagnosing newborns extra difficult because they don't interact in a helpful way.

One of the times he was in the ER, Roque had the full work-up, the spinal tap, etc. It was rough. Watching people hold him down, stick needles in his fragile doughy body, hearing him scream. *I wish it could be me instead.*

We lived in the hospital room for about three weeks. I remember watching the NFC championship game in the hospital with our friends Brian and Jess, Seahawks vs. 49ers before Colin Kaepernick decided to kneel. Rebeca's parents were over a lot. My parents came up once I asked, wanting to give me space. *I want Mom and Dad here. I need someone steady, something consistent.* And it was a relief to have two people who were so steadfast and calm in a situation so fraught with uncertainty.

We were at Children's Hospital of Wisconsin, which is a nationally ranked hospital housing many top specialists. It is a somber "destination" for parents all over the Midwest seeking expert advice and care. The staff were excellent. The expression "bedside manner" really means something when you wonder if your child is dying or will have a lifelong affliction. It is also a teaching hospital, meaning that the adjacent Medical College of Wisconsin sent over multitudes of residents, first year to supervising level, to observe and lead our circle huddles in our room, update case notes, ask questions … This was 24/7, so Rebeca and I were often woken up for these "rounds."

After the meeting, I would usually go down to Café West, which was the little restaurant and store by the main entrance. Café West had good coffee 24/7 (because business hours don't exist in a hospital) and hot paninis, nutritious snacks like granola and fresh fruit, and guilty-pleasure desserts like ice cream. Once or twice a day, I would go down and drop like $10–20. I also would hit up the kitchenette in our unit for ice cream cups like three times a day. If I could cheer myself up with a quality coffee and bring Rebeca a hot meal, well, I would have paid $20–40 a day for that. Anything to warm up her February day in Wisconsin. Our friends and family would often bring food too, which was absolutely amazing. In hard times, food is solace, food is distraction. *As for me, how soon is too soon to ask a nurse for another ice cream cup?*

The "*doctor*-doctor," the person at the top of the expert chain, would come once a day. Eventually, they identified that the problem had something to do with his urinary system. Even so, the urologist visited infrequently. The medical residents foreshadowed his visits during rounds, so it was like the messiah arriving when he came to talk to us. These 10–15 minutes face-to-face conversations were a lot of pressure. We would take notes on what our questions were, and felt we had to ask them in just the right way, because we wouldn't see this guy again for a week. We were one more brief conversation in his day, but at that dark time, he held such tremendous power. We hung on his every word. He could have broken our spirit or sent us home skipping all the way to the parking lot. Each meeting, the urologist was the judge, but we weren't sure if there would be a verdict that day; only that there would be one, hopefully soon. He was responsible not for account management, or dining service, but for keeping children alive. I underestimated the composure needed to counter the distress of a family. A doctor needs to deliver news kindly and truthfully. It's not always going to be alright.

After a week, it began to dawn on me that I was using sick days to be here at the hospital. Pretty soon, I'd have used up my year's supply. I had spoken to my supervisor when our son was admitted to the hospital, but that was a standard out-for-family emergency call. I had kept him updated, but we did not discuss how this would play out in terms of benefits. We were a small organization with seven or eight employees total, not big enough to have a defined plan for this or to qualify under the Family Medical Leave Act. I knew that my absence, however justifiable, was causing hardship with programming and hiring. I think I was out for 7–10 workdays. The following 7–10 days, I slept at the hospital and commuted to work from there.

I had to ask my boss how we could handle the time, whether taking an advance on future sick/flex time or taking unpaid leave. Neither option seemed good. Following these two months of paid leave for Rebeca, she was planning on taking a third month of unpaid leave, which now for sure was going to happen. In my apprehension before the benefits call, I considered the cost of all this for the first time. The bills from Roque's delivery had just started to trickle in. Medical bills always kick you when you're down. I wasn't sure what I could even say. My merit was irrelevant here. It was a powerless feeling. *You and your savings account thought you were hot shit.*

"Oh, Brett. Please … don't worry about it." I felt a sensation I had read in a book; relief washed over me. I was amazed. I was going to get paid time off, all of it. *I am valued.*

On my way back to the hospital after going home to feed the dog, I stopped at Noodles & Company for our dinner. As I walked out, I observed the man, older than me, wiping down tables. *I'm not easily replaced.* My supervisor's discretion was crucial, of course. He didn't have to make that compassionate decision, but he did anyway. All the same, categorically, I *was* a professional who was not easily replaced. If I were a custodian, they could have found another guy without a sick child. Or I would have been back at work after two days, unable to ask questions of the urologist, unable to tend to Rebeca, her own health deteriorating further every day that her baby continued to rely on an IV, in limbo, struggling with postpartum depression, and complications from a difficult childbirth.

The diagnosis was vesicoureteral reflux, a severe grade "plumbing issue" that could be resolved with surgery when Roque was older. It would require daily antibiotics until then. All in all, it could have been so much worse; almost every day we saw a child in chemotherapy in the hallway or elevator.

Our medical bills trickled in over the next six months. Just when you think you're done, another one shows up. *Imagine if you didn't have any disability insurance, and that was you in the hospital. F**k.* We had at least $5,000 in the bank at the time this started. I felt great about it, but now I knew why so many people living on the street were carried there by medical bills, or by avoiding treatment and consequently becoming unemployable. Rebeca not earning for a month meant about $1,500. Altogether, after a "good" and "low deductible" health insurance plan, we had about $8,000 in medical bills due for Roque's stay. Plus, all the labor and delivery bills. "Tests" are the most expensive, and hospital "services" are not included. In an era when many of us say we can't afford to save $100 a month, chance will call on some of us to do whatever is necessary. Prepared or not.

Our experience was relatively minor. We lived near our specialist, so we didn't have to travel or stay in a hotel. We were there for weeks, not months. Our supervisors supported us, and we had jobs when we came back. Not everyone is so fortunate. The helplessness affects all parents regardless.

To date, I've advised several expecting couples into parenthood, as one voice along the way. Some couples will ask me, looking for reassurance as much as a calculation, "Can we afford a child? Are we prepared?" The short answer is, "You won't know till you try, but humans have been rising to the occasion for thousands of years." In the absence of serious and immediate challenges, most parents are as ready as they're ever going to be by the time they turn 30, and probably by their late twenties.

We weren't. How could anyone be? Waiting longer simply lowers your probability of conceiving and delivering safely.

Four years after this experience, our son had surgery to correct the issue, got off antibiotics for good, and has been doing great ever since. Around this time, as a new-ish financial advisor, I gave a talk on financial literacy to a group of AmeriCorps members in Chicago, and I remember telling them, "I would kill someone for my child." I have no idea how I got there, but the intensity of that statement brought a pause to low chatter in the room. That was a part of myself that arrived only in fatherhood, a primal voice I hadn't heard before. All our emotions are magnified through our children: hurt and joy, enthusiasm and sadness. I would have given anything to take the place of my son in the hospital, to take that spinal tap on his behalf. The innate motivation makes parents rise to the occasion, and most of us will do whatever it takes. I used to bring that intensity to youth work at Lake Valley Camp, wearing my soul on my sleeve. Once I felt I had to choose between them and my own son, I began to withdraw.

As a parent, you begin to learn advocacy in a new way. Saving and spending on your child is an act of love. Getting your own house in order is an act of logic. That perfect nursery will be lost along with the house if the mortgage isn't paid. Like an oxygen mask on the plane—put yours on first before assisting others. And sometimes that means swallowing your pride.

Our second child Rio was born in January 2018. Other than sub-zero weather, it was as smooth as could be, no complications for mother or baby. The medical bills piled up regardless…During this time, Rebeca worked with me in my practice. We were both self-employed, together, and money was tight. When we work less, we earn less. So, she was logged on for client service an hour per day just one week after delivering. I was working full-time just days after. *Choose your own hours, they said.*

You won't have a boss, they said. For the first time since AmeriCorps, we qualified for financial assistance. We had 80% of the bill waived. And the remainder could be paid on interest-free monthly payments. Not all hospitals do this, but this nonprofit one did.

The waiver was 80% of around $7,000. That's a big number, just wiped clean. This was not advertised. For me, growing up with my dad's phenomenal federal employee plan and $15 co-pay, these bills and options were new, so I would never have thought to ask. For many Millennials, our parents' healthcare was better and cheaper, so we shouldn't compare ourselves to them. Being more accustomed to hardship in general, Rebeca was the one who said, "Let's call and ask for assistance. There are measures we can take." I was too proud to ask for help.

What I see often with clients just starting out in adulthood is they avoid, stall, or hide if they can't pay, lowering their credit in the process, which affects their future car interest rate. It's hard to get off the grid. They'll find you. Where possible, these clients might pay it all, because the bills say the balance is due, but they use credit cards or their entire emergency fund to smooth out the remaining bills. A payment plan at no interest would be way cheaper. The hard part is telling the human being on the phone that you can't afford to pay your bill. For me, I knew we could find a way, so this was difficult for me to accept. But then you realize that billing service reps get calls like this all the time. Sending them our income statements was a small price to pay. Fortunately, they accepted recent pay stubs on the financial aid application, giving us a legal loophole to wait, not pay the bill on time, and use two recent paystubs that were very low. Thankfully, we dodged the scrutiny of two years of tax returns, which is the requirement for most lending/credit applications for self-employed people. It pays to know the system.

It can look far worse. My father-in-law Jorge fainted on his 60th birthday in El Salvador with his family. He went to the hospital.

He stayed in the hospital. No one knew what was wrong. We all waited, helpless again. Eventually, they told my mother-in-law to get him back to the US for testing. The doctors in El Salvador said, "We can't help you." Imagine how that feels … So, my sister-in-law, the oldest child advocate, flew down there to bring him back, their mother seemingly paralyzed with indecision. Arriving in El Salvador, my sister-in-law reported back to us that the situation was bad.

On their return, I took the day off to shuttle them back from O'Hare Airport during early rush hour. They helped Jorge into the car. His eyes were bulging out of his sockets like a Halloween decoration. He couldn't speak. He soiled himself when we arrived home. For someone so recently full of life, Rebeca and I looked at each other later that day, and expected him to die.

Stage 4 lymphoma. He was in the ICU for weeks, and the cancer unit for a month more. His illness brought family closer together. Illness will do that, remind us of forgiveness.

Keeping the house out of foreclosure was another story. This is America. Bills don't stop when someone gets sick. He had some money. Who knows what he owed where … And let the games begin.

Getting government benefits takes some skill and persistence at the worst time. Rebeca, as a licensed Medicare agent, knew enough to get started. She spent hours and hours and hours on the phone, on hold, doing research and forms to get her dad on Medicaid while he was unable to work. His medical bills were hundreds of thousands of dollars.

I learned, in a scary moment with a Medicaid spend down attorney, that putting assets in an irrevocable trust for the spouse could shield them from Medicaid estate recovery. He got life insurance a few years before, and it seemed that the money would have gone to repay the state of Wisconsin for their "loan" of healthcare costs in his final days. His widow would keep one residence and a vehicle. The rest was up for grabs to be reclaimed by the state. *Nothing is certain but death and taxes.* The system always keeps score.

The attorney said not to pay Jorge's credit cards or back taxes for now, because they were used to getting left hanging. *What is actually required then? What a racket.* Rebeca had to get her mom as co-signer on things. We had to have my father-in-law sign things while barely coherent in the hospital. We searched the house for passwords. We were holding it together as a team effort. He had disability insurance through work, which then messed with his Medicaid. *Think of all those without a support system like us. We can make calls during work. What if I was a sandwich artist?*

Healthcare is expensive. Four years after Jorge was in the ICU, our daughter Nahlia was born and went into the NICU. Again, it looked super expensive. Again, I would have said, "Whatever. Send us the bill. We will figure out it later. Do what is necessary to save my baby girl." If a loved one has an acute illness or injury, I'd want them here. Medicaid, a health insurance company, or you will pay for it.

When my father-in-law was dying in the hospital in El Salvador, they turned off the lights at night and went home. In the US, you'll pay until you're broke, and beyond. I'm not saying healthcare should be done cheaply. I'm saying who pays for what is debatable in a wealthy country like ours. Is healthcare a human right? I think so. As it stands now, we are asking many people in the midst of a traumatic illness or injury to add a layer of financial trauma, compounding the effect. Individuals under stress must negotiate against the government and insurance companies, two organized, highly resourced entities. The medical team is committed to preserving life, but there isn't a financial team committed to preserving your dollars.

Just the opposite. When we're sleep deprived, raw, and vulnerable, a bill arrives along with junk mail, casually asking for thousands of dollars upon receipt. Is it due or not? Due date is a tactic to prompt action. I believed you had to pay-in-full the bills mailed to you because that's what was written on them. Silly me.

Leveraging human suffering for financial gain is the worst side of a free market system. In the US, being unhealthy is expensive, and unhealthy people are very profitable. That's better than no treatment, but that profit motive ... Pushing opioids as non-addictive, to disincentivizing preventative care because acute care bills more, to commercials suggesting "ask your doctor if ______ is right for you."

Parents will absolutely delay self-care, and health care, if they believe it will take money away from their kids. For those barely making ends meet, the choice is definitely getting a bill for treatment or maybe recovering on our own and buying new school clothes instead. Toughing it out works, until suddenly it doesn't. If randomized rewards are proven to be more motivating, does that mean randomized punishments are more debilitating? What if we didn't have health insurance? A former student of mine racked up $800,000 of medical debt without it. Another former student was dismissed at the ER twice with antibiotics before being rushed to a better hospital for emergency surgery the third time. What if I was a gig economy delivery person with no benefits and no salary? What if my choice was to be with my family or lose my job?

I felt overwhelming relief when my boss Jim said, "Don't worry about it." And gratitude. Most aren't so lucky. And their newborn is worth just as much as ours.

"so, you're leaving the kids to be a ... financial guy?"

As the weather warmed in 2014, my resident camp responsibilities loomed larger than ever. This would be my third summer as Resident Camp and Expedition Programs Director. The kids hadn't changed, but I had as a father. The work wasn't harder, but the opportunity cost was more poignant, the choices tougher because of it.

Spring was always a busy time for me, and more stressful in lower staff retention years. Hiring for summer required a lot of judgment calls, because we needed people on a deadline, but had to maintain standards. This was such a year for me. We were also behind, in part because I had been out of the office for a few weeks when Roque was in the hospital in January. I had also recently let go of a full-time staff member, which I'd never done before. It had been emotionally draining, since I was the one who had co-hired and supervised him.

My relationship with my boss was feeling more strained, too. I had a stretch-goal action plan that we'd set up after I had asked for the second raise, so confident that I was underpaid. I was now managing school year programs, including high school curriculum. I was firing on all cylinders with good instincts, but I dragged my feet on this action plan … even with money on the line. Jim told me explicitly that he couldn't present my request for a raise to the board without proving that I went above and beyond my current responsibilities. Fair enough, but I had an emotional block to earning that raise—of about $5,000, up to $58,000. I just … couldn't do it. I was inwardly furious that we couldn't measure quality better. I was handling all my current responsibilities *well. Wasn't that worth something? I can juggle all these things at once. Isn't that saving the organization some money elsewhere?* Jim and I went back and forth on what would be appropriate. He heard me out, but it just felt like semantics. Almost subconsciously, I resisted the procedure to get the raise. He laid it out plainly, and I left money on the table. *What's wrong with you?* I felt so slighted by these "hoops to jump through" that I couldn't get started.

My camp director debut in 2012 was a peak life experience for me. I was in the zone for three months, an incredible feeling, surrounded by the right leadership team. It was a culmination of years of institutional knowledge, training, and refinement through trial and error. Jim built this entire organization from scratch, and handing off the crown jewel program to an original summer hire (me) took a lot of trust.

Going into 2014, we had worked together closely year-round for five years. We knew each other's styles and preferences. We had a passion for Lake Valley Camp as an organization, and experiential education as a vehicle for growth and change in youth. I think we felt there was no one else on the team as committed to the organization. Although we disagreed on tactics often, we were bound by a shared commitment level. LVC came first. Our lives and our wives worked around the program schedule. It was nonprofit martyrdom compounded with small startup obsession.

But 2014 felt different, and the trust seemed to erode slightly. In any long-term relationship, dynamics evolve, almost imperceptibly. As I was working on the bonus, Jim funded a professional coach for me. I spent most of my time with that coach, asking for help on how to communicate with Jim. Yes, this nonprofit paid over a thousand dollars for a personal coach over four months, and I was still grumpy. Privilege at work, I know. Which I admitted to myself, and that only made it more vexing. Frustration paired with self-loathing. Blend with strong work ethic and idealism, and you've got the nonprofit mindset signature cocktail.

I had to miss my good friend Adam's wedding because I was leading staff training that Saturday in early June. It couldn't have fallen on a worse day. It stung a bit more than past weddings I'd missed. I didn't even try to ask about that one: I'd already asked for five days off during the first week of programming. Also a tough week to miss, but some of our best friends were getting married. They met while we were all in AmeriCorps together and new to Seattle. They were renting a beach house in Michigan for the bridal party and close family for the week leading up to it. This would be a—dare I say it—summer vacation, something I hadn't had since high school.

This did not go over well with Jim, and belief in my commitment waned further. With good reason. Every other program director there before me with kids had ended up leaving. I had a hunch at one point I was being groomed to replace Jim as the executive director, so he could create from scratch again elsewhere. I wanted to believe that, at least. Executive Director, in his image, meant not taking time off the first week of camp. To "non-camp" people this may seem like just another time-off request, but camp culture is fragile, and a day of rapport at camp feels like a week in the rest of the world, especially during the first week of setting precedent and cultural norms. *The Army doesn't allow time off during Basic Training.* I understood the magnitude of my request.

This was a turning point for me, and I knew it. As a dad all of six months, I was choosing to spend quality time with my family and friends, to eat, drink and be merry for four days, and to spend time with my six-month old son, who I knew I would miss terribly the rest of the summer. I was choosing that over spending another five days making the world a better place.

Or was I? If I didn't go, I knew I would be bitter. I chose my personal life. Jim responded by taking back direct ownership of the summer resident camp program. Not a pay decrease, but I was no longer directly supervising the leadership staff or operations, which stung more, and he knew it. I couldn't make decisions while I was gone at a critical juncture, and it would be hard, we thought, to transition back and forth between us. So, he took back "operational command," and I could see why. My ego was bruised. He offered me the chance to not take the time, and keep ownership, but I went.

And it was sublime. I couldn't relax much because I was the primary babysitter, and I was still taking staff calls for expedition teen programs. But I had a taste. It wasn't a stellar summer for staff or for us. Jim and I were "co-managers" (remember that episode of *The Office*?), and I lost that extra 10% of effort, reducing 13-hour workdays so I could talk to my family more. I was scheduled to be at camp until 5:00 pm the day of the Fourth of July fireworks in Milwaukee, putting me home around 8:00 pm. Rebeca wanted me home by late afternoon to eat with the extended family. I could hear it in her voice. I *may* have given her false hope a few weeks earlier. I asked Jim, and he was clearly irritated by the request to leave three hours early, even though it was a slow day, when I didn't see any practical reason why I needed to stay. He said no. There was a precedent that could be set.

I left his office and fumed for a bit, then called Rebeca to say I couldn't leave. She was upset too. She didn't think the request was unreasonable, after all I'd given them over the years, often going above and beyond. "Tell him it's a family emergency?" she halfheartedly suggested. What she really wanted was for me to grow a pair and tell my work dad what I needed. She made it clear I'd have bigger problems than him if I didn't leave soon. *My people-pleaser strategy is not working today.* I paced the gravel road.

I mustered up some courage, went back in, and told him, "If I can't leave early, I'm giving my two weeks' notice." He gave me a blank look, and after a few seconds, said something like, "Well, I guess you're leaving early then," then swiveled back toward the window without another word. I walked out, drove home. Something big had happened. That weekend, I started to think about what I could do for LVC by working out of the Milwaukee office, leading a more normal life.

I've always been resistant to authority, and don't take orders easily. What I loved about summer 2012 was that I called all the shots. Jim was about 13 or 14 years older than me, and like me, just about all his work experience was in youth work and summer camps. When things were good, we brainstormed, joked, and connected on a deep level. He said on many occasions that he didn't like "being the boss," and wanted a collaborative environment. In tough times, it was never that way, because he was ultimately accountable.

In August, when things slowed down after resident camp, I reached out to JB, and I resumed the interview process to become a financial advisor with his firm. As we had wrapped things up the year before, he had asked me to think about doing what he did. At that time, it sounded so absurd. I declined, but I was humbled by the compliment that he felt I'd be good at it. It just seemed like a faraway world of numbers and suits, not a place this sweaty t-shirt camp director could occupy. It was the antithesis of my mission and worldview. But JB was different. As a favor to him, I went to the office for an initial interview with the recruiter. The building, elevator, and office were gleaming. The names on the doors seemed male and White. The recruiter focused on how much money I could make, which was a big mistake. None of this was what I was used to. The encounter fulfilled every stereotype I could imagine of that world.

I told JB that, and he countered with something like, "That's why we need people like you." I had to admit he was right. I was reacting to a future values conflict, not dismissing the importance of the work itself. When it came to financial expertise, the people with the knowledge often weren't trusted, and those who were trusted often weren't knowledgeable.

That year, I delivered the junior and senior high school curriculum, and we had one workshop on financial literacy, taught by me. I had borrowed some great content from Secure Futures, which is a nonprofit that uses volunteers to promote financial literacy in schools. A former summer co-worker of mine had some good stuff from the University of Wisconsin financial aid office, but it was the naive teaching the clueless. The only real difference between me and my 18-year-old audience was nine more years of life experience and White privilege. I was no expert, and what I could offer in an hour was woefully inadequate in the face of an onslaught of commercials and offers, leading to consumer debt and institutionalized racism that made it harder to navigate. Not to mention the haters trying to keep them in the neighborhood. They knew almost nothing about how money worked, and frankly neither did I. I talked through a slide on compound interest, and they could tell even I felt it was pretty much magic. I mean, they knew I was a teacher, working there, with them. I had no indicators of personal wealth whatsoever. What did I know about money?

With less satisfaction at work, I began to think more and more about what being a financial advisor could look like. I started to take a bird's eye view of my current situation. First, there wasn't much room for growth. A few years earlier, I wanted to be the executive director eventually, but it seemed less likely all the time. I spent more time thinking about how to present ideas to Jim than on the ideas themselves. I met Jim in 2005 as a 19-year-old, filling a spot as a camp counselor in the first year. Lake Valley Camp had given me so many firsts (including my first time, if you know what I mean) that it felt impossible for me to redefine myself "as an adult" in his eyes. If I came in as a late-twenties youth worker, I could've started fresh.

A reset meant running the risk of alienating Jim, since after all I thought I could be the executive director eventually, and I was wary of doing that because he was my only real advocate and only critic. Other than him, there was one other director, three or four program staff, and two or three administrative staff. The Board of Directors counted on reporting through Jim alone to evaluate my worth. I was stuck.

Second, Lake Valley Camp, despite annual programming, still did summer camp best. I had to be away in the summer with the action or accept a lesser position. I began to realize that I had been bringing an entrepreneurial mindset to a salaried job, but the extra effort wasn't being quantified, and I didn't "own" the results anyway. It would be one thing to put in more time and work at a critical moment, to enjoy the fruits of my labor by relaxing longer when I could afford it, as a business owner would. However, I was pushing to get results when it mattered most, working 110 hours a week instead of 100, and then limiting my vacation days to the off-season regardless of work ethic or results. There just weren't enough people or scale to withdraw from direct service and supervision.

In August 2014, for example, we had three staff and 15 kids on a college and service-learning tour in Illinois and Missouri. Unrest in response to the police shooting of Michael Brown, Jr. in Ferguson, Missouri was unfolding as they approached St. Louis, so I spent that night researching options, and talking with the lead staff. A young startup was innovative and exciting, and I loved it. I couldn't unplug, though. I would always be needed to make judgment calls in new situations.

There would also be routine Saturday programs, Sunday family reunions, overnight retreats, and after-school programs. I didn't own my time. I would always be working when other parents were not. See the long-term issue here? I realized freedom was more important than income to me. If our kid had a soccer game five years from now, I was going to f**king be there.

Third, I wasn't teaching much, but I was supervising programs year-round. And planning them. And hiring or training for them. And more. I was falling into a linear promotion model that we all knew wasn't effective, but didn't have time to work around. I did well as a counselor, so I became a program director. I showed results as a program director, so I became a senior director of several programs. I didn't feel like I was doing anything well. I had been an exceptional counselor, trainer, and teacher, but was clawing my way to mediocrity as an administrator. I missed being a counselor. As camp director, what I loved doing the most was:

(a) Talking with kids who were making negative choices (and their parents) about their actions, as the last stop on the bad behavior escalation train. This included written contracts with kids around their behavior, and often conferences with their parents in the fall. I also coached counselors very specifically on behavior management strategies, and coached young people to find and nurture their unique abilities, and maintain an environment they could grow in.

(b) Group staff training on counseling and teaching, and one-on-one coaching, with team leaders and instructors. I loved hearing their struggles, answering scenario questions, and working through management challenges that "front line" managers were experiencing. Many of them were 21- to 25-years-old and supervising near-peers for the first time. They were spreading their wings and figuring out who they were as people. One even lay down for some his coaching sessions, admitting with a laugh it was therapy for him.

(c) Speaking about how to contextualize our shared experience: to the staff of 40 before the kids arrived, to a group of 20 teens, to the entire community of 150. I liked connecting the dots. I stayed up late crafting these secular sermons, scribbling lines on scratch paper radiating out across the desk.

Common theme? Coaching and counseling. Around this time, I read *Good to Great*, which is a bestselling business book, the first I'd ever read. The author, Jim Collins, stressed how critical it is for businesses, nonprofits, and people to identify and understand our value proposition. *Self-help for organizations, okay.* What do we do better than anyone else in the world? Not what can we or should we offer, but what can we be the very best at? To his credit, my boss pushed me to try to figure this out for myself. He wanted to know what I was thinking and wanted me to find my passion.

When I had interviewed from Seattle to return to LVC, Jim had asked me to take Tom Rath's StrengthsFinder assessment. He wanted me to play to my strengths and wanted to make sure we complemented each other. Mine were Connectedness, Learner, Ideation, Strategic, and Achiever. I was a good counselor, I realized. *No, you're a great counselor.* So, I should spend more time doing that. I called JB again.

I returned to interview with the managing partner of the financial group. I brought out the suit I'd bought at Kohl's in my senior year of college for job interviews and had worn only once to a job fair. Now that I cared about the outcome, I noticed how gleaming the elevator was, how well appointed the lobby. I grew more self-conscious of my three buttons and cheap red tie, like a 14-year-old little brother at a wedding, dressing up for the first time. I don't remember much about that first interview, except it was different from any I'd had before. I was confident, I knew I could do this, I knew JB believed in me, but this was a corner office. The managing partner Steve was wearing a very expensive suit.

As I settled into our conversation, I began to see how this was not a job interview; this was an opportunity assessment. He didn't look at my resume at all during the meeting. Steve asked questions and waited for the answer. Questions about what I wanted in life, questions about what mattered most to me. I told him that I would not be able to provide my children with the childhood my parents gave me, if I continued on the path I was on. Summer vacations and child-centered weekend routines all seemed unreachable. As I spoke, I kept looking across the table out of his 23rd floor window, toward the Hoan Bridge where the mid-morning sun was reflecting on Lake Michigan. Beautiful places move us toward our truth. He talked about how this career had helped him think bigger for himself, and that it could do the same for me if I was coachable and worked hard. He certainly seemed pretty slick, and I knew that his role was to recruit someone like me. That didn't change the fact that he sincerely asked me what I wanted, and listened to the answer.

I left with homework, to conduct 15 surveys with individuals about how they felt about money, and what they would look for in a financial advisor. I interviewed five friends, five acquaintances, and five others who were referred by friends as open to doing the survey. Could I get people to sit down with me? Would they refer my character and process to people they knew? Steve said that success in this career mostly depended on just meeting with people. This I could do. As it turned out, I loved doing the surveys, even though three of them were pretty skeptical. This was counseling, facilitation.

There was a science to client-building. I'd never had objectives that were consistent and clear before. *My impact would be measurable.* The art to client-building I knew I could handle. I wasn't coming from some dull corporate go-through-the-motions job. I was used to risks and improvisation. *You perform better under pressure.*

My parents came to visit one weekend, and I told them that I was very seriously considering being a financial advisor, with no experience, no salary, no guarantees of any kind. In my family, most things are said very deliberately. My parents knew I wouldn't bring that up on a whim. My dad, the same guy who wouldn't speak to me a few years earlier, said matter-of-factly, "I think you'd be good at it." Prompted further, he told me I got along well with people, was easy to talk to, a good fit. I don't think he'll ever know how much confidence his words gave me in that moment. He knew me, he'd been around longer than me, he was a natural skeptic, and he wouldn't lie to me.

My mom looked at the floor, nodded her head thoughtfully and said "hmmm." Maybe that was my imagination, but I seemed to remember this reaction when I asked for something outlandish as a teenager. She was worried. I think she wanted to shield me from failure.

Failure was not only possible but likely, something like one in six new advisors with the firm made it to a sustainable practice. JB was with me every step of the way. He stressed to me over and over how hard it would be for the first five years. I was expecting something hard, to take one step back before three steps forward. The key was that I was willing to bet on myself, and always had been. If I failed, it would be my fault.

I could control my schedule, my own thought process, my own course for the future.

At some point, Steve showed me an income projection, using the information I shared about my network and some other factors. It was so much that I scoffed in my head. Unlike the recruiter almost a year ago, Steve knew that I wasn't in it for the money, but he also wasn't afraid to show me that this career could get me the quality of life I wanted. *It's okay to want what money can bring to my family.*

He invited Rebeca to join us at the second or third meeting. I was shocked because inviting the spouse had never occurred to me. Once Steve pointed out that I wasn't doing anything without her approval, much less give up a salary, it appeared obvious. One of the firm's core values was family. She came to his office, and he answered her questions. I couldn't tell if this was feminism or good salesmanship. *Why can't it be both?*

I accepted Steve's offer to join the firm in August, and gave my notice to Lake Valley Camp that month, about three months before I had planned to leave. *You're leaving the kids.* As I'd grown into more responsibility there, I had become more worried about retention, staff satisfaction, and making the kids' experience exceptional. I worried about people's safety, and our liability. *Now you just worry about yourself, just another suit.* I'd grown up fast, and the kids, teens, staff, and parents trusted me. Jim had given me the chance to prove myself. Now there wasn't a long enough career runway at LVC to engage in bold decision-making. I needed a fresh start, with complete ownership over my results. Being a big fish in a small pond felt great, but I needed to become the office noob again to stretch my comfort zone.

Armed with the knowledge that personalized coaching and counseling were my gift and joy, this bleeding-heart nonprofit Millennial caricature went to work helping people figure out how to get money to work for them, not just the other way around.

I realized that I was an entrepreneur stuck in a salaried job. It wasn't just about the money. Nonprofit youth work to financial advising was an identity shift. When I said I managed a summer camp for at-risk youth, people thought I was wonderful, no questions asked. Maybe too nice. Financial advising, it was the opposite. *I left the kids to chase money.* A handful of people that I hired at Lake Valley Camp met with me as prospective clients. Some became clients. Others assumed I was using my rapport to take advantage of them. I was using my rapport, for sure, but to mutual benefit, I hoped. I was the same person, just operating under a different occupational stereotype. I understand they didn't want to see a role model from their past tarnished, a memory tainted. I stewed on those rejections for a while, as I did with friends who didn't hear me out. "Big B's not a teacher anymore?"

Change is painful. It took ten months of reflection to be ready. But I knew I'd rather experience the pain of growth than of regret. I volunteered for change because I desired a quality of life I wasn't getting in the present.

The two poles of behavior change are fear and desire. Worrying and wanting, the less extreme versions, affect our daily mindset, but tend to fall short of sparking behavior change. If you haven't experienced financial fear or desire, you aren't alone. Many people stay in the worry-want continuum their entire lives, vaguely complaining and wishing without any action. *I wish I had a nicer place. I want to move. I'm worried about my loans.* Falling in love or running for our lives activates a motivation that lies dormant within us most of the time. How can we activate that?

My desire to be a fatherly role model for the staff and participants at camp was my catalyst for years. It became more of a want once our own son was born. One summer of that, and I knew my impact would wither. My fear as a new parent was that I wouldn't be able to provide the lifestyle that I experienced as a child. My new desire was independence. I wanted to own my results, and my time. I would grind until I did.

Setting my own schedule has been better than I ever thought. Always having the choice to say "I don't want to work this afternoon" is an absolute joy. However, the total amount of work to earn that privilege is a grind, and not for everyone. It took years of working constantly to get there. What kept me going on the most desperate days was fear and desire. *You won't afford club soccer for your son. You couldn't take time off work to see him play anyway. You know how hard this is. You are building passive income and clientele over time. Imagine the choices you'll have in 10 years, for vacation, for hobbies, for volunteering …* Without those defined, I might have given up long ago.

But if it were easy, everyone would do it. And like singing or cooking, those who are good at selling make it look effortless. For example, I became very good at selling the benefits of being a resident camp counselor for LVC. Selling a teen on the benefits of a positive attitude. My program team said I could be very persuasive. And that isn't hard when you have conviction. I went from whining about the need to document my $5,000 bonus to opportunities for making that amount in a single meeting. I had experience selling relationships, building trust, and coaching for growth. It was money that weirded me out.

Upon joining the firm that winter, I had to give financial advice, by law and by moral code, as if I didn't care what the prospective client's response was, although that outcome meant a great deal for our family. I chose a period of financial insecurity working on commission. In return, like at LVC, I learned how to perform under pressure, this time around my apparent Achilles' heel: money.

Hard to say in hindsight, but I'm glad I'm through it. Hopefully. At all levels of business ownership, many of us will use the self-made narrative as a means of claiming superiority over the salaried, and characterizing a hand-up as a handout. We say we never got a handout, scrapped for every penny, and so on. This biased belief affects politics and policy. Every one of us got help along the way, but some want to pull up the ladder behind us. Now, surviving that experience is trial by fire for most. The only thing that made it tolerable in the darkest moments was the fear of being a quitter and remembering why I did it in the first place: the desire to grow into my gift for coaching and counseling.

My gift was hidden in plain sight. I was trapped in limiting beliefs about categories: education and business, selling and teaching. I didn't recognize that what I enjoyed had become out-of-sync with the linear path I was on. Once I course-corrected and became a financial advisor, I could tolerate financial hardship because I was cultivating my gift, with no limit on where it could take me. Oppression and negativity stifle so many gifts before they blossom. That's what I always wanted for the children and staff at Lake Valley Camp: a fair shot at growing their gifts. That's what I want for my own children now. It's what I want for my clients. And for you.

chapter thirty-one

"I can't afford not to"

As a new advisor, I needed to take on clients right out of the gate, and I was afraid of making a mistake. I knew I had to learn and act now. This conflict was agonizing. My strategic personality wasn't a natural fit for this type of a blur.

They kept saying "prospect up," meaning meet with higher-income earners. They wanted me to succeed. They also knew I'd be less likely to leave if I was making money. They didn't know me that well though. After all, I was focused on financial literacy first. My "natural market" in Milwaukee was almost entirely nonprofit professionals, and first-generation college grads. I had to start there, I suppose, but being a competence-equals-confidence personality, I shied away from approaching people who were better off, believing falsely that they would be there when I was ready, and that my near-peers "needed" more help. *Rich people get enough help.* I knew this was judge-y, as all people need help, but I was still in martyr mode all the way. Or I was afraid. Or both. Every hour, I had to choose between a nonprofit action and a "for-profit" action. My heart (and my experience) was in nonprofit work.

Without a doubt I felt like an advocate. I came across some scary numbers. Payday loan stores can charge up to 500% interest. You could get a $1,000 advance and pay back like $4,000 over the next six months. *How could this be legal?* I started to notice how needing money could be leveraged against you … The furniture store that promises no credit check. The no-money-down offer. Living in poverty meant getting through today, and there were plenty of ways to make today easier, or just possible. These places knew you weren't going to lawyer up two years later. It was all in the fine print anyway.

An intern mentee and I met with a prospective client, a Spanish speaker with no papers. She had bought a car from a corner lot dealer and was paying 17% interest on a seven-year lease. She had no idea. Since she had an infant, a reliable car was a necessity. What's the monthly payment? That's where the uninitiated might stop asking questions, fearing that's the best they can do.

The issue was that consumer lending, debt counseling, investing, and insurance typically happened in silos, cordoned off from each other. Here I was, earning money only by selling insurance and investments, spending the bulk of my time doing credit and budget counseling. For free. *You said you wanted to help people. Look at you now.* And there was lots of free information out there, but the unfortunate perception of anything free is that it isn't high quality.

Moreover, the trust built within a financial literacy program, often from a personal mentor or book or whatever, is not with you when you go to implement this stuff. Meaning I could tell someone, "With your credit score, you should be able to get this interest rate from the bank you have now. The dealer will ask you to finance, and if they can't match this rate, go to the bank to finance." The problem is when that person goes there, they bring up what we've discussed and the finance manager says, "Well, what Brett doesn't know is that blah, blah, blah ..." And I'm not there to respond, "You scheming prick. That's total bullshit."

Sometimes I felt like a first responder trying to mitigate a situation that is already bleak. Financial advisors, loan officers, personal bankers, attorneys, and insurance agents usually aren't trained in trauma-informed care or family counseling. We can learn through trial and error, but our relational "errors" can have numerical impacts. If we offend while delivering an accurate financial message in an effective way, our prospect will seek out a receptive place that reinforces an inaccurate financial message. For instance, I once received a credit card offer titled "prestige without the price." *Wow, this mail is so respectful, only they understand how hard I work.*

Again and again, I found myself interpreting a financial transaction already made by the client, and explaining how it worked. "Yes, there was no money down, and low monthly payment, but look, this is how much you pay in interest." They got a low payment, but the interest was like an ocean undertow, making each step twice as hard. *This is sneaky as f**k. And everyone wants to believe it. We're all failing the marshmallow test, buying shit we can't afford.*

The tragedy is that when things aren't looking so good, and you have to deal with all this stuff, retail therapy can look better and better. Especially when it's on credit. Luxury cars in the hood have the temp sticker as often as a license plate. "No payments till next year? Well, I might be in jail by then so whatever."

Years ago, I was in the classroom of a middle-school teacher, a wonderful new mother who cared deeply for her family and students, but who was "raised broke" as she put it. I explained some of this interest as a current stuff. "So, investing is like a reverse credit card?" Yes, it is. The current carries some of us forward, and pushes others back.

When a client sees a compound interest calculator, it may blow their f**king mind. I would use the app to show them that $200 a month for 10 years earning 6% interest equals … 20 years equals … 40 years equals … Another world became possible. A world of generational wealth, most easily accessed by the young people, with the most time to leave their dollars in the interest current.

As a new financial advisor, I met with a lot of young people. I knew that: (a) they probably hadn't done anything yet, (b) they weren't as informed and therefore gave me some "credibility cushion," (c) talking about life with young people was my thing, and (d) they weren't deciding whether or not to retire yet, so the stakes were lower. This was more about motivation than strategy. For most people in their twenties, I just had to demonstrate that shit happens, and compound interest is awesome. For 90% of client meetings in my first year, the message was more or less the same: disability insurance if you rely on all your income; term life insurance if you have little kids without a safety net; a Roth IRA, as long as you're getting your retirement match at work; have three months of expenses saved; don't have high-interest credit card debt. Not easy, but simple.

Is it some luck too, though? In the last several decades, the workforce has become more fluid, and employee benefits are getting worse. Defined benefit pensions (employee payout is the responsibility of the employer) are being replaced with defined contribution 401k and 403b plans (investment performance risk lies with the employee). Still incredibly useful, and studies show that about 30% of total compensation comes in the form of benefits with large employers. So, where you work, when it comes to developing habits, has a lot to do with chance.

Let's say your first job out of college gives you a 6% 401k match, and you sign up only because HR says so. And let's say your salary is $50,000 then, so the company's 6% is $3,000 per year, if only you put in your own $3,000 per year. Do that from age 23 to 26, that equals $18,000 in the account. If that grows an average of 6% for next 40 years, when you're 66, without adding more to it, you'd have $185,142 to spend before taxes.

On the other hand, if your friend doesn't have a retirement plan, and doesn't have me on their case, they will likely spend that same $250 per month on "stuff" and 40 years from now their purchases will have gone from being their favorite, to storage in the basement, to Goodwill, to landfill. Their things depreciated in value as fast as yours appreciated. By riding the interest current, you can actually buy a lot more things, if you just wait it out. Many studies have shown that opting-out versus opting-in default settings increase savings rates.

Saving is about habits more than choice. I didn't floss as a child, so I don't now, but I know I should. I've tried to start, but I just don't. By contrast, I started giving $35 per month to Children International in my early twenties, and I haven't stopped, even when I needed the money. Many of us accumulate significant value in home equity, just because paying the mortgage isn't optional. Only the psychology of habits can explain it. The compounding effect of small actions taken consistently, like water dripping in a cave to form stalactites and stalagmites.

The interest current at full force is hard to stop. Another analogy: have you ever seen a video of an avalanche flattening trees? I hear from clients, "My parents helped me out with $5,000 in this emergency" or "$15,000 for down payment and I'm paying them back." At their parents' age, the compound interest train is full steam ahead. Forty years of 401k matching can realistically add up to $500,000 at age 60. And that amount can realistically grow 5% in a year, say invested in 60% stocks and 40% bonds. That is $25,000 created out of thin air. The parent giving $10,000 to junior isn't the achievement. The foresight of the parent, or the parent's aunt, or company HR manager, or friend decades ago, is the real achievement. We can't buy more time. *Why do they nod and agree, and then not change a thing?!* Bearing witness to avoidance and short-term thinking is hard.

At first learning this, I couldn't believe it was real. The more I spoke to others, the more passionate I became about at least sharing the math of compound interest. So, why wasn't I making any money by revealing this to anyone, anytime, anywhere for six straight months? *I made a career change to avoid burnout. WTF? OMG, Michael Scott was right … You have to play to win, but you also … have to win to play.*

I realized I was trained as a river rafting guide, to navigate interest current. I was paid to steer a raft that already had momentum and speed, using my expertise to avoid danger, foreshadow during the calm stretches, project confidence in the rapids, and celebrate wins afterward. I couldn't earn a living helping people who were afraid of water, or were paddling upstream, straining desperately to maintain. You don't need a guide for that experience. You need a therapist. *You need to prospect up. But you're good at being a therapist. Yeah but that doesn't pay our bills.*

The thing about compound interest, whether you're swimming against the current or it's pulling you along: the current takes a while to gain steam, like the Colorado River becoming roaring rapids in the Grand Canyon. You have to know how rivers work to ever believe that the mountain stream you're looking at will turn into something else. You need to know about rainfall and gravity. In your view of the murmuring mountain stream at your feet, you know that you can jog faster alongside it than the water moves in it. For this reason, many people have their bank account alone, because it's the only feature on their map. The checking account is their pond, all self-contained and visible. *It was not a loan.*

In July of 2015, I had been a financial advisor for six months. I could savor summer with family for the first time. My sister-in-law invited us to join them on a family vacation, but I had to admit we couldn't afford it. I was getting desperate. I hadn't made any money in June. By July, I was faced for the first time in my life with not having enough income to pay our bills. Where would the money come from? *Not from all these appreciative, kind, hard-working, but broke people I'm spending time with. I can't borrow my way out of this. I can't quit either. Everyone I know was so surprised I'm doing this. It would be such a public failure.*

I had been paired with a veteran advisor mentor when I first started, and we met about once a month. There wasn't really any structure to it. He was more of a sounding board for what I was struggling with, and he always had digestible, useful, and immediately applicable information. I was so grateful for Chuck's ability to listen and coach well, not to mention his generosity volunteering his time.

One day, I met him at 6:30 am (this office norm was to get up super early, a culture shock for me) at a Starbucks at Red Arrow Park in Milwaukee. It was quiet at the outdoor table, birds chirping, sun shining. A beautiful summer day. Chuck sat down and, seeing the strained expression on my face, asked, "How can I be helpful today?" We had a conversation, and I was vulnerable about my situation. I respected Chuck's intentions, and his track record spoke for itself. He was only five or six years older than me, with young kids, so he was relatable. He had about ten years' experience as an advisor by this time. "I'll ask you what I would ask a client: do I have your permission to challenge you?"

"Yes."

"Is your intention to continue with this work? Despite this short-term situation?"

"Yes."

"Can I tell you what you need to hear instead of what you want to hear?"

Chuck challenged me to further reinvest in my business to push through this dry spell. "You're not sure you can afford to. That's what your clients say, right?"

"I can't afford not to."

Changing my mind would have a cost, too. I spent weeks studying for exams, having conversations with prospects about long-term goals, and planting seeds for the future. I had future income to harvest, and I needed to stay in the current of momentum to collect.

Chuck had a 7:30 am meeting and left with a knowing twinkle in his eye. His advice landed because he had done what I intended to do. A guide has been there before. He looked me in the eye and—without words—said, "Don't freeze now. Keep paddling."

In the end, I did it, crossing a threshold personally, and learning an important lesson professionally: my own financial decisions and my recommendations for my clients did not have to be dry and formulaic all the time. If I was to be a financial advisor, I would have to give life advice. I would have to be a catalyst for forming good habits. Habits are so hard to start, increasingly easy to maintain, eventually automatic.

As motivational speaker Les Brown has said, "Do what is easy, and your life will be hard." That message is best received from a near-peer: someone who has done what you want to do, but has done it recently enough to remember and relate. If a 60-year-old with a billion dollars under management gave me the same advice, it would still be true, but it wouldn't ring true in the same way.

As we age, we tend to hang out with people at similar income levels. I don't give free budget counseling at 7:00 pm on weeknights anymore. I am committed to connecting every person ready for that conversation to a financial advisor on our team, who will be their near-peer catalyst for change.

Chuck was a near-peer for me. He was my guide in the rapids of financial advising. The water was moving faster than ever. And in this career, and in life, sometimes the best advice is to paddle harder, because the easiest way out is through.

Les Brown also said, "You can only escape what's behind you by running toward what's in front of you." If you've ever been on a guided whitewater rafting trip in rough water, you'll know the guide will say, "Look ahead where you want to go, not at what you want to avoid." Eyes up, paddle hard. The safest place to be is off on the side in the eddy, just floating calmly, going nowhere. The fastest part of the river is where the action is. But are you paddling with the current or against it? Do you have a guide? Wealth begets wealth. Poverty begets poverty. The working-class family that will scrounge up cash to help each other out? Best intentions, doing the best they can. Yet the picture is of a better swimmer trying to save their friend without a flotation device. The rescue is tiring at best, dragging both under at times.

Maybe that's why I wasn't making any money. Out of loyalty, I was moving at their level, not mine. We went rafting in Colorado once with family. Rebeca was pregnant at the time, so for baby's safety we did a stretch with only Class II rapids in an eight-person raft. And it was nice to be drifting through the mountains. But having previously done "throw you out of the boat" Class V rapids, it was lame as hell. No offense. I love my family. This was just not my ideal rafting group. And while I believed everyone there would do everything in their power to help me if I needed it, I didn't want any of them as my guide on this river, because Class II was their comfort level. Skills and experience were worth ten times more than effort here.

One thing all people have in common when it comes to money: we don't want to be surprised. That's why a guide is helpful: the guide explains what to expect up ahead and steers a course accordingly. You still have to do the work. You don't pay a guide to watch you paddle across a flat lake. You pay a guide for judgment in fast-moving situations and tough spots. A guide won't freeze like a deer in the headlights. Unlike a celebrity paid for a cryptocurrency ad, a paid guide has liability.

In my first year, I was just calling people to get offshore. I spend more time guiding clients through the rapids now. New referrals often reach out to me once their current picks up speed. We hit rocks, but we are moving downstream quickly for the most part. Similarities also emerge in different spheres. For example, the lottery is popular because the worst-case scenario is losing the ticket price. The daydream alone is worth it for many. The probability of winning is irrelevant. And while that may be looked down upon by some, it's not too different than a stock option—worst case is an unused premium when the option isn't exercised. But guess which has a higher probability of winning. The culture of finance is different, but human behavior not all that much.

That's how some people "magically" acquire a financial tailwind and others don't. Some of us found the current after floating aimlessly for a while. Others are stuck without a paddle. As the magnitude of the interest current sunk in, I fought to educate everyone about it, whether they appreciated it or not. At the same time, veterans of financial advising gave me this financial advice: meet with "better people." *All people have value.* What they really meant was: meet with people who have financial problems that we are compensated to solve, people who need guidance heading fast downriver. Not the ones still fearfully dipping their toe in the water from shore. That advice was correct financially but stung personally.

Surging through the rapids with friends and a guide is fun. Paddling furiously and getting nowhere is exhausting. And when attempting a water rescue, you can drown yourself if you're not careful.

That year, despite more financial pressure than ever, we paid our mortgage, and deliberately saved long-term for our future financial security. I kept our boat out in the water, at a time when I really didn't want to get wet. And years later, we've been splashed and jostled, and even tipped over a few times, but that mindset remains, carrying us downstream. We can't afford to stop paddling. *Thanks, Chuck.*

running errands

When asked to describe their ideal future, prospective and existing clients in their twenties will often describe a lifestyle above that of the average American household. That same person will often look to their average peers to guide their decision. How does that add up? You can't beat the average outcome with average habits. Every behavior and ritual earns or charges interest in the game of life. I'll see better results getting 30 minutes of cardio daily versus a once-a-week visit to the gym. Financial wellness is a process, not a New Year's resolution.

While money, effort, and habits have a compounding effect, I realized quickly as a new financial advisor that time does not. We all get the same damn amount. I got home about 8:00 pm after a busy workday. I had ventured across town that day, which I don't like doing and typically avoid. I love to travel, but driving around to meet people? That, I dislike. First, venturing outside our home or office means unexpected things come up. We might pay for parking, feel obligated to buy a coffee when we already consumed an entire pot at home (not that I've ever done that), or otherwise spend time "getting settled" when we have a place where we are "settled" already.

On this particular day, I had about five meetings. This was when I had been a full-time financial advisor for around three or four months, when Rebeca was still at City Year. *Living that soft salaried life.* That day, I had one internal meeting at our office downtown at 7:30 am, then a prospect meeting at a coffee shop by the mall, then a few client meetings at the office, then a volunteer community organizing event in the early evening. In between meetings, I was setting up other appointments, preparing for the recommendations I made that day, getting some investment paperwork sorted out … Busy.

Every day was stressful at that time. I was finding my income meeting by meeting, and our bills didn't stop coming, so the clock was always ticking. I felt like I couldn't afford to take care of myself. *Two hours with no work and no parenting? Ain't got time for that.* The fight-flight-freeze adrenaline was constant. I suddenly stopped putting my seatbelt on until the first red light. Like I didn't have the time …

It's common to see people who are living in financial insecurity showing very risky behaviors, and now I was one of them. Never had I been so keenly aware that time is money. Because it was. Every call or text message could lead to a client in some way, shape or form. Although it was a good day, I was grumpy because I had to drive out to the mall. It was about a 25-minute drive each way, plus about 10 minutes walking each way to my parking spot downtown. So, an hour in my piece-of-shit car with no AC and no Bluetooth, sweating through my cheap suit. Beyond that, I just don't like malls in general. I always try to get in and out, which is tough because, like a grocery store, the whole place is designed to keep you in.

The guy I was meeting said he was running late by about 20 minutes, but I had already driven out there, and he said he was coming … I waited, till I received a new text: "Sorry, let's reschedule." *This is what I've been reduced to, the once-mighty camp director.*

So, I got home well after dark, tired and drained. Optimistic that I was building rapport, gaining credibility, but nonetheless aware that I had just spent 13 fast-paced hours without technically making any money. The realization that I was hungry surfaced once I saw the fridge, so I went through four or five random things in there and in the pantry that required absolutely zero prep time. I moved on to leftovers, not knowing if I was even hungry anymore. A release.

During this stress blur, Rebeca came sauntering down from upstairs. She said, "We need to go to the mall on Saturday for _____, and I don't want to go there with Roque by myself." Then she walked into the living room. She didn't even break her stride.

*What the f**k?! Saturday? All three of us, when it's packed, on the day when I can finally get away from people briefly?* I just wanted to go to the park with our son and forget about the rest of the world. I just couldn't get on board with that. I can't even remember what it was we "needed," but I do remember "needed" was in quotes as far as I was concerned. It was something that most people have or do, something totally reason-able, something that I wouldn't object to normally. Except that I WAS JUST THERE. AT THAT MALL. WAITING. It could have been done, and now it was going to suck the life out of a precious Saturday. *I need to be working or recharging.*

In the moment, I was sulky, and passive aggressive. I couldn't actually express my feelings. My reaction was not supportive or helpful. From her vantage point, she must have been thinking: "Um, okay, you chose to work even more than before for way less money, and the last pay run you didn't make anything, and I'm trying to maintain our family life and do things that normal people do, and I do not want to haul this growing child around when clearly you are a human pack mule."

Maybe we both were too tired to really be angry, just deflated. We did have faith in each other that we were each doing our best, but there was a rift widening. *She supports me, but how could she understand?*

Feeling the pressure to get a lot done, all I could think about was the redundant wasted time. Wasted? Spending time on a little family outing? How could that be a waste? Well, that's how I felt. As a business owner, I suddenly realized that time spent doing something—anything—always had an opportunity cost: giving up the opportunity to do something else, something better. Would it be a family trip to the mall? Well, yeah, but it could have been a family walk in the park instead. My own reaction caught me off guard a little bit, because acts of service is my primary love language, like my parents. But this was so inefficient, so avoidable. *I'll have to watch consumers spend money. Oooof. Get me away from people.*

The constant urgency to meet opportunity as it presented itself, to streamline, to scale, this was new to me. I forgot that Rebeca was still living in the salaried world I'd been working in until the previous year. When I was at Habitat, some volunteer, coming upon a group of people talking, would always say, "What is this, a government job?" *Ha!* When there's little financial incentive for efficiency, you do end up with people standing around, and everyone is paid the same. On the other hand, the roofers that Habitat contracted for our development were clearly paid by the job, and they were hauling ass to get to the next one to make more money. Hauling ass so quickly, in fact, that one morning we found human excrement on the floor, and frankly it didn't look like an "emergency" turd. Getting out and back into a harness was apparently too much time to waste—no pun intended. They needed to put food on the table. If they were undocumented, they couldn't qualify for food assistance like me.

One day in this first year, I was checking in with my managing partner, Steve. He asked about my weekend. I must have reported mowing the lawn, because I remember him telling me I shouldn't be mowing my own lawn. Mowing the lawn is pretty much the only chore I've ever liked, so this got my attention. *What do you mean, Steve?* Here's what he meant …

If you take how much you make in a year, estimate how many hours you worked, you can calculate your hourly rate. If that is higher than what you pay someone else to mow it, then you shouldn't be doing it. Really? You shouldn't be doing anything someone else can do for you? *Maybe I can't afford not to.*

Back in my cubicle, I did my own math. My final salary was $53,000. Resident Camp hours were hard to calculate, so I just said I averaged 50 hours a week, times 49 weeks equals 2,450 hours. 53,000 divided by 2,450 equaled $21.63 per hour, pre-tax. A lot less than I would've guessed, *and* still more than I needed to pay a neighborhood kid to mow the lawn for 45 minutes. Dammit, he was right. Maybe the push-back from the private sector was not completely because they were evil or trying to take advantage. That government job joke is a blue-collar classic for a reason. Maybe it was just because the government moves slowly and has no immediate reason to speed up. Businesses don't want to waste time. And many government employees, secure in their benefits and a culture that does not incentivize speed, are in a run-out-the-clock situation each and every day.

But really, don't mow the lawn? I'm not bougie. I don't need to pay someone to do something I can do myself. That's ridiculous. The middle-class ethos was strong in me. I wasn't a senior citizen living alone. I wasn't out of town. I could do it myself, like any self-respecting homeowner would.

Yet Steve's point about the freed-up time really stuck with me. Going to the grocery store just for milk? That, I could live without. I began to realize that some of the veteran advisors in the firm, those making \$200,000–300,000 a year, they seemed like pretty regular people, *but* they were intentional with time. Every day was a new opportunity. I learned there was a contrast between my middle-class roots and my newfound finance observations: while middle-class folks tend to be self-reliant in as many aspects of their life as they can be, often stubbornly so, higher-income earners were quick to delegate things they didn't understand, didn't have time for, or just didn't want to do. The thought process was, "Well, my hourly rate is about \$120 this year, and the landscaping service is \$50/hour, and when I get home, I want to spend quality time with my kids. I'm not mowing the lawn ever again."

I like to get things done, and I like to run errands by myself. I drive faster, I listen to the music I choose, I walk faster, I get in and get out. On this occasion, we went to the mall together, and it was just fine. We sat and watched our son toddle around the play area. But since then, Rebeca and I continue to work on how get the menial things done as quickly as possible. There are many things I will pay for, and I am happy to support local businesses. Our spending is their earning, after all.

One day I had a lapse in judgment and went to the store on short notice without clear directives. I was staring blankly at a grocery list with broad categories like "tortilla chips," "bread," "milk," so I showed the 16-year-old clerk the picture of the label. I text her back and get a follow-up question the kid can't answer, and he's like, "Dude, just get yogurt," and I'm like, "You really think I'm the one who will only accept a single brand/flavor/fat content combination?"

How much is an hour of our time worth? Well, in a growing business, the number goes up all the time. And if it's not, then you aren't really growing. Our potential is infinite, but time is limited.

I have learned helplessness at the store. I don't mind going. It's the small decisions that stress me out. Now we use a shopping delivery service all the time. Even the local organic coop is on there now. This is fantastic for me, because Rebeca chooses the specific items herself, the shopper selects them, and any mishaps are their fault, not mine! The COVID pandemic accelerated trends already in motion. Online delivery of all things is one of them.

So, if I'm not wandering around the grocery store, I have to use the time saved productively. That's the key. Not on binge-watching. Repurpose that mental effort. A choice that is priceless is being present with our kids. They won't think I'm cool much longer. A choice that is time-value focused is writing, volunteering, working with clients—things that I am uniquely positioned to do. I have a value to the marketplace, which is totally unrelated to the value I have to my family or community. I may have an "hourly rate" higher than the neighbor kid, but that doesn't mean I'm better than him. It does mean that he can earn from mowing while I spend the day playing with the kids inside. I can't do both at the same time. The dark side of capitalism wants us to believe that we need to grind and hustle endlessly to prove our worth as people, measured by our income and our possessions. An insidious lie. Those who believe the lie will see their value to their family and community fall, even as their market dollar value rises.

Therefore, I'm not assuming that I should always buy back time to work more. Maybe you meditate. Maybe you write a heartfelt letter to your brother or childhood friend. Put something positive online instead of negative. Get lemons and make lemonade. Experience the restorative power of doing nothing for an afternoon. Create a vision board. As Denzel Washington said in a commencement address, "Just because you're doing a lot more doesn't mean you're getting a lot more done. Don't confuse movement with progress."

Capitalism organizes and streamlines through specialization. I've come to realize that I'm not great at doing tasks; I am good at creating them. The person who shops all the time will inevitably get more efficient than someone who doesn't. (The gig economy is real work. They need real employee benefits.) A single trip to the store is a mental shift to a new skill, and all cognitive transitions take mental energy, and therefore time. The time spent changing gears adds up over time.

Hopefully, you weren't about to cry me a river. Rebeca and her family were extremely supportive. I was healthy. Still terrified of debt, our fixed bills were low. Rebeca accepted that it would be hard starting out, and worth it in the long run. Stories of entrepreneurship require faith and time. These larger-than-life stories often involve sleeping in the lab, or leaving family behind, or being on the road chasing a dream. They require time, every spare minute of it. That's what was so deflating about the mall on a Saturday.

Around me, then and since, I observed the barriers to entrepreneurship, including growing a financial planning clientele. First, access to capital. Who do you know and who will bet on you? I may have been new, but I did look the part of "financial advisor stock photo." Second, the amount of time to work. I have a friend who worked long hours for SpaceX, and then left to take care of his ailing father, because he couldn't do both. The more people need you, the harder it is to get going. And third, the amount of money you need to earn, and by when. We all have a different runway. The entrepreneur who can live on a friend's couch has an advantage over one who is already hosting those in need. Juggling all that creates a drag for financial advisors, which is why financial advisors and entrepreneurs have historically been mostly White and male, like me.

Self-care is the hardest for me. On commission, I felt like I couldn't afford to take care of myself. On weekend afternoons when I'm with our kids, in the yard, the park, whatever, I do wish I had more time to mountain bike, read, watch a two-hour drama uninterrupted like the old times. But by witnessing all the little moments now and caring about the Lego, or the rock, or another rock, seeing their personalities grow, it will make my outlets three times better when I can take them with me. Relationships, like assets, usually appreciate in value when nurtured. As Chris McCandless wrote shortly before his death in the remote Alaskan wilderness, "Happiness is only real when shared." Professional success with estranged children is not in my vision.

I feel the self-imposed pressure to fulfill my potential, to keep the sail out, and to use the tailwind I've been given. I feel the pressure to be responsible, and uphold middle-class values, while understanding more and more how wealth is built with assets as much as work. If middle-income Americans identify with responsibility and hard work, and often look down on lower-income Americans as lacking these virtues, then higher-income Americans identify with delegation and strategy, and find them missing in middle-class culture. Even now, I find it hard to delegate. It feels out of character. My brain knows it's right, but it's hard.

Generally, Americans work hard even though we live in a nation of abundance. Nothing is more motivating than survival, and being a financially comfortable American is a pretty plush existence. America became a superpower through innovation, conquest, and a little luck. But I'm not sure we're thinking hard. What innovation can I work on that will be useful 20 years from now? What skill do I have that I can share with my neighbors? How can I convert that Saturday mall visit into a strategy to be more valuable at work and get promoted? Can I take free online classes in a new subject? *If I buy back my time, how will I spend it?*

If you don't have goals, you will always work for someone who does. Every day, we are given 24 hours of time. We decide, through our goals and our values, how much is poured into sleep, our family, our hobbies, our health. They don't get the same amount every day, but if we don't decide, all the buckets will leak into TikTok. Unless you have a TikTok influencer goal, that corrodes your progress.

As with most important questions, when we look to others for comparison, it's a false choice. Each day, we fill those time buckets in ways that serve us and our loved ones, allowing us to develop and thrive. I will use delegation and strategy, being disciplined with the time I buy back. Once old enough, our kids will mow, rake, shovel, and clean. Their hourly rate is a great deal. Teaching the value of hard work is always worth the time.

the definition of negligence

In my first year as a financial advisor, I was summoned for jury duty. I felt panicked that I had to step away from growing my business with no reliable income yet. Like every American I've ever met, I hoped I wouldn't be picked for the trial. *I can't afford to miss work. I'm only eight months into this.*

I was in a line-up of 100 people summoned for this trial. After "check-in," you go to another room, where you meet the judge, attorneys, plaintiffs, and defendants. We could sense this was a big deal. There was media attention. There was palpable tension. I learned the trial was expected to last a month. *What is this about? This might actually be interesting.* And my internal conflict mounted: work to earn or do my civic duty?

The plaintiffs, two police officers badly shot while on duty, were suing Badger Guns, a dealer, for negligence in the sale of a gun to the teenager that shot them.

Jury selection alone took two days. For that, you sit in the courtroom all day until you're called. I waited my turn to be interviewed privately by attorneys for both sides with the judge presiding. People told me to say my brother was a cop or say something extreme like no citizen should own guns or something like that. And they didn't even know this case was about cops and guns. What does that tell you about how tense this was? People thought I could look biased and be dismissed for a connection to cops or guns. I didn't say anything untrue, though, and I was picked. *You'll miss weeks of work. You can't have your phone during the trial. You'll have to do two meetings each night. Admit it. You're excited. This is democracy in action, high stakes conflict. You're a social studies nerd.*

Opening arguments, and we were off. Sort of. The pressure of trial law is immense. Performing under pressure consistently leads to high financial compensation. I witnessed the pressure and stakes in this case. Basically, after a lifetime of joking about how lawyers suck and get paid too much, I saw how difficult and important their role can be to our society.

The amount of stress, pain, and money poured into both sides of this conflict had mounted for years already. *Like a dam ready to burst, but whose house will be washed away?* The oral arguments and line of questioning were deliberate, measured, and a little dull. The high-profile attorneys and the elected circuit court judge were under a media microscope even in the courtroom. The jury, silent day after day, wouldn't have a spotlight until our verdict was delivered. I was interviewed on national television. To get there, we had the pressure of making a sound decision, based on weeks of testimony and evidence. That was not entertainment. A lot of it was boring.

The boring stuff was there to verify the tragic past and unsettling present: images of a police officer's fractured skull; video deposition from a young man, filmed in prison, dark skin and bright orange suit in a room of gray; completed paperwork to buy a firearm, with writing at a second or third grade level; security camera footage of an employee waiting for two guys to come up with the cash to buy a deadly weapon. Except for the merchandise itself, it looked like two nine-year-old kids pooling change to buy candy at the corner store. And echoing throughout, the classic defendant refrain, "I can't recall ... I can't recall ... I can't recall."

In a busy store, I wouldn't expect an employee or owner to recall every transaction. Which is why process and procedure, or lack thereof, was in question early on. It seemed the defendants didn't have much and didn't apologize for that approach. They were just selling weapons the way they would sell secondhand furniture. Using their "best judgment" because "every sale is different."

A young man filled with anger asked another young man who was just old enough—but who could barely read—to buy him a gun, while he was standing next him. The 18-year-old picked the one he wanted, handed over cash to the slightly older straw buyer, who struggled to fill out a basic one-page form for half an hour. Then the true buyer started trouble when high school got out, was chased by two cops, and ultimately shot both.

When are more safeguards required in a transaction? Human judgment is flawed, and conflicts of interest abound. It seems like whenever money, legal contracts, and human agendas converge, we find an environment rife with bias. The defense attorney reiterated repeatedly that there was no basis for holding a gun dealer liable for what the gun was used for after the sale. I agree with that statement. They shouldn't be held liable if they follow the existing law. If the defendants *had* followed the *existing* law, then the Second Amendment would have been under attack, because the potential liability would be too expensive for a gun dealer to cover. But that wasn't what the trial was about. Powerful and persuasive opinions are used to obscure the facts at hand all the time. *We the jury are the voters. We know the least but are strangely in charge.*

After the trial was over, the media framed the trial in terms of gun control and the Second Amendment. Our verdict, and that of the judge, was described through each media source's lens on that issue. But this was a case about the legal definition of negligence and understanding the law as it is written. The judge uses judgment to interpret the law, but the judge doesn't write the law. Congress does. And we the people vote for them. *The law is the rulebook. If we the voters are the crowd, then our response to the game may change the rules.*

Our judge's admonition to the jury at every break in the trial was "do not discuss this case with anyone and do not read any news … to do so may cause this case to become a mistrial at significant expense to the taxpayers." He read the full statement and maintained his enthusiasm over the full month. We all started to chuckle by the end, even the attorneys. He knew correctly that personal anecdotes, hearsay, and news coverage did not constitute facts. That was so critical. This was a civil trial, and we weren't sequestered in a hotel. The choices and criminal charges against the two young men happened years ago. Badger Guns had been operating ever since. The judge is the referee, keeping the bias and the emotions in check. *The referee doesn't make the rules during the game.*

In 2015, I learned things about gun sales that are totally legal and alarming. No skills test. No drug test. You could snort a line of coke in the parking lot and pick up your handgun ten minutes later. Criminal background check and ID proving you're 21 or older are the only requirements, but everyone has a first time … In a "straw purchase" like this one, any person could just shop, then give a friend money to go buy what they want. The law required the seller to stop the sale if there were signs it was being purchased for someone else. That responsibility is in conflict with an immediate profit, with only a moral compass and a potential lawsuit to keep that temptation in check.

I thought the judge was there to preserve order when things got heated. Then I realized I'd only seen judges on TV before. The judge here, a veteran close to retirement, interpreted the law. That requires both knowledge and perspective. The judge's interpretation of what we the jury could know, the line of questioning, all of it, was by the book. He never cut corners. He never editorialized.

The attorneys went into the judge's chambers. This always seemed to happen when we approached business practices and succession planning. It was always a bummer for us because it would follow two or three objections, just when things were heating up. We were only allowed to know the events leading up to the day of the shooting, nothing after. This was tricky for everyone. *The attorneys are like the players, jockeying for any advantage. They're in a timeout, drawing up plays. And the referee has to know if they're legal first, because once something is said, and we hear it, there's no taking it back.*

After the closing arguments, it was time for the jury to vote. The judge gave us a booklet listing the specific charges. It was like ten pages long, and nowhere did it say anything about gun control or the Second Amendment. We were given, I think, 17 individual charges to deliberate and decide guilty or not guilty, separated into three groups: negligence, negligence in the sale, and conspiracy. In addition, we also had to vote on a dollar amount of damages paid to the officers for pain and suffering. We heard hours of testimony from the plaintiffs' psychiatrist, neurologist, surgeon, you name it, everyone who had a first-hand role in treating their physical and mental injuries. On top of that, the prosecuting attorney said more than a million in punitive damages "would send a message" to other bad apple gun dealers.

Just like in the movies, we the jury faced each other in this small bland room with expressions ranging from anger to apathy. As a group of voters, I'd say about half of us really tried to discuss the law objectively, others made it clear which team they were on from the start, and one or two were just waiting to tack their vote onto the winning side so we could leave and not come back. We were all imperfect with our triggers and beliefs.

"C'mon, let's just get it over with today, and get outta here!" Shortly after that opening comment, I was elected jury foreperson. I had to focus the group. I like mediation in general. For me, if I'm working in any way, then the more pressure, intensity, and adrenaline I have, the better I'll perform. I love to chill, don't get me wrong, but if the law says I have jury duty, well then … let's make it a memorable, quality experience. It makes the time pass, it makes me better mentally, and it is my duty as an informed citizen regardless. *You're a soccer referee again, and it's a close game. You have a responsibility, so focus. It's not a game, focus.*

We spent eight or nine hours talking through it. We had to break for the day and return the next. *People need to get back to work. I know he watches his kids and works second shift. Maybe that's why he wants to wrap up.*

Pain and suffering were hard to quantify, so each person voted for an amount of damages, and we averaged them out in our decision. A few jurors said $0. Shit happens. As a financial advisor, even I found the quantifying part fuzzy. It sounded like a lot all at once. But considering how lives were changed, it seemed fair. In a civil trial, a jury needs nine votes to reach a verdict. We voted on 17 individual charges. On each negligence charge, between eight and eleven jurors voted guilty.

We like to talk about our emotions. We are motivated by them. But financial outcomes in this country are dictated by contracts and laws. While you focus on buying the car or the timeshare, a contract is operating in the background, often hoping you won't read it too carefully.

In the absence of a military draft, jury duty remains an essential element of democracy, and serves as a fundamental leveler. You are judged by a jury of your peers: our jury was diverse by gender, age, and race, and likely by income. We weren't lawyers. We were paid just $17 per day to be there. But as fellow citizens, we owed it to all parties involved to do our very best. Sometimes the urgent matters must wait for the important ones. Or so most of us felt, including me. A few just wanted to leave. Maybe the urgent things in their life loomed larger than the important responsibility before us. In their defense, our government doesn't subsidize democracy enough. Jury duty is costly to the juror: childcare costs and lost wages grow. The law gives us leave of absence only.

If, however, we take for granted our democratic responsibilities, like voting and jury duty, we won't be democratic much longer. If we don't pay attention to how judges are appointed or elected, we waive our right as voters. I often show up in the primary election booth not knowing a thing about the circuit court judges on the ballot. Shame on me. This experience proved to me I should be informed, and yet I'm still not.

I spoke to the prosecuting attorney a few days later. He said he wanted me on the jury because, being in my profession, I would understand process and procedure, and the importance of due diligence. The CFP® certification mandates oversight of my actions as a fiduciary. As a registered investment advisor and insurance agent, I have significant licensing and continuing education requirements, as I should. I carry liability insurance in case I make a mistake, and the contracts I use are reviewed by lawyers. Giving advice on someone's life savings is no small matter. Neither is selling a gun to a young man who can barely read, with his teenage "friend" looking over his shoulder.

This jury experience reminded me of how grossly oversimplified news headlines are. This was a case involving gun sales, Black men, White cops, and the Second Amendment. Every facet was complex and polarizing. But our task, for an entire month, was to dispassionately interpret the definition of negligence, and willfully ignore our feelings on all of that.

People at my office connected the dots between my jury duty and the news. My family, my professor, everybody shared how they "felt" about our verdict in terms of gun control, not negligence.

Defining each term takes time. In my Philosophy of Ethics undergrad class, the professor (who had a rotation of exactly three shirts and two pairs of corduroys, unless he had duplicates) stressed how the basis of philosophy was defining terms before arguing. The majority of jury deliberation was understanding the law. We spent the last month hearing the facts. We weren't there to decide if it was right or wrong. We had to determine if the law was broken—the law as it exists, regardless of what we think the law should be. Which is boring. Sometimes the hardest thing to do is to focus on a tedious task, to get it right by blocking out your emotions amid a storm. *Don't look at them. Just re-read the definition of negligence one more time before calling a vote.*

Elected politicians are the architects of the law. Laws often need updating. If we hear a verdict we don't like because of political implications, we must remember that judges only interpret. Congress makes it, so go to the source; take it up with Congress. And remember, they too will play to our opinions to obscure the facts. Better yet, focus on getting the money out of politics altogether. If we don't pay jurors more than $17 a day, then we shouldn't allow wealthy donors to send more than $17 a day to their political candidate of choice. Being on that jury made me proud to be an American. And because I witnessed how important impartiality is, it reinforced how critical it is as citizens that we do our best to improve our judicial system. Humans already have all forms of personal bias, so the least we can do is remove the bias of money. Even when it's not the main reason for a decision, money is always present.

The gun dealer who sold the crime weapon negligently to make a quick buck started this tsunami of tragedy. We justify our actions by distance from their effect. Sometimes our actions with money become so routine that our negligence, deliberate or not, sneaks up on us. We wonder how we got there. We end up saying "I don't recall" in court next to a hundred boxes of documents. Sometimes our actions with money are so impactful, meaning one jury decision could mandate an exchange of millions of dollars between parties, and have a ripple of consequences, deliberate or not.

With great power comes great responsibility. The bigger the consequence, the more deliberation is warranted. We ended up awarding nearly $5 million in damages to the police officers, and we awarded $1 million in punitive damages against Badger Guns. It was the first time a jury found a gun dealer negligent. An interview clip of me made national news. *Camera adds 40 pounds, in my case.*

The media speculated about the future and tightening gun control. But the evidence was so damning that negligence under current law was obvious. The current law made buying a gun easy. This case was beyond easy.

In court, everyone is equal under the law. But outside, only $17 a day meant more to some than others, and that reality didn't reinforce the need for careful consideration. It reinforced searching online "how to get out of jury duty," making a jury of true peers less likely. Freedom isn't free.

to lease or to own, that is the question

I love to drive. I hate cars. No, I love cars, but knowing what I know now, I hate thinking about what to get, when, and how. At age 30, I finally had to buy a car. Being on a tiiiight budget and trying to balance a myriad of emotions and scenarios made this pretty difficult.

Cars are so dumb and so important at the same time. There were two reasons that now was the right time to buy: one meaningful, one mostly ego-driven. Buying a car would mean that we would give Rebeca's two-door Toyota Yaris to her mom. Her mom and dad were down to one car, and they had done a lot for us in the last few years. Back when we lived in Seattle, her dad took over the payments on the Yaris for a year because we only needed one car, which amounted to about $3,000. Rebeca's mom watched Roque two or three days a week, and being able to give her some more mobility was worth it. That car, in great condition, but by anyone's account a barebones car, was her Mother's Day present in 2016.

While I loved the parallel parking ability, I did not like to drive that car publicly. *This isn't Europe. You look ridiculous.* I had two colleagues at Lake Valley Camp call it a "clown car" and a "street-legal go kart" respectively. It had worked for a sporty, sexy Latina in her twenties. It did not work for a burly White guy in his thirties wearing a bad suit.

The more ego-driven reason was a mounting pressure to have a legitimate car to make public appearances in, for social or professional reasons. In January of that year, we had driven the Ford Taurus to a family weekend retreat in Wisconsin Dells. I had to qualify to go, so only the more prominent members of the firm where there, and Rebeca, Roque and I shared a cabin with other promising newcomers and families in our downtown office, including the managing partner. We had a great time, and everyone was so welcoming and generous. Of course, the only parking space left when we arrived was right in front of the entrance, the big dents in the side in plain view, alongside the Lincoln and the Audi and the Mercedes and the ... you get the idea. *My scarlet letter.*

I knew enough to know that cars depreciate rapidly. Their value drops so fast it's misleading to call them an asset, like real estate or a business or stock. You're really owning a means of transportation primarily. It's unlimited access to a service: a box of metal that can move people quickly and precisely. If that is your only reason: get me from point A to point B, then it makes sense to buy. But when we consider our car is also an experience rooted in identity and status signals, it gets a little more complicated.

I knew the most cost-effective way to have a car was buying a gently used vehicle, because most of the depreciation in sales price comes off in the first few years. Or was it? I also knew that our staff accountant, a CPA, leased cars, as did some other advisors in our firm who I respected and who seemed to know the system of money. So, I started to dig into the leasing versus owning question. Perhaps it wasn't one size fits all.

My parents had had practical cars because they were practical people, which I mean as a high compliment. *So, why can't you just be practical?* They seemed to buy cars and keep them until they died, or they had a kid turning 16. If that's the plan, owning still makes sense.

I am my parents' son. I can't lease a car like a sucker. I would buy a gently used car, *except* … I didn't want to front the cash. I could get it, but not easily, and even $2,500 down (10% of the purchase price) would have made me very nervous being without a base salary. Plus, I wasn't sure we would want this car for 15 years, or even 10. I didn't know how many kids we would have. I didn't know where we would live, or what our commute or access to public transportation would be like.

With those unknowns, I didn't know how long two cars would be necessary in Milwaukee. I didn't know how long it would be before money wasn't tight, and then, given the option, if we would think differently. We were paycheck-to-paycheck, but we didn't want to be cheap and have a car maintenance headache later. I didn't know if Rebeca and I could both like the same family car equally, and want to keep it. To put it more directly, this would be "Rebeca's car" that I would drive when our family was all together. Meaning she had to like it now, and I would likely have to love it when the family car was upgraded. It might be my hand-me-down. What if the price of gas goes up? I overanalyzed and cross-examined my hypothetical future self for about a year before we acted. Worth it? Not sure.

We leased a 2016 Subaru Forester through our credit union. A payment can be problematic, of course, but so can owning a shitty car. First, there wasn't any cash down in our case. The monthly payments just began, which relieved a lot of pressure on me for finding a down payment. Second, we were able to drive a newer car, and honestly this was important. Even my practical dad had said that about the Taurus one day when I pulled in at their house, "You really shouldn't be driving that car for business" and something like "people will wonder." And this from the guy wearing clothes born before I was. He was not concerned about appearances personally, but he understood the nature of my work enough to point out it was an issue. Our cars were pretty average for our neighborhood, but when I made a house call in an affluent area, I would often park a block away and slink around the corner, detached from my scarlet letter. "Ha ha, yeah, I read the address wrong when I pulled up, go figure … well, we're here now!" I feared they would judge me, and more importantly, it affected my confidence, which affected my income, which affected my ability to buy a better car. I had to break the identity cycle.

We signed a four-year lease, meaning we committed to payments for that time, and when it expired, we could renew (based on a new appraisal of the car's worth), walk away without a penalty to make a new decision based on new circumstances, or buy the car outright, in cash or financing it through the same credit union. We—*gasp!*—borrowed a car for the time being.

I knew a *lot* would change in four years. *It better. It has to.* I also knew that a lot of indecision with my clients was rooted in not knowing how life would change. They knew the present, but they had a fear of commitment, worried they couldn't adjust later. Perhaps the greatest gap between the world I started a family in compared to my parents' generation is the rate of change. Technology and globalization have made drastic changes faster and easier. Why would I buy a gasoline car in cash when there will be more electric options soon, self-driving cars in 10 years, and hovercraft in 20? Keeping your options open—or put another way, the convenience of change—always carries an extra cost. Buying isn't always better, but committing to keeping a car is where the value lies in the long term. It usually does with money. Investing for retirement is tax-deferred, whereas keeping your options open and investing for anything has taxable gains. Same idea: commitment pays off. I've learned the value of delegation and thinking bigger, but another pathway to financial security is a simple rule: buy what you'll use and use what you buy.

The longer you own a car payment-free, the better it looks financially. Even on a typical 5–7 year financing plan, that means you are driving a car without a payment for 7–10 years at least if you keep up with routine maintenance. We still have my grandparents' dressers in our house, and they passed away 14 years ago. I remember those dressers in their bedrooms when I was a little boy. That's a pretty good return on investment. They hold underwear just as well as they did 40 years ago when they were new.

What if you're not sure you want that car for 10–15 years? Indecision always has a cost because transactions always have a cost. The math on a trade-in or sale isn't very good after you've owned a car for a few years, because many cars are sold for half the original value after only 3–5 years. After that, the rate of depreciation slows down gradually. As the car passes into the "you can't pass this off as new anymore" territory, the price has more to do with mileage and cosmetic defects because the car is reduced to its essential function: the utility value of unlimited access from point A to point B.

Selling after buying new also works against you because the interest on financing is front-loaded. Cars, mortgages, student loans alike, the interest is front-loaded because the lender wants to make sure they're paid first. So, the resale value of the car drops fastest in the early years, *and* you pay the least toward the principal (your balance) of the loan in the early years. Interest on a seven-year car loan or 30-year mortgage will be, all else equal, higher than on a four-year car loan or 15-year mortgage. Ever wonder why your income-based payment plan on your student loan has the amount you owe going *up*? Or how someone could "buy" a car and soon owe *more* than it's worth after an accident? Or what "underwater" on the mortgage means? A lower monthly payment always means more total interest, i.e., the total cost is higher. If you borrow $10,000 and agree to pay it back over ten years, you're technically borrowing $1,000 of it for one year, $1,000 of it for four years, and $1,000 of it for 10 years. The lender fronts the money, and the borrower fronts the interest.

If we financed the $25,000 over seven years, it meant a payment of $414 per month, which includes $3,351 of interest charge. That same amount financed over four years is a monthly payment of $598 but total interest of $2,220. So, if someone can part with another $184 each month *now*, they'll save $1,131 on interest, and get to a $0 monthly payment three years faster.

It might be worth it anyway. *Anything to lower that monthly bill or get out of the clown car.* Transactions should be front-loaded. Years later, I paid $7 for a drink along the Inca Trail in the Andes Mountains in Peru. Hiking uphill at that altitude wiped me out. The markup was steep, but then again, the local woman hauled all of these 20 oz. Gatorades up the mountain while I just carried extra socks and a rain poncho. Well worth it. The seller carries the risk because there's no guarantee we'll buy. The lender charges interest first because there's no guarantee you'll finish payments.

When the Federal Reserve (those bland government money people who make boring news only one friend of yours cares about) lowers the interest rate, they are increasing the volume of transactions in the economy. It's like heat causing water molecules to move faster: ice, water, gas. We are connected, so my car financing means the lender is hiring, the employee is earning, and their family is staying in their home. With all transactions and services, the seller or provider stands ready to deliver the second you arrive. They are fronting the cost of standing at the ready, and therefore they are paid first.

Your lease payment matches the rate of depreciation (i.e., lost value) on your vehicle, plus interest and fees charged.

So, making a 2016 decision that suited us perfectly was okay, if we could reassess no strings attached in 2020. *Things will be better by then.* The payment was based on a depreciation schedule and interest. We assumed an estimated 10,000 miles a year. This was low but was pretty accurate for us at the time. We didn't often drive very far, which is why a lease made sense. We didn't pay a penalty if we went over mileage, which is common in leases and a major deterrent for drivers who plan to drive a lot. Borrowing and renting keeps options open. With cars, higher mileage means lower resale value, because they are more likely to need repairs. But cars are a depreciating asset either way. More frequent use means more return on your dollars as the buyer. *You don't use that bike trainer in the basement, but those hand-me-down dressers do hold your underwear just as well as your grandpa's, every damn day.*

We would, however, owe more on the car at the four-year mark, because all else being equal, a 2016 Subaru with 40,000 miles on it is worth more than one with 60,000. We would owe that difference under appraisal value. I was willing to figure that out in the future. If the car was $25,000 new, and the estimated appraisal four years later, with 40,000 miles and normal wear and tear, was $18,000, that would equal a monthly payment of $300 to buy it.

The cost of borrowing is almost never free, but it was at near record-lows at the time. At work, I was routinely seeing 3–4% mortgages. A few years later, during the pandemic, 2% mortgages appeared. As a Millennial making moves in this decade, I found it hard to fathom that mortgages used to be 12% interest. Or that a guaranteed certificate of deposit (CD) at the bank could ever earn more than 2%. Or that government savings bonds used to be popular. Anyway, our credit was good, and we paid 1.9% interest for the lease from a credit union. That's less than the inflation increase in 2016.

Therefore, a financial robot would say this was a no-brainer. Even if we could pay $25,000 in cash, we'd be better off putting a minimum down and buying a five-year CD earning 3–4%, or putting more into our retirement account, or college fund for Roque. Those would grow at a faster rate than the drag created by paying interest. All money in circulation has a time value. When a client wants to prioritize paying off debt, I remind them that while debt payoff will *save* them money, investing or doing something else productive will *earn* them money, often more than they would save by accelerated debt payments. Or buying something else they really want or need. If you want it bad enough *and* long enough, then it's often worth it, even when it's numerically illogical. Self-esteem often is.

Our new $250 monthly payment could be defined as a $50 gift to my mother-in-law, $100 keeping Rebeca happy with a nice four-door family car, and $100 for my self-esteem. Four years later, we financed the car for the same amount of its resale value. In the end, we paid $250 to rent a car. Worth it to not be embarrassed. Which is where I was in the Taurus: driving a 13-year-old car that ran just fine, but didn't fulfill my "experience/identity" needs. It bothered me more than a car payment would. *I'm paying $250 a month in embarrassment right now.*

The inherent beauty of capitalism is that free market ambition, creativity, and agility solve problems faster than any mandated system. The inherent flaw of capitalism is: where no problems exist, advertising will create them, and further invest in the perception of problems. Which then creates real problems. The supply and demand loop can accelerate faster and faster. How much will you use it? For how long? How important is it to love what you drive? To appear well-off? Supply and demand affect price, but originate in culture. *Ugh, the 2016 Subaru has Bluetooth instead of Apple CarPlay. Might as well be a CD player.*

It is easier for us to buy a puzzle online with a few clicks and get it the next day than remember to ask my mom if she has saved any kids puzzles, then wait for our next visit. Capitalism makes it easy to buy, easy to say yes. Seems to me, the "reduce" part is harder for Americans than "reuse" or "recycle", because reducing our consumption involves saying no. It means admitting that the dresser isn't the color we would choose, but it still can hold underwear, so we don't need another one.

When things are disposable, their value is fleeting. Why do people buy cheap things? Sometimes all we care about is that lower payment, even if it means replacing it more often. Those who can afford to buy and maintain nice things will see them hold value.

Four years later, I financed a gently used car. It had 10,000 miles on it as the previous year's model. One year reduced the price from about $32,000 to $25,000. I wanted to buy this vehicle to counterweigh the Subaru lease. Interest rates were even lower now. I knew myself, sentimental sap that I am. After months of debate about what type of car best defined me as a person and would balance our family's needs, I got a black Toyota Camry Hybrid. Reliable, good mileage, more fun to drive than anything I'd had since my black Toyota Camry, age 16–24. The connection to my past meant I would keep this one. *The Black Pearl II.* See? I'm just as irrational as everyone else.

Material objects have an energy. Things made lovingly, with beautiful materials, foster an aura of respect. For me at least, they do. Machines make life better, but the energy of a skyscraper or a car comes from the assembly and construction workers who used machines. A smoothed wooden block has a different energy than a neon piece of plastic, both from the creation and the original material. As Michael Pollan (and countless others with a lower profile) has pointed out, "real food" we can recognize is better for us than something packaged and processed. Trying to masquerade margarine as butter is bad energy. And how could something called cream cheese be low-fat? The energy of an event or endeavor exists in the object. The energy of the endeavor shows up in processed food that requires advertising in the absence of quality, as it does in your favorite stall at the farmers' market, through a local connection.

We will often pay top dollar at the time of sale, but the value has more to do with how much and how long we use it. Here's my message. You can't always be cheap. Be strategically cheap. And when you do spend, spend intentionally and joyfully. Leasing means you'll always have a car payment, which is no fun. As the sharing economy gains steam, maybe question the conventional wisdom of the 20th century. Driving a car you hate isn't ideal either. There are no tax benefits to car ownership after all, unlike homeownership or college savings or kids. Commitment isn't for everyone.

Financing to own a car, and leasing to borrow a car, both exist because they both have merit. Beware of a claim that a well-known option or product is always bad or always good. Nothing sells like simplicity, but the truth is it always depends. If one was better 100% of time, the other would cease to exist. Know thyself, too. Is the compounding effect of a lower or no car payment more important than the compounding effect of something new every four years, and the pleasure derived from that? If your monthly payment goes down, then your total payment goes up. Or vice versa. There's no right or wrong, just reality.

Turns out, getting a car is super easy. My spending is another's earning, so they make it easy. Getting a car in the best way for your unique situation might take a year of furrowed brows and FOMO angst, but I'm used to that by now. I have the forehead wrinkle to prove it.

The most recent iteration? The minivan in 2022. Is the compounding effect of a higher car payment worth ending the compounding effect of three kids untangling seat belts across the back seat of the sedan, Pokémon-based arguments escalating in the rearview mirror? *What will the business revenue look like? Will the electric vehicle tax credit improve or stay the same? Does leasing credit apply to loan or in cash back? Should we wait for more EV options? An SUV can tow. Is that worth giving up sliding doors? Only little kids in back seat? When are used car prices expected to fall? How long will delivery take? Should I make estimated tax payments or wait, since credit isn't refundable? How important is an entertainment system when we don't drive that much? If I'm shuttling kids more, will we swap cars all the time? How long have I been down here squinting at my phone reading car blogs? Go to bed.*

All money has a time value. Our thoughts do, too. Both involve tradeoffs. You can spend them here or spend them there. I can ruminate with the best of them, and the fact is, maybe buying or leasing ended up being a thousand bucks more expensive. Maybe I got it right, maybe not. But I could have made a thousand bucks using the time spent roiling alone in analysis paralysis, a cyclical browser history echoing in my head. It's a financial truth I still struggle with personally: it's best to decide quickly, and change your mind slowly, if at all. Life's too short to stress much about a car that works anyway. I hear they're a terrible investment.

cheese boy hands

One summer when I was still a new financial advisor, we put up a small retaining wall and privacy fence around our backyard. The yard is about two feet above the sidewalk. Up to this point, we had some pretty ugly hedges growing over and around a string of battered chicken wire. It kept the dog in, but the many passersby had an unobstructed view into our yard. Between the bus stop, the school, the ability to drag race down our side street, and foot traffic from the Walmart down the road, it was busy. Really more like our front yard. If we were sitting out there with our son toddling along the hedge side, I could imagine some crackhead just snatching him up and yelling at me for cash, threatening to break his arm. The joys of parenthood... Nothing brings leverage like the safety of your kids. *I guess that's why daycare is expensive.*

Privacy in our own home is important. On one of the first truly warm days that spring, I was out without a shirt on, and some girls gave me a look that reminded me I'm old now. And to think I was in a good mood before that.

The Layton Boulevard West Neighborhood Association (since renamed VIA CDC) had a program for $1,000 matching grants—regardless of applicant income—for home improvement projects facing the street. That was just a little more incentive for doing the fences. I figured the whole project would be about $2,000, so it worked out perfectly. I set to work that spring measuring and penciling plans on a sheet of paper, rekindling my eighth-grade architect phase. Doing this was an outlet from so much stress at work: unlike reorganizing money, this was tangible.

But beyond reading a tape measure, I didn't really know what I was doing. I walked into the store with extra conviction, and not quite enough confidence. My enthusiasm dissipated with some detail that derailed my purpose, like three block options instead of two, or the sales pitch walking past the cable service kiosk.

I remember working through projects with my grandpa as a kid. He would proclaim some project, janky as it may be, good enough to proceed to the next step and still work.

Same thing at Habitat for Humanity when I was a construction lead. I vividly remember my group had framed a whole wall out of line. I thought we'd have to tear it out and start over. I asked my boss Mike, the site supervisor, and he looked at the measurement, looked at me, looked at the measurement again. Then he whaled on it with his hammer like five times, moving the corner a half inch, which in this case was "enough." Confidence that comes with experience. Doing that had occurred to me, but I didn't have the expertise or the experience to make a judgment call.

The feeling I get with home repairs is 90% confident, 10% terrified. I'm alone in the basement at night with the furnace, thinking … *I can't blow up the house, can I? They wouldn't, like, make that possible, right?*

The project ran from March, when I was out measuring, to July, when we finished in the heat of the summer. I'd guess it took about 100 hours of my own work time, plus 100 hours of other people's time. Rebeca's brothers and dad put in some hard labor at the end when the fence went up. I hired a neighborhood kid to help me lay brick in the retaining wall after I leveled the dirt, the only thing I really knew how to do myself. My father-in-law supervised the fence itself, placing posts, pouring concrete, measurements, all that. In the Latin tradition, our family was so supportive. They knew why the fence was important, they knew we didn't want to pay contractors, and they rose to the occasion in exchange for a steady supply of food and heartfelt thanks.

My father-in-law's opinion gave me the confidence to get it done. He was a facilities director for a large nonprofit youth center, so he did this type of low budget "that's good enough" project all the time. He was crucial because he was in his element the way my grandpa was. The supporting cast of characters was not. It did bring us closer, as all barn-raising does. But at what cost? Their time was valuable!

And what about the time spent in my head? Without confidence, doubt creeps in. As I drank my ice-cold beer, basking in the satisfaction of a job well done and calories burned, my thoughts would turn later that day to potential mistakes, cosmetic defects, and negative self-talk about how I should have been able to figure things out myself. There was actual time and mental time. I may have spent another 100 mental hours thinking about this. How much was that time worth, applied elsewhere?

Amid the unpredictability of being self-employed, this type of physical labor appealed to me more than ever before, even as I knew I should focus on growing my practice. *I just need to finish something for once. Something tangible.* After all, Rebeca always said I had soft "cheese boy hands," but I did know something about landscaping. Andrew the neighborhood kid and I were out there hard at work, doing essentially the same job. He was a 16-year-old high school dropout with a good work ethic. I was a 30-year-old with a mortgage. Although the property was mine, we were doing identical work. Therefore, I was "earning" the same $10 an hour that he was. That did make me wonder. *Steve said don't mow your own lawn. I don't see people on Lake Drive doing this shit.*

Pride in our home can be a personal refuge and a financial Achilles' heel. We've heard it said a man's house is his castle. I am not above these feelings. I gardened, landscaped, raked leaves, and mowed the lawn. Doing something on your own is immensely satisfying. But is it a hobby, or a job?

Figuring out a problem and saving money are satisfying too. How much time am I willing to spend? The sight of a crisp lawn was gratifying. Trying to decipher the error code on a washing machine was less so. Again, I needed someone with the confidence to tell me to either repair it or replace it. For me to pursue that knowledge myself on a weeknight—when the kids seem to be out of clean underwear—isn't realistic. I could pay $200 for a technician to come out and say, "Yup, get a new one." Or spend an hour getting more confused online, and then call a technician anyway. And then I feel like an idiot and stare at my cheese boy hands.

When my father-in-law found the problem and a part for the washer, he saved us $500, and his face just lit up. He made fixes like that countless times, with a discount on parts and no charge for labor, always with love and a smile. In every corner of the country, there's an immigrant like him, grateful to work hard and live in the United States, because there is more opportunity than back home. And there's a native-born American like me who benefits from their support. *Don't take it for granted.*

The cost savings of having family and friends who know how to do things is immense over time. There is financial security in having a personal network. Their willingness to help, even years later, is a testament to the power of relationships. And it speaks to a human truth: helping people we care about does as much for us as it does for them.

And yet, financial abundance doesn't come from self-reliance at all costs. If that 90% confidence is enough to move forward and accept that the 10% chance of error is tolerable, great. You may add 50% more time to fix the mistake later, but if it's a hobby, no big deal. That's you, all you DINK home DIY-ers that are "so busy." When the consequences are higher, or it's not something you enjoy, that's when people get really f**king stuck. The hobby becomes a job once you're shooing toddlers away. When a prospective client meets with me for the first time, they often remind me of me: a capable person apprehensively staring at the furnace. With my experience, I can calmly and quickly troubleshoot a problem that has them frozen with anxiety. Often, they were on the right track anyway, but the last 10% of confidence kept them from acting. And action is all that matters.

Asking for help takes a lot of confidence, because we must admit we have no confidence in our own ability.

As my confidence grows, my questions become more idiotic. As I was writing this, our dryer lost power. Checked the fuse box, nothing. Called Jorge, he came over later, found the breaker in another room. Problem solved. *Wait! Are a fuse and a breaker the same thing? Have I been saying it wrong my whole life? Should I look it up to get it right for the book?* I had to reconcile two conflicting parts of my identity: I was not an idiot; yet I was and would remain totally clueless about many things. Jorge used to try to teach me what he was doing and why. Now we both accept I'll stay clueless.

The dominant culture of middle and working-class Americans is steeped in self-reliance. I've heard people mock more affluent people as clueless. I did it myself at Habitat, "Yeah, they don't even know how to ______." That makes sense, if you feel that your income is entirely reliant on your boss/interviewer/public policy, and so on. In that case, thinking more about work wouldn't help you earn more no matter what you did: read, research, therapy, classes. So, you might as well save money by reading the dryer owner's manual. I could spend days learning about dryers, and still not ID the problem.

The culture of wealth is steeped in growing your gift—the thing that you can do better than most people—whether that's your caregiving or your career. I had to let go to grow. And the more I grew my own gifts, the more I came to appreciate others'. My grandfathers were so different but had a mutual respect. Our nation needs engineering and artistry, blue-collar and white-collar work. It needs to recognize all gifts to thrive.

At any rate, homeownership turns a part of our focus inward. Our thoughts and emotions build momentum over time, until the compounding effect of our consciousness ends in hoarding or serenity. Homeownership makes us care about things we never cared about before, like carpeting and weeds, and pulls us away from the things that bring the most financial value to our lives (like mastering our craft to earn more money), or the most joy (playing a game with our kids), or recharge our batteries (a mental health day). If we aren't careful, we'll be retired, muttering to ourselves about home maintenance—the lawn, the paint—while tuning out what matters most. We'll ignore the growth around that keeps us young: our nephew introducing his fiancé from Italy for the first time, a new craze the kids are doing, a new hobby to keep us sharp. Maintenance alone might preserve the value of your home, but it won't keep you young. Helping others will.

If I go out to the back yard, and put down some paving stones myself, gritting my teeth and getting it done, maybe my son sees my hard work and my determination to do it and do it right. Couldn't I role model that exact same task while volunteering with Habitat for Humanity? The regular retired volunteers on the Habitat job site in Seattle were vigorous and healthy, and that was no accident. They had purpose. Service to others has inherent value, and he would see me interacting with others, and he would meet people of different skin tones, different personalities, different ages, instead of just being in our yard.

When we move from our home, or pass away, the next owners with a different vision will just repaint and remodel anyway. What I need to do is remember that home is a refuge, but ultimately temporary, as all material things are. We may nurture and maintain our home in lieu of a lost relationship beyond our walls. Home is where the heart is, but only because memories are made there. Families come together. They pitch in. It's helping each other that sustains us. Once upon a time, I thought I needed to know how to do everything. But if I wanted to prove these cheese boy hands could do heavy grunt work, I should have taken my son to provide hurricane relief and haul sandbags.

It's possible to obsess over a home to no end. Just remember that for every repair, renovation, and design question, there is someone else who can do it faster, better, and more easily from years honing their craft. For a price, or as a favor, both ways connect people with each other. I'll never get the time back I spent measuring and planning that retaining wall. At the time, I couldn't afford help, and many of us can't now. I would challenge everyone to connect and collaborate with other people regardless of what we can afford. Chat with the contractors on how they do things. Ask your friend with a flair for color what they think. Pay someone you know could use the money. Coerce your cousins to help move. Crowdsource ideas online. Pay in dollars or pay with a return favor. Keep only what you love or what you must.

We aren't meant to die alone in our homes, forgotten by the wide world. We are designed to grow in wisdom even as our bodies slow down. Human connection keeps us young. I don't want my kids to remember me as a guy who was fixated on something he owned. My legacy is to share and grow my gifts. And I can do that with cheese boy hands.

think and grow rich

My initial impression of "success literature" was to lump it in with huckster prosperity gospel garbage. Mention a "motivational speaker" to me in my twenties, and my reaction was "there's a charismatic, brilliant speaker, who charges broke desperate people money they can't afford for the illusion of success, a glimpse of greatness." Then I read a book that made such an impression that I began to think differently. This book, written nearly a century ago, described faith as an emotion, an emotion that can exist apart from religion. Still skeptical of the title, that caught my attention. It rang true, and the more I read and re-read the pages, the more I began to see that success in any endeavor was more formula than luck. Luck always helps, but enduring success can't be built on luck on alone.

Napoleon Hill's book *Think and Grow Rich* has stood the test of time. Before airplanes or internet, its "steps to riches" make sense even now, because while technology is changing, the human mind is built the same way. Researched over 20 years and published in the Great Depression, it spoke very openly of money like an oasis in the desert. As I began to read it shortly after my 30th birthday, I thought it was a little out there. The title was so off-putting, over the top. *Admit it. It drew you in.* But it really wasn't much different from modern social psychology. I knew psychology from counseling others. Now I was counseling myself through the most difficult mental endeavor of my life.

The book was commissioned by steel magnate Andrew Carnegie to study the habits of successful millionaires, regardless of their field, to summarize the collective wisdom and habits for others. Many of these habits were illogical, irrational some would say. I dog-eared page after page, astounded that such a book had eluded me. I was even more astounded that I loved reading a book with "grow rich" in the frickin' title.

Interviews with successful people about how they "made it" often feature the words: *vision, focus,* and *faith.* In such interviews, we sometimes also hear: *higher power, the universe,* and *God* as well. The first three terms are inextricable from all earned success. The last three are ways of understanding the first three. When a person commits to a vision, it requires focus to get going, and faith to sustain. We all interpret that in different ways. I do not believe that faith and science are opposed, because faith is an emotion that can be applied to anything. If we define faith as complete trust in someone or something without explicit proof, then faith can be cultivated and held by the Christian and the atheist alike. After all, faith in yourself is required to fulfill your potential.

Think and Grow Rich applies a qualitative research lens to test why some people achieve improbable things and others don't. A conclusion the author reaches is that religion doesn't do a good job of explaining how to grow your faith. We have religious people who accomplish very little, and selfish, evil people who accomplish a great deal. Decouple the emotion of faith from the framework of religion for a minute.

Let's go back further to the very start. I think that human beings, like animals, respond to fear (survival, rejection, pain) and to desire (reproduction, power, pleasure). We are social, and so we need to be likable enough to survive. In our modern lives, we may go a long time without activating fear or desire as a catalyst. We need to do things that make us come alive. If we don't activate a deep desire in our hearts, human beings will shuffle through life committing slow spiritual suicide, not pursuing anything but creature comforts they have already achieved: food, shelter, electricity, Wi-Fi … When we have no purpose beyond the creature comforts, we languish. As a varsity high school athlete, I practiced constantly, all seasons. I had a desire to be an All-State selection, team MVP, co-captain. Not as noble as world peace, but that desire made me come alive and achieve.

As I've said, deliberate, consistent, massive actions are galvanized by fear or desire. Not worry or want. Everyone worries and wants things. Not everyone can articulate what they fear and what they desire.

When I meet a couple in my office for the first time and ask what's coming up for them, why are they looking to meet with a financial advisor, most of the time they provide worries and wants. By that I mean, the things they think about often, but are not "musts." There is often a life event signal that draws their attention, like turning 30 or buying a house, but only a minority are ostensibly fueled by something deeper: a fear or a desire. Fears and desires compel us to act in the face of adversity and stagnation alike. My role is to draw them out, uncover those deeper motives. What does the peak of your career look like? What experiences do you want your children to have? Are you hoping to emulate your parents financially or break the family mold?

Indeed, our biology is designed to keep us alive with minimal effort, in case we need to escape a lion in five minutes. There are biological reasons to exercise. I want to look good so my wife will respect me and reproduce with me—a *very* powerful motivator, and no different from any other animal. Yet my body is telling me on the early morning jog, *"Dude, we aren't running from a lion, chill out. It's Tuesday morning, and the kids have soccer and homework tonight, and there's no way you're getting laid today even if this run magically restores your abs from age 18 by the time you get home. Forget it. Just walk home now."* Guess what. The book talks about "sex transmutation" in a way that sounds more like a textbook than relationship advice, much less business advice. *How can this feel relevant 90 years later?* Harnessing deepest desires and fears into actionable momentum is the first step.

Our souls yearn for more if we listen. People love grit, persistence, and risk-taking in movies, but not in real life. Why not? Why do we admire the power of those qualities in fiction, but deny that power in our own lives? Why wait for circumstances to demand greatness? Find your challenge and meet it. If we respond to the well-worn story of our heroine facing her greatest setback, gritting her teeth, and emerging victorious, then why are we shopping at IKEA, and hoping for a cost-of-living raise? At a company training, I heard national leader John McTigue say, "There is no passion in reasonable goals."

But what if you're all set? Blessed and comfortable, your goal is to maintain the security you've worked hard to build. Good for you, but look at what motivated you in the first place, and craft a vision with even more of that. All actions have a current. You cannot preserve what you've built by treading water. If we stay in the continuum of worries and wants, shielding our heart from the rougher waters of desire and fear, we run the risk of slowly sinking into complacency. Life most likely keeps our status quo, and we take the path of least resistance, and rationalize why that's best. We all have worries and wants. That's universal. But not many people can describe their one-, five- or ten-year vision. If a client can articulate exactly what they want, they get a much more precise financial plan.

That's the starting point of my planning process with prospective clients. What is your vision for success—personally, professionally, financially? We don't achieve anything difficult by accident. It's easier to articulate what we don't want, but the best way to break free of your past is to run forward. What is the finish line for you? You don't have to know what your marathon time is when you start; just put one foot in front of the other. You don't have to run to win, but you do need a finish line somewhere.

As a new advisor, I had to make money to pay our mortgage. If I quit, it would be a public failure. It was such a drastic departure from youth work that I had to make it work or publicly admit I'd made a huge miscalculation. *It was not a loan.* Fear kept me going early on. I was not a person who identified with failure. Fear can be very useful. Pushing beyond the survival stage of starting out, I needed to find fear's counterpart: desire. I had to define what I desired so much that I would persevere to secure it. I wrote it down and read it aloud every day. I'd been given that advice when I first started. And it helped. Call it prayer or meditation or vision planning, by expressing my burning desire to achieve my vision, fully present, and with an engaged heart and mind, it began to feel real. It became an eventuality instead of a wish. A when instead of an if.

I used to teach goal-setting, specifically SMART goals, as part of the teen social-emotional learning curriculum at Lake Valley Camp. SMART is an acronym for Specific, Measurable, Attainable, Relevant, and Time-based. Yes, I attempted to get kids in chaotic homes focused on the basics, to get into this on the weekend. I had it all wrong. The *Think and Grow Rich* version said the hell with attainable. You can start small, but don't settle. I should have worked on identifying your deepest calling, and then how to obsess about it heart and soul. Goal-setting should feel more like a vivid daydream than school. What we think about, read about, talk about, we become.

Vision requires visualization. Watch athletes with a routine, rituals, headphones in, eyes closed, visualizing the performance to come. Young children can visualize being a singer, actor, or athlete because the "vision" is public for us to see. A clear vision provides a decision-making framework. In high school, I did sit-ups and push-ups in the basement, visualizing the future game. That was the motivation.

The athlete and the addict have goal clarity: the benefit of a clear, measurable vision of success. I might worry about over-spending/over-partying/over-eating/anything. The vision becomes the litmus test, the guiding light to measure all decisions. I desire to be an involved father who takes my kids on vacations and attends their activities. A commitment to that vision addresses many small choices about seemingly unrelated things, like how much I work. The average person must create their own practice schedule, finish line, season. Consider doctors, who make excellent money. They generally are called to heal the body, and they enjoy the diagnostics. They have to in order to endure med school and residency. There are other ways to make money. Yes, prestige and earning comes at the end, but the journey to get there is a sacrifice. Mothers must leave the house at bedtime, or delay starting a family. Spouses are left alone while studying for boards. It's brutal. I can't believe the residency expectations are even legal. So, why do approximately 84% of med school students graduate, and over 80% of residents finish? They've been given a vision…

Aspiring medics can see practicing surgeons or family practice docs now. They can gauge future earnings and hours clearly. They can see how they will be treated, observe tough hospital bedside talks, and goofy toddler well visits. The vision is clear, like winning the championship. You just have to put in the work, then hang in there. Failure is not an option when the vision is compelling, and based on your personal values.

After reading the book in August 2016, I paused for a while and asked myself some bigger questions about what I really desired from this career. I desired *enough* money, not maximum money. I mainly desired *influence* to create a more equitable world. That hadn't changed since high school. I started writing thoughts on scratch paper in the Green Door Tavern in Chicago while waiting for my client meeting at 4:30 pm. The idea of writing a book seemed to … materialize. Once the seed was planted, I never doubted I would do it. I added it to my vision statement. I told people that I was writing it, just so they would ask me how it was going. I leveraged my fear of disappointing others into motivation. I referred to specific chapters. I set a deadline to finish it. (And another. And another. And another.) It never left my core vision, even when I wasn't making progress. I took moments alone to visualize. *You can do this. If not you, who?*

In hindsight, I realized that progress doesn't always represent more words on the page. My vision of writing a book about personal cause and financial effect consumed me. It was like a generator running in the background, an ever-present humming. With the vision clear, bits and pieces of the how and what came into focus: while I was driving, watching TV, or showering, just like everyone else's best ideas. We all get good ideas. Your vision is the filter through which mundane choices are made.

Get started. You don't have all the answers, and that's alright. Introduce a part of your day when you are wholeheartedly pursuing a dream, be it community theater production, dog-grooming, car restoration, or blogging about workplace equity. Just start. Think big but start small. Your path will be revealed to you through feedback along the way. Mark Zuckerberg said as much. He didn't know what Facebook would become; he just started and course-corrected along the way.

This is easier said than done. It's hard to stay focused. Harder if you're working three jobs to make ends meet. Every minute of every day is a chance to pursue your vision, or to do something else productive, or to waste time. And we live in a country of such material abundance that there are countless ways to waste time. The sheer volume of shows and movies streaming online is staggering. If you cut out one hour of screen time a day, and replaced it with quiet reflection and research on your vision, you would see results. What we say no to is just as important as what we say yes to, because we all get the same amount of time. As life gets more comfortable, it becomes easier to distract with consumerism, to get a quick hit. It takes focus to maintain that initial passion and hunger when you no longer have to. Humans are designed to relax when we can afford it. And pursuing a lofty vision is uncomfortable.

Not only that, but others will do everything they can to rattle you. I watched the documentary series *The Last Dance* about Michael Jordan and the six-time champion Chicago Bulls in the 1990s. I remember watching these game-winning shots live as a little boy. What I notice now is how, at every opportunity, reporters ask Jordan about off-court drama: Rodman's antics, beef with the owner, trade rumors, how he will handle the next series, and so on. Such and such happens. And Jordan, without fail, would deflect, and say, "I'm focused on preparing for our next game." It's true that negativity sells. Focus delivers success, which sells even better.

If your personal circle isn't thinking big for themselves, they will dismiss and distract you from your unique vision as a way to shield themselves. You'll be told to "get a real job," or "look out for yourself," or something to that effect. You will be asked to waste time with all sorts of foolishness. Crabs in a barrel will drag each other down. I've spoken to many young people raised in poverty who just need to shake off the doubters long enough to spread their wings. Clients who should leave toxic work environments. We don't exist in isolation. Prioritizing healthy relationships that support your vision and honor your focus is critical.

Think and Grow Rich explicitly names vices that promote poverty instead of riches, like greed and dishonesty. The author knows that—in life, as in sports—no one wants to hear excuses. *Of all the teens, staff, and clients you've coached, the whiners never gave themselves permission to shine. They all lived in scarcity, some with more home stability than others. But they didn't achieve the same things. Poverty is a circumstance* and *a mindset.*

In Carol Dweck's book *Mindset*, which talks about grit, she quotes legendary basketball coach John Wooden, "You're only a failure when you begin to blame." *Think and Grow Rich*, and all the inspirers since, have known that excuses don't get results. They might be valid. Other stories in this book explain how valid they are. But using them doesn't help. The first enemy is within. It's so much easier to say what we don't want than describe what we do. Abraham Lincoln issued the Emancipation Proclamation. He was imperfect, but he was woke AF for the 1860s. Canceling him won't end racism.

Forgiveness cultivates abundance. We must let go of a feeling that doesn't serve us to make room for one that does. It's another burden the historically oppressed face; they have more to forgive. *Yes, prospective client, I hear you. You have every right to be angered by the past. And your financial present is not your fault. But only actions in the present will create change from your dollars.*

Blame is an obstacle to financial progress, individually and collectively. How can we as a nation acknowledge the past, reconcile, forgive, and focus on building a better future? Only a shared vision, rooted in a common fear or desire, can move us forward. The reason is that money is nothing more than bookkeeping, a way of tallying what you owe the community versus what it owes you. Blaming means you feel you have been cheated, wronged, or shorted. A person projecting that energy is not open to abundance; they are fixated on the past.

Using vision, focus, and faith to achieve is not only the domain of Mahatma Gandhi, Abraham Lincoln, and Oprah Winfrey. It is also the method of dictators. The latter felt they needed to prey on others, that they could only win at another's expense. The former experienced hardship as well, but rejected bitterness, and maintained that everyone could be elevated together. All of them had vision, focus, and faith. The difference was the mindset of abundance instead of scarcity. We cannot change the past, but we can run toward our vision for the future. The path to lasting abundance is providing more value to others than you expect in return. And doing that requires a deep trust that your efforts will ultimately be acknowledged or rewarded in the long run.

Which brings us back to faith, defined as trust or confidence in the absence of proof. The more improbable your vision, the more faith is required. Faith in yourself requires self-esteem. What religion gives so many people worldwide is faith in the future even when the observable data shows struggle. According to my good friend Pastor Tim Ophus, the gospel of Jesus Christ is thriving in the global South as it recedes in the most affluent countries. Faith steps in when realism is hard.

Political scientist Fareed Zakaria observed in an interview, "The New Testament seems to pretty much say give to the poor and don't care about material things." Yet, we have more "golden idols" than ever. In the absence of vision, consumption fills the void. Success does not always mean wealth. Successful people are fulfilled and have community. Money without fulfillment is hollow satisfaction that always needs more, like an addiction. Corporate greed is one symptom of a vision of power.

Faith keeps us going in the absence of encouragement, working toward an outcome that may not even exist yet. A business that's growing has no cash on hand. All of it is reinvested. Think about that. Many of the most popular publicly traded stocks aren't paying dividends, which are a surplus shared with investors. Meaning they are appreciating in value but aren't turning a profit. The billionaires we read about have most or all their net worth as ownership shares in their company. You better believe they need faith in some form to manage that pressure. Or consider the parent who drives their child all over the state to play competitive hockey because his coach thinks he's got a shot at the NHL. That parent is buoyed by their faith in him. They are "reinvesting" to "appreciate the asset," and that first professional contract is the eruption. Money, like the water from a geyser, will usually burst forth after a long period of building focused pressure in one direction.

The key is a willingness to bet on yourself, even if the odds are against you. If you want to be more than average, then they are against you. At a commencement speech, David Sedaris counseled graduates to be all-in, and not have a fallback plan. Yes, that David Sedaris, the self-deprecating author who made a career out of describing his ineptitude, not some chiseled titan of industry. There will always be a new priority or a new trend. But those who commit to a lasting vision, and faithfully stay on the path toward it, tend to get better outcomes. Like so much in life, the work is front-loaded. Oftentimes, those who care most about you will counsel the safer, easier path to spare you from the pain of hardship. And pain is more likely than reward; that's why faith is needed to keep pushing *through* the pain *until* the reward.

Identify deeply rooted fears and desires. Use them to craft a compelling vision, one that feels real and relevant every day. Focus on it and use it as a litmus test for all choices big and small. Does this support my vision or not? Pursue the vision with faith.

It was not a loan. It was a mistake. We can only grow when we are honest about our mistakes. You're a teacher. Teach what you've learned. All this cognitive dissonance about money, use this perspective. This vision was given to you.

I read the book at age 30 because a colleague said I should. What I have found since is that interviews and books focused on success are very similar: vision, focus, faith. This was all unknown to me until

I found myself in a company culture where abundance and ambition were valued together—with plenty of room for both. *Idealism can pay the bills if I want it bad enough. You have permission to dream big.* There aren't any numbers in this chapter. Wealth isn't only measured in money after all. But when you commit to pursuing your vision authentically, the numbers tend to fall into place.

chapter thirty-seven
"I'm in grad school"

"**I'm in law school.**" "I'm in medical school." "I'm in grad school."

Two of these conjure images of academic exclusivity, professional esteem, and financial success. The third evokes … all kinds of things, including avoidance and irrelevance.

The difference between them is that law and medicine have a clear application. Knowledge is not power. Applied knowledge is. But the tuition is due whether you apply it or not.

Really knowing a given subject is to have intuition toward answers others don't. I loved the themes in different periods of history: the labor movement, the trust busting, emancipation in America. A lot of them were terrible, but the intersection always made sense to me. Like my dad could figure out my math homework even though the steps or calculations were taught differently when he learned it. When you have the instincts, you can apply known principles, narrow the range of possible solutions, and make an educated guess. Then a multiple-choice test isn't about knowing the correct answer out of four; it's about assessing the probability of each answer based on context.

Anyway, back in Milwaukee post-AmeriCorps, my $5,600-ish Segal Education Award was burning a hole in my pocket. I had $1,000 of professional development money to spend annually, too. Admittedly, I wanted to return to university and really engage with the material in a way I didn't in undergrad. I also took the GRE and was compelled to use it. I had more life experience and specificity about what I wanted to learn: social psychology. My enduring curiosity had always been human behavior.

I found the Educational Psychology program at the University of Wisconsin-Milwaukee. UWM is a research institution, right in the city, the second largest public university in Wisconsin. It is unique because most public universities of this size (about 20,000 students) are in "college towns," and somewhat sequestered in the so-called "ivory tower" of academia.

A huge percentage of UWM students work full-time, and attend part-time, at the undergrad and graduate levels. Like the rest of the country, graduate programs offer lots of night classes and flex scheduling. And like the rest of the country, graduate programs are full of adults looking to differentiate and develop themselves, and under-grad programs are full of children making bad choices. Generalization, but not judgment. In my youth work experience, I observed many students, or friends and family of students, working and going to school. Twelve credit hours and 30 work hours. Nine credits and 40 hours. Nineteen-year-olds doing just three credits and 60 hours of work like me. The nine-year plan for a four-year degree.

Developing our college access program, I also knew that the research on first-generation and low-income college students demonstrated that attending college part-time was correlated with lower graduation rates.

Our social networks and environment influence our priorities, intentions, demands, and needs. And higher education is about delayed gratification. Knowledge can be found in books, but higher education curates that information into something applied. In my case, at the cost of $2,400 per three-credit course. Others pay much more. What's the rate of return on the cost of higher education in 21st century America?

I especially loved my advisor Chris Lawson and his colleague Jackie Nguyen. The discussion in their courses was particularly thought-provoking. The cool thing about a graduate program like mine was that I could dictate the subject of my writing in many cases. I had heard so many friends and acquaintances say they wanted to go to grad school, and far fewer who thought through the reason why. I suspected that for many it was a way to delay growing up, delay commitment. I was damn sure that I didn't want to do something that I couldn't apply to my career and/or life. I also felt that a graduate degree alone could never conceal a lack of value in an interview. I suspected some of my classmates felt that it could.

I finished my two-year program in the fall of 2017, after starting in the fall of 2012. I used grant money, I used professional development, I used cash, I used a loan, I accepted a gift from my parents. *Education still a core value.* Altogether, taking 30 credits over five years cost about $24,000. Had I done it in two semesters, it would've been more like $20,000, I think. Bulk discount, just like anything else.

And that tuition at UWM, and most other places, is pretty much level regardless of program. Art history to aerospace engineering, MSW to MBA, the cost wasn't much different. The future income? That varied a bit. I had financial planning clients who borrowed for undergrad (no scholarship or help from middle-income parents), and then got a master's in social work (for a raise), to be mid-twenties with $60,000 in loan debt earning $48,000 a year doing a job that was miserable. Ask yourself what

28-year-old woman wants to spend her life working for Child Protective Services doing home visits in dangerous neighborhoods at odd hours … when she also has a responsibility as a mother? I may want to be a child advocate, but in my life, the only thing more important than principle is the welfare of my own child. The martyr parent is hard to find. Why would she continue when she could earn more with less stress doing something else? Let's say she married a guy who has the same debt, but STEM sexism being what it is, he is an engineer making $70,000 with upward mobility in a work culture that respects 9:00 to 5:00? She leaves social work. When the baby comes, her salary just barely equals the cost of childcare. Using the degree is painful emotionally. Not using it is painful financially. If she's not a social worker, why did she get the degree? There's an ugly reality in the job market: higher tuition doesn't equal more earnings when the work is underfunded and unappreciated to begin with. And it's the compounding effect of being underappreciated that makes the long-term career choice for most.

My classmates represented a mixture of narratives all with great intentions, and our group discussions had brilliant flashes of ethical dialogue and a real enthusiasm. We cared deeply about our city. We were troubled by the social ills that plagued it. We all cared enough not to think too much about the student loan coming due five years from now. That would be a problem for later. There's nothing more seductive than no money down. That caring did not always translate to focus in the weekly classroom session, however.

Professors know a lot of stuff. They are like a living museum, search engine, and bibliography all in one. But we shuffled into class with 50% energy most days. Some people were on Facebook, because no one takes notes on paper anymore; screens are the new norm. And when you're tired, it's just too easy to click over. Some people asked logistical questions that had already been answered, didn't do the assigned reading, didn't have much to say when the professor asked for reactions. The ones who did were often the few full-time doctoral students.

Now I think being a student should be a full-time occupation if you're paying tuition yourself. Otherwise, we might be paying for a credential instead of applicable knowledge. Not challenging the professor or using office hours or doing all the reading is like buying a flight to Cancun and not seeing the beach. But who wants to talk about urban poverty when you've spent the day overwhelmed by urban poverty? And you're thinking about the time spent away from your own kids, having doubts about your decision to do this program instead of picking them up from school and making dinner like a *Leave It to Beaver* family from the 1950s. Maybe that isn't possible anymore. Maybe you're living in urban poverty already, and don't need a class to explain the issues.

Teachers, social workers, and nonprofit professionals (like me at the time) are people generally working 50 plus hours a week already. Walking into a 2.5 hour class at 5:00 pm after a long day, braving the long, dark Milwaukee winter was not always the most appealing.

Hierarchy of needs comes into play with the continuing education adult learner. I went to class under pressure for a deadline, or skipped lunch, and just missed my wife and kids. The realities were grueling; the tuition cost was the same no matter what knowledge I retained. And busy with life, I too wanted to do the minimum.

In the early years, sometimes I was late. Probably once a semester, I would skip. Another time, I would have a legitimate conflict. In addition to that, there was a "spring break" and maybe a holiday in there, and the professor might have a conflict like a conference or something. Every single one seemed to move up the final exams week, so it ended up being like 9–10 classroom sessions. *Aren't I paying for 13–14 classes either way? This is like a container of yoghurt with a surprise indentation in the bottom, it's not as much as I thought.*

The university's funding was getting slashed in the state budget, so I suppose the only way to raise revenue was to increase tuition. Universities that attract students from wealthier families have a huge advantage. Solid financial footing for the undergrad means they can attend full-time, not balance generating current income to help the family or pay as you go. Students from wealthier families are more likely to graduate, even if for the wrong reasons, make more money, and then donate to the university. Elite universities benefit from exclusivity and wealth. Wealth can insulate the student from all the roadblocks of poverty that can detour the working student endlessly. The longer the road from student borrowing to student earning, the harder it is to persevere.

UWM lacked some community because a lot of them were part-time like me. I got a great education, but I have no sentimentality attached to the place like I do with my undergrad at U of I. I was there to get shit done and get out, not loiter on the quad or make memories. I had access to the fitness center, subsidized study-abroad opportunities, free concerts, all that. I had time for none of it. At U of I, I enjoyed a lot of campus services but not all, like a laptop with most of the software unused. Like so many other things over the years, I could have squeezed more value from it. And going back to the research, many students never finished. And therefore, would never donate. And you know what's more expensive than an advanced degree? Starting one and not finishing. Every college wants to admit first-generation students. Graduating them is another story. The school pockets the tuition up front, after all.

I took a break from graduate school when I started as a financial advisor. Eighteen months later, I returned to finish with a newfound appreciation for time and money. I didn't skip anymore. I was on time. Not only did I not have any guaranteed income now, but I was paying. So, now I was calculating the cost *per hour*. If we started late, I was irritated.

We had a class on the night of Tuesday, November 8th, 2016. Our class was canceled so we could watch the presidential election results. The tension was palpable. But we wasted our tuition money that week to go home and stare at the TV, and fuel the media-election complex, reinforcing the campaign style and strategy that we didn't like in the first place. Instead of having class to apply material to current events, we were distracted. And distraction is always costly.

When I started the course, the subject matter appealed to me in and of itself. At the time, I wanted to be an expert in behavior management. I had a unique opportunity with the resident camp to control environmental variables, and an emotionally safe place to do some qualitative work, made possible by existing relationships with parents and some trust in the organization.

Now I knew what I wanted: to apply cognitive research on decision-making to how people make financial decisions and plans, bringing some science into a field that seemed to be dominated by the calculators and sales only. *You really could write a book. It's not just an idea in your notepad.* I also wanted to take every opportunity to apply my studies to my work with clients. I would read articles and could immediately think of how this looked in real life. Naturally, I was more engaged because I had a specific application for the knowledge. I began to structure my client presentation meetings based on how the brain learns.

Unfortunately, many people go to grad school without a plan. It was only after finding a plan that I knew what it could and should feel like. I started studying learning and development in educational psychology to design better programs for kids over a 10-year span, and adult staff learners of all ages. As I moved into financial advising, I tended to focus more on stereotyping, prejudice, and social psych, along with heuristics for decision-making. I asked questions in class like, "Can you explain how temporal discounting might affect retirement savings rates?" And the published psychologist and professor would just answer my question, happy that a student was engaged in the material. Suddenly, like a law or medical student, I could focus on the present because I had the application in mind.

Plan or no plan, the working parents in graduate school just needed to finish. My last three-credit course was an online summer class. It was a total joke: open book online quizzes and an exam. It was so easy and fast; the entire course probably took me about 10 hours of time. The conflict? I was thrilled that I got my credits, meaning more time with my son and wife, more time to work in my financial planning practice. *I thought this would take weeks! But I paid $2,400 for that? $240 per hour? For a textbook and an online quiz?*

And with this pressure to get the degree, and with society becoming more litigious, a B is the new C, a C the new D. Universities need tuition for payroll and bills. If the grad student taking night classes drops out, no more tuition. If the undergrad flunks out, no more tuition. Classes for the former are made more convenient (*Online! Flexible schedule! Accelerated program!*), and the classes for the latter are sold as part of campus life (*Greek life! Extracurriculars! Waterpark in the student union!*). I don't fault universities, public or private, for doing their best to attract students. I do want to point out that they are selling a product: a (likely) degree, a (maybe) job, and the experience (individual results may vary) along the way. Any quality control measures are entirely upon the student.

If that's the case, we need to look at supply and demand in economics and the labor market as the basis for counseling teenagers. If the student decides more immediate financial security is important, a union job in the trades looks pretty damn good.

You could do what I did for undergrad, which was study teaching, and know that you would be generally employable for reasonable pay. While there, you could soak up every aspect of campus life, as I did, and emerge a more informed and well-rounded employee and person.

You could sacrifice your sleep and freedom now with challenging school for a financial windfall later, the way doctors, dentists, and lawyers do. They take on six figures of debt, and are underpaid for years, for a pot of gold later. Their compensation flows from an ability to perform under pressure.

Or you could try to anticipate. The hockey legend Wayne Gretzky said, "I skate to where the puck is going to be, not where it has been." In life and in money, if you anticipate what's coming, you have much to gain.

Consider the old joke about a philosophy major not having a job, despite being intelligent and interesting, which only holds up if the student learns the past without a plan for future application. If I met a philosophy major who told me their plan was to become the world's foremost authority on the ethics of CRISPR (gene editing technology), and they planned to build a consulting business on that, I would listen up. That's a unique and forward-thinking goal. That's bold. Remember, there is no passion in reasonable goals. But that's a hard road, with years of delaying the payoff, if it ever comes. It is higher risk, higher reward. Their compensation will flow from a unique ability or insight that others didn't have.

Contrast that with how many lower-income students enter college. *Everyone says I should go, that it's the key to success, right? But I've always hated school, and my family needs me to help with the bills, and none of my friends are going.* Two semesters and $10,000 later, they're back where they started. The added burden of the first-generation college student is that their family often needs them, pulling them away from school. They need to earn something now.

In investing, we measure risk-adjusted returns. In other words, how well did we do given the probability things could have gone badly? When we discuss this with the investor, we cover the range of possible outcomes, and even more importantly, the intended time for withdrawal, when they plan to exit the interest current and head for shore. Will you cash out in a year? A decade? Thirty years? So, staying the course along the way is essential for the investment to play out as expected. The return on college—measured as total tuition cost and loan interest versus cumulative earned income for the graduate—could be negative 30% or positive 50% at any point in time, depending on the moment. At age 23, after one year salary and one year loan payment? Negative return. So negative. How about after five years, with one raise, halfway through loan payment? Better. How about when you reconnect with college classmates, and create a startup that takes off? Pretty good. With investing in all its forms, a safety net increases the likelihood of success. A safety net gets you from point A to point B unscathed, without life derailing the investment.

Any amount of tuition with no degree is financially a bad choice. A degree without the ability or courage to leverage it fully is less so. Applying the knowledge is a good choice. There was a multiple-choice question on the CERTIFIED FINANCIAL PLANNER™ exam. It coldly and rationally asks for a calculation: "When is the breakeven point on this student's decision to attend graduate school?" I was given current salary lost during school, tuition amount, and future annual earnings after graduation. This is a time value of money equation, no different than a car lease or home mortgage or pension contribution. *Everything is connected.*

Culturally, we tell young people to "invest in their education" but good investing is unemotional. If someone wants to make a decent living, it's not that complicated. Not all careers are created equal financially. Money's not the only thing. But it's a bigger thing than most undergrads realize.

Some go to grad school to study something they like. I absolutely love school, but it's expensive to go based on that alone. Like "uneducated" Will says to the pretentious pony-tail Harvard snob in the film *Good Will Hunting*, "Yeah, I read that one too" for "late charges at the public library."

Go to grad school with the destination in mind for your career, life etc. If your employer pays or helps with grad school so you'll apply new skills and get a promotion, that's great too. The "Executive MBA" is packaged accordingly with a short-term application. An application for the knowledge, which acts as a filter for every class and assignment, is critical. If you're seeking knowledge on your own, I recommend you go full-time. It may cost more sooner, but it will be less per credit hour, and the return on your experience and level of engagement will be way higher. A client of mine moved to London to get her master's in public policy in 18 months, for less tuition. She got a degree, and an experience along with her studies.

As a rare breed financial advisor/grad school student, I saw the "before" and "after" picture in one day. I sat next to the hopeful student in class mid-day, then consoled the indebted graduate as a client that night, trying to create a workable loan reduction plan. We can live to work, or we can work to live. I'm not judging, and I don't think every 18-year-old freshman knows what their career will be. Just don't change your mind halfway through anything without good reason. The grass will always be greener on the other side. Commitment pays off.

When you have an application for your learning in mind, that commitment is easier. My tuition was the down payment for my career. *I missed work to go to class and write essays. I chose to write this.* I might as well use what I bought. *Ugh, my personal marshmallow test.*

chapter thirty-eight

"you ran the red light"

In late 2018, we sold my grandpa's car, the 2003 Ford Taurus, to a foreign exchange host family tired of driving their Hungarian hockey phenom around to games. It was hard for me to let go because it was a memory of my grandpa, thoughtfully preserved by my folks. The car itself I always loathed: beige, ugly, clunky. After it was gone, I never looked back. Letting go of things creates room for new things to come. My grandpa would want it to be appreciated, and more importantly, for me to grow.

A few months prior, I had committed to being a bike commuter, and selling the car was part of that "burn the bridge" strategy for forming the habit. I was complaining about not being able to bike enough, about gaining weight, and about the cost of parking downtown. Lo and behold, I finally connected the dots. I had tried biking to work the summer before, and the summer before that. But the clothes, the changing, the weather made it a hassle. It was just too easy to say, "I'm running behind, so I'll drive." I'm not some sleek, hairless hipster who can jump off a bike without swamp-ass. I needed a system. So, I went all-in: a sturdy commuter bike, lights, a waterproof backpack.

A game changer was finding a tiny locker room tucked away in the basement bowels of our office skyscraper, back by the equipment and custodial rooms. It hadn't been updated since the building was built in the 1980s, I'm sure. It had that retro blast-force water pressure shower, which felt incredible after biking in zero-degree weather. With trial and error, I created a system: I either drove once a week, or more often dropped off clean dress shirts and dry cleaning on a Saturday when out and about. I bought a fat tire bike for unplowed snow days. (Well, that's why I claimed I bought it.) I was ready for anything. And with the car gone, I had to be ready. Ride share came in handy a few times, like when I took the train to Chicago and didn't have a locker room to change. Overall, maintenance and occasional ride share was waaaay less than car insurance and parking costs. If you work in Milwaukee's 100 East Wisconsin building, I can give you all the tips and tricks to make your bike commuting a success.

The universe has a way of testing our resolve. The first winter, I got three flat tires within my first month of full-time riding. I had to cancel a client meeting once. I almost gave up. But when your principles and values are clear, the choices are easy. *I had to do this.* I wanted to support biking as healthy for me and good for the environment. An unforeseen benefit was the smug sense of superiority I felt over the soft, insulated car drivers that surrounded me, sipping their tea like wusses in the dark winter mornings. Truly, gearing up on cold days, including ski goggles and balaclava on the coldest days, rekindled the sense of extreme adventure I felt was slipping away as I inched further into middle-aged, white-collar fatherhood. This was badass, and it was practical exercise.

Commuting by bike isn't without risks. I had several variables converge that made it possible for me personally, including being big enough for someone to think twice about mugging me. I carried a switchblade on me. Biking exists on a spectrum, as does anything. Ask someone if they "like going fast" or if they "mountain bike," and it's hard to know their skill level without seeing it.

When I bike to work and around town, I bike as fast as I think is safe. I'm cautious. I always wear a helmet. I acknowledge, as a motorcycle rider as well, that falls have consequences on a different level than in a car. I got my front wheel caught in the streetcar rail one slippery afternoon. I bit it hard in the middle of the street. I fishtailed going up the parking ramp entrance. That's part of it. Every time I see a noob on a Bublr Bike ride out into the crosswalk without looking over their left shoulder for cars turning right, I wish they would at least get a scare, a reminder. "Hey, this is the f**king street you're on. Wake up!" I follow the rules of the road, as one does when biking in the road. Other than rolling stop signs, I signal, follow traffic lights, and turn left just as a car would.

And I have to hope that cars around me will also follow the rules of the road. When I'm driving among other drivers, we enter into an agreement to follow rules that allow us to move fast. Systems that facilitate movement are built on structure.

I know that drivers don't always do that, so I ride defensively. I'm used to it now, but I recall first moving to Milwaukee and realizing yellow lights meant hurry up, and turn signals were optional. Milwaukee driving was sloppier than the freeway driving I'd come to know as a visitor from Chicagoland. Tailgating is dangerous, but so is inexplicably slowing down while merging into the freeway on-ramp. Biking was risky but biking in a city during rush hour was riskier.

One day I was heading west to the credit union for an errand as board treasurer. A gray day, in the 30s, just a blah Midwestern winter

Wednesday. This wasn't a common route for me. I found myself turning left from 35th Street onto State Street. It was a busy intersection, one with two lanes each way, a few blocks from the Miller-Coors headquarters, where a mass shooting happened seven weeks later.

Milwaukee red lights really are laughable. Just when you think the last oncoming car will stop, they cruise on through. I was used to that, and I idled in the intersection, balancing up on the pedals, waiting. *Light is turning red … my lights are on …* I had a white bike and orange helmet. The last car passed at full speed, and I started to bear weight down on the pedals turning to clear the intersection, when an oncoming car hit the gas after it had been slowing down.

The human body is amazing, and fragile. I had at least a full second to register that I would be hit by this sedan heading toward me at 20-something miles per hour. It felt longer. *You've got to survive. I don't think you'll be killed. It could be bad. Just survive.* I recalled reading that tension makes impact worse. That's why the sober driver is often killed while the drunk driver is not. I remember thinking, *Get on top of the car, get high on the pedals, and try to loosen up. You'll be hit and break a leg. Don't get run over by trying to get out of the way.*

I remember being hit at 90 degrees from the right, I remember the impact on my right heel, and hitting the hood of the car, but not the street after that. I woke up on the curb later with the paramedics. The driver of the car had stayed and given his phone number—by choice or because of witnesses, I didn't know. *Holy shit, you were unconscious lying in that intersection till paramedics came. Four lanes each way.* He apologized, and I just said something a wholesome Midwestern boy would say like, "No worries."

When the adrenaline kicks in, nothing hurts as much. Our body wants us to get out of danger first and lick our wounds later. I could remember my name and address, but had no idea where I was headed.

The short-term memory loss freaked me out. Eventually, I remembered I had a client meeting later that day, so I texted "hit by car on bike need to reschedule."

Along the way, the paramedics asked, "Where do you want to be taken?" I said, "Huh?" "For insurance, do you have a preference?" So, those are the conditions in which patients are making financial decisions: en route to the trauma wing of the ER with possible brain bleeding.

The EMTs also asked, "Who should we call?" To which I replied something like, "If I'm not dying, figure out what's wrong with me before you panic my wife, please." I couldn't raise my left arm. Upon arrival, since I had head trauma, they cut my clothes off and x-rayed wherever "I had pain," which was everywhere but my right arm. I was very aware of the expensive equipment, of the man fighting for his life on the other side of the curtain. After they confirmed I didn't have internal bleeding or rupturing, I was left alone to listen to his struggle and the intercom arrival countdown for the next trauma patient. *What a fragile world we live in. All your plans can be taken away in an instant.*

I waited to be moved to the "regular" ER, where I watched *Avatar* until Rebeca arrived. I was dismissed four or five hours after I got there, arm in a sling and a handout for concussions. The aches kicked in when the adrenaline wore off. The next morning my body felt 100 years old. I was grateful to be alive. This was a week after Rebeca gave birth to our third son, a miscarriage at 16 weeks. It can always get harder, I guess.

My in-laws helped with the kids even more than usual, and my parents drove up several days in a row to shovel the sidewalk, buy groceries, everything a one-armed dad of two would need help getting done. (Rebeca had gone away to process our loss with her best friend, who herself had a full-term still birth on the same day our first son was born.) I had a phenomenal support system. Many people don't.

It took me a few more days to be like: *WTF? That guy must have been on his phone, looked up saw the red and figured, "I can make it." He sped up after I began to turn. WTF?* I texted the driver to see if he had insurance. He said no. I asked how I could know that for sure. He just apologized. "That doesn't answer my question," I replied. "Are you okay?" he asked.

I was alive, but my bills were mounting. I couldn't work and didn't have any paid leave so … "okay" is one word that could be used.

I had no idea what I should or could do. I had to wait a week to get the police report, so I pinned all my hopes on that. I didn't have a chance to talk to them the day of the accident. *Surely, there were witnesses. Clearly, he was at fault.* All would be revealed. I hadn't been going anywhere as I kept getting dizzy, so Rebeca drove me to the police station. We got the police report, which cost 25 cents per page. Naively, I assumed this was my evidence. In essence, it said Unit 1 struck Unit 2 at approximately 3:30 pm with a shit stick figure diagram. *Worthless.* For the first time, I experienced the feeling of being completely overlooked by the systems created to protect me. I had no advocate. No one cared. I had followed the rules. *WTF?* I wasn't used to this because I have privilege in so many ways. Many others don't. *Of course this isn't a high priority case but … WTF.*

Rebeca came to my defense. "You need to call a lawyer. At least see what you can do." My instinct was to suck it up, to grin and bear it. I would recover. I could manage. Things happen. I'm not a complainer. *Hard work can fix anything.* But then again, I needed an advocate and an expert. I didn't know what to do. I planned to follow the rules, but they failed me. I wouldn't even know how to bend or break them.

The more I thought about it, the more I realized this wasn't me being reckless. The guy was totally at fault. When Rebeca drove me around now, I was gripping the door handle, on edge.

The year before I had taken on a wonderful family as clients. The dad was a personal injury attorney, so I sent him a message saying, "Hey, here's what happened. Do you think I have a case?" It helped immensely to know him personally before calling. I had heard him and his wife talk about their goals and concerns, joke about parenting and spending. At such a vulnerable time like this, the human instinct is either to withdraw or to lash out. And sadly, most professional service providers, including financial planners and injury attorneys, don't know trauma-informed care.

My personal instinct was to retreat, to suffer inwardly. The hurt person either pushes away or is difficult to work with. Their guard may be up the rest of their lives after getting burned once. The last thing I needed was to be brushed off again. Or deemed unfit to make a claim in the first place. If my attorney said, "Well, you should have looked before you turned," I would have a grudge against attorneys, as many do. Being a White male, in finance, and well-connected all meant rejection was less likely. But a rejection at this low point would be so painful that I almost never asked for help.

But we did it. Rebeca and I went to meet the attorney in his office. I experienced what it feels like on the client side of the table: "Tell me your story. How do you feel about it? How has this affected your life?" To have an advocate is a wonderful feeling. "This is tough. We will do everything we can on your behalf." To hear him say this was so reassuring.

Later, when I started physical therapy, I had the peace of mind that another expert was guiding me in a difficult time. If I worked my rotator cuff alone at home, I'd have no idea whether the pain was rebuilding range of motion or reaggravating my shoulder that needed rest. Experts help us make decisions in context. Experts apply knowledge and organize resources. That's the thing about capitalism. It organizes expertise and resources. I can buy anything or hire anyone if I know where to look. In the case of the attorney, I didn't have to pay unless I won, so our interests were aligned. The specialized knowledge knew what to do when I was at a loss.

I focus on that raw memory when I meet prospective clients for the first time. They're asking for help. Admitting they aren't experts. Attempting to trust a person they've just heard about. A person in my role may resurface painful memories or recommend sacrifice on the path to financial security. Vulnerability is always difficult. Even more so when you don't know if the sacrifice will be worth it. My shoulder recovery required me to allow a physical therapist to put my arm in pain twice a week for months. *Jenna, this can't be right! Are you sure?* Improvement always requires sacrifice somewhere.

My car insurance had $10,000 of my own medical payments included. The bills from the emergency room only, which started coming weeks later, totaled about $24,000. That in-network ambulance ride they asked me about? Four grand for a two-mile trip.

Imagine a single working parent making $13 an hour seeing these bills arrive for thousands of dollars, all "due upon receipt." While that's happening, they're fired from work because they've missed too many days, and they don't have short- or long-term disability insurance. Workers' compensation insurance doesn't apply because they weren't hurt at work. And things spiral from there.

As a client of an attorney, I had an advocate. When I went to the orthopedic specialist and they asked for payment, I said, like on TV, "Call my lawyer," because the attorney's office takes over. They deal with the insurance companies. It was my lawyer versus the driver's insurance, not the driver himself. Turns out, there was insurance on the car, so my conscience was clear. *Giddy up. Let's go for the jugular.* His firm is compensated only if we win a settlement. Sharing a third of it with a law firm was better than keeping 100% of the $0 I had now. I read the form to confirm and signed it. I had followed the rules, been hurt anyway, and then been forgotten by the system. *How many millions of people experience that reality in America their whole lives?* Here, I found a new set of rules:

a web of contracts and liability only accessed because I made one call. That's all.

Allowing others to help me was a difficult lesson in my self-care journey. Without Rebeca's influence, my sacrificial pride may have gotten in the way. Without my professional experience, I wouldn't be as aware or know the people who could help. Eleven months after the accident, I did receive a settlement, which compensated me for lost time at work, as well as pain and suffering. For risking rejection, I got a rate of return I still can't believe. I almost never called, not feeling I deserved it. We can't make excuses when we screw up. But when we hit a true setback, ask around and ask often. As the expression goes, the squeaky wheel gets the grease. I keep my mangled front bike wheel as a reminder of that.

chapter thirty-nine

stimulus

Money has the properties of water. Strong and flexible, focused and meandering. Water in a river, like money in our economy, will trend in one direction, seeking the path of least resistance, and gaining momentum, along the way. A river will have calm spots and bottlenecks; the shape of the land affects the force of the current. That current can be redirected, but it takes monumental effort. If you've stood in any river current with the water above your knees, you know that water is more powerful than it looks. Size matters. When the river floods, some things are built or have grown to withstand it and adapt. Smaller things are swept away, their fate left to the forces of the current. Water under enough pressure will eventually burst through. You either harness the power of the current with irrigation or boats or a dam. Or you roll the dice.

It reflects our shared optimism. Your purchase from her food truck allows her to buy a new car, which allows the car dealer to buy his mom flowers for Mother's Day, and so on. Your spending optimism lifts me up; your pessimism drags me down. In economics, my spending is your earning. My humanity is tied to yours. Unless you bought land and materials in cash and live off the land, off the grid, declining medicine and mechanics alike, we are connected. In cities, even more so. Temperature increases the rate that water molecules move. Cities have long been the hub of economic activity because that's where the market is. People, ideas, products, and dollars are colliding at a rapid rate. When the Federal Reserve lowers the interest rate, they are stimulating the economy by encouraging more of those collisions.

In March 2020, the markets froze into a block of ice. It was a big, fast economic contraction because everything closed overnight. It was way faster than 2008, and it was my first as a financial planner. And while nearly all my clients have kept their jobs, I absorbed client anxiety one conversation at a time, week after week, from Seattle to New York, counseling patience, calm, and optimism. After the initial panic wore off, a lot of people, including our family, received checks that were appreciated but not needed. Our intractable two-party political environment made something more nuanced than a check with an income phase-out impossible. These client check-ins so often went like this:

"Given the state of the world, how are doing? How are you feeling?"

"Well, personally not so great. Virtual kindergarten is a lost cause. Juggling work has been tough, but my boss is understanding. Financially … [long pause] we're doing just fine." *They're embarrassed to say they're better than ever financially.*

A lot of computer-based workers like us, secure in our financial outlook, took one or more of these actions with their stimulus checks and extra spending money. First, we spent it shopping while masked and online, boosting the values of big tech and homewares stocks even further, and fueling this bizarre dichotomy of struggling families in crisis and a booming stock market. *It may be the apocalypse, but this Home Depot is at capacity.* I'm worried for the country, but I have to admit we invested extra money in the stock market. When it first happened, my colleagues and I hung in the hallway, wondering what this would all mean, and buying stock in airlines and hospitality companies on the cheap. We also borrowed money, induced by low interest rates, to buy a more expensive house or reinvest in our business. So, those who could afford a better, nicer home often got one. I took an "Economic Injury Disaster Loan" for my business, with low interest, subsidized by the taxpayers, in order to expand. It was stimulus for sure. But I wasn't injured economically.

What do these three actions have in common? They increase the valuation of property, in company stock and real estate that we own. Remember, the asset gap is far wider than the income gap. We made money because we rode the current to our advantage. Government stimulus did stimulate, but stimulus and relief have different meanings. Relief is a painkiller; stimulus is adrenaline. For Americans who needed the money as relief, they purchased essentials. While that juiced the economy, if they didn't own stock in the company they purchased from, their finances didn't appreciate like ours did. Asset inequality spread further. And we end up with billionaires in space and homelessness flooding city streets.

The story of COVID, in the United States and globally, is that there are clear short-term winners and losers. My clients aren't a representative sample of the whole country. They tend to live in cities and suburbs, make decent money, work for large employers, and can work online remotely if needed. Software engineers may have lost a loved one to COVID, but their finances are just fine. Like heavy rainfall in the river, COVID accelerated trends that already existed. And one of those trends in the United States is that the rich are getting richer, and the poor are getting poorer. I am grateful that I haven't lost anyone close to me to

COVID's many variants, as of writing this. Most of my COVID stress came from seeing so clearly how some people gained and some lost. The divergence of dollar value from human value is so unsettling. I serve people, through the medium of money. We come to love what we serve, and our failure to cooperate is so disheartening.

Present in our shared American DNA—before, during, and after COVID—is a rugged sense of self-reliance and independence, and therefore a proportional distrust of elitism and expertise. Mask-wearing as a symbol of authoritarian compliance is sadly ideological. We accept wearing seatbelts, after all. What's the difference? I dislike wearing both.

It is interdependence that allows us to get a pool skimmer, groceries, and essential oils shipped to our door within a day. We are all vibrating at a fever pitch. The free market innovates to make that happen faster and better than the government can. But some things only the government can solve. The American experience, in this vast nation, is multifaceted. We contain multitudes. Taxes buy civilization. Someone can argue their tax dollars are wasted, and if so, get involved. That's what democracy is. But no taxes? Then no road repairs, food-processing, health inspections, public schools … We are all connected.

Big government is for solving big problems. Not little ones. Let the free market do that. It's more nimble and responsive. But the biggest problems require cooperation: national security, healthcare, pandemics … Socialism is about sharing. During the Great Depression, the New Deal legislation expanded social safety nets and public works. I've been in beautiful stone lodges built back then, now nearly a hundred years ago. We put people to work building things that last. We were in a rut in the Great Depression, and action helped. Responding aggressively to a seismic threat got us out of it. Government can tell the private sector: "I am ordering you by law to stop what you're doing and do this instead." World War II was the last chapter in American history where everyone—I mean everyone—sacrificed for an urgent, patriotic cause. We made tanks instead of cars. We bought war bonds, letting the government borrow our savings to spend it fighting fascism. And by uniting in the face of an existential threat in Nazi Germany, we did thoroughly kick ass. The enemy had a face, unlike a virus.

And all that (*gasp!*) deficit spending and post-war middle-class policy support ushered in a period of relative prosperity for Americans. But over the last 40 years, the size of government has contracted or expanded depending on who you ask to measure. What is clear: trust in government has declined. Agency funding has been cut, making them less effective, which then reinforces the point that they are a waste. A self-fulfilling prophecy. A good leader, in any capacity, has vision. The best presidents, Republican and Democrat, have cast a bold vision based on principles. The principles may be timeless, but an effective vision must exist in the future.

During COVID, all politicians could manage was to buy us off, throwing us a "stimulus" instead of a plan. If you've ever had a perpetually broke friend or family member ask you for help, knowing full well that you have the money, you know that a few hundred bucks might get them through the week, but it won't reform them. It's all the more painful, because they know you can afford it, and you know it won't change anything.

Government action during COVID, in a spirit of cooperation, could have galvanized the free market to problem-solve for the public good, instead of standing flat-footed waiting for a policy decree from on high. In the 1950s, the interstate highway system was funded by taxes championed by Republican President Eisenhower, and catapulted shipping and commerce forward. (We bulldozed poor urban communities and created segregation lines still present today too. That doesn't change my point that vision can lead to lasting change.)

We could pay unemployed teens to build garden plots in food deserts. We could offer tax incentives for healthy food vendors in such areas too. We could pay manufacturers to retool to PPE. We could offer scholarships to study infectious disease. We could hire tens of thousands of people to install broadband internet in rural areas, since the internet is likely the "city market" of the 21st century. We could … Sigh. In a fast-moving current, your answer can't be to stay in the same place. You have to look downstream and pick a spot to head toward.

Now and through history, we have had public figures who choose to cast a vision of what's upstream from where we are now. In other words, the past, what we have already floated past on the current. Even if you personally want to return to that place, you'll be swimming against the current to get there. It's the past for a reason. Time to let go. Honor your grandfather the coal miner by becoming an engineer for renewable energy. Times have changed, but we should honor the legacy of coal miners, who risked and sacrificed their health to propel trains across the continent.

Economists generally agree that deficit spending is sometimes necessary. Macro and microeconomics are not the same, but economists allow me to simplify here. Many voters feel we should not fund initiatives or growth spending while we are paying interest on debt. *The government is spending money we don't have? Why? How irresponsible.* I would counter. Did you pay for your house or your college degree in cash up front? If not, you're doing the same thing. I won't deny that government spending can be wasteful; I have proof in the news all the time. How tempting it must be to just print money. Until inflation inevitably results from creating more money without adding more productivity.

Sometimes we must act and invest in the future in a targeted way. I certainly hope our next infrastructure bill does that. The public had more faith in government during and after World War II, in large part because there was oversight to make sure our money wasn't wasted. Notably, the Truman Committee was dedicated to minimizing waste, inefficiency, and profiteering in war manufacturing. Optimism for a vision is what deficit spending is all about. If we create the right circumstances for growth by watering the crops in spring, then we will harvest in fall. If we borrow $100 now and earn $200 later, isn't it worth it? The effort is always front-loaded. Effort we don't want to make if we don't have faith in the vision. That composure under pressure is what gets human and dollar results.

While most of my clients are individuals and couples, a handful own small businesses. Unlike direct payments to households, business relief was a little harder to figure out. When news of massive wealthy companies getting Payroll Protection Program (PPP) loans came out, people were understandably outraged. Those companies could afford to wait until mom-and-pop corner stores were served. Knowing how money moves, I wasn't surprised. When someone can breathe financially, and steps out of survival mode, they can focus on future opportunities. They can claim distress while investing in a drive-up ordering app, then emerge stronger than ever. The government kept millions employed, and enhanced unemployment benefits for others, and absolutely helped millions tread water. But it kept the status quo.

Bigger fish employ specialized experts in law, accounting, public relations, you name it. They are in the river with the equipment in hand already. The better you can absorb a setback, the better you can seize an opportunity. They have the raft and paddles to navigate.

Smaller fish in a small business looks like four people trying to do ten things well. In this case, looking for a raft after the COVID-19 iceberg tore a hole in their boat. Larger fish immediately researched the Coronavirus Aid, Relief, and Economic Security Act (CARES Act), applied it with due diligence, and were hyper-responsive and organized.

Smaller fish did not. Those wary of the government did not. I, too, was upset because the smaller fish have the smaller margins and needed it most. I hope the American public realizes that everyone in business isn't flush with cash. These PPP loans were forgiven for the most part. This was another windfall gift from the federal government, considering that many PPP recipients made more money during COVID.

It became clear that our government prioritizes corporate interests. Corporations are "too big to fail" primarily because there aren't enough baseline employee protections. Being attached to a large employer was useful during COVID. Being a gig worker was not, because so many benefits in the United States are still linked to employment, even as it becomes clear that employment is increasingly fluid, and all Americans are increasingly interconnected. Based on what I've read, funding some form of universal basic income with a tax on ubiquitous technology that we all use would be an improvement on the status quo. But we must look downstream for that conversation.

Okay, so everyone could apply, but why did the big fish get it first? Well, the government mandates low interest, but interest is how banks make money. Two percent of a million dollars is $20,000. Two percent of $10,000 is $200. *I wonder which application will get processed first.* Your interest charged is another's income earned. Capital can get organized and pivot very quickly. Consider how amazing it is that multiple drug companies developed a vaccine for a novel disease in under a year. Goal clarity coupled with financial incentive is powerful.

What if they hoarded vaccines for the highest bidder? We need government to keep our worst human impulses in check. The worst human impulse is profiting from human misery. Profiteering exists on a spectrum. If I consider buying rural land in Wisconsin with farmable land and access to water, part of my brain is thinking, not hoping, that human displacement and scarcity caused by climate change will make my property more valuable. Before COVID closed the US, some guy started hoarding hand sanitizer, and was shamed into giving it up. Financially, it was brilliant. That's how leverage works. *If we forgot to pack diapers, I'll pay whatever they cost on the road.* The more basic the human need, the more we will pay to meet the need. All financial decisions are built on a hierarchy of needs. The pandemic is a human story unfolding in a world of financial tradeoffs.

First, being poor or isolated or both is bad for your health. Chronic stress and financial insecurity make being poor, all else equal, much harder. If you live in an under-resourced neighborhood, that is also bad for your health. In October 2020, the then-president was flown in a helicopter and given COVID treatment not available to the general public. So, clearly money and power are correlated to quality of healthcare.

Second, the politics of pandemic policy in America obscure a bipartisan reality: those who can financially afford to limit COVID exposure have done so, and those who cannot have not. An IT worker who is fully remote can afford to not leave the house. A plumber cannot. All financial decisions are about risk tolerance. For the comfortable, we might say, "I won't risk catching COVID and putting my family in jeopardy." For the delivery service gig worker without benefits, they might say, "No matter what happens, I won't risk missing a pay period and putting my family in jeopardy." For some, the calculation is taking a low-probability, high-severity health risk. For others, it's taking a certain economic risk (missing a paycheck or being replaced by someone else) in exchange for that same health risk. In that risk calculation, everyone had to choose, and then confirmation bias led us to seek information to validate our choice and judge others for theirs. Not an easy call for many.

Frontline workers deserve every penny of hazard pay, whether a nurse or a delivery driver. I work with an ICU nurse who thinks he has PTSD from watching so many people die. I used to feel awkward watching a somber employee drop shopping bags in my trunk through the rearview mirror. I don't anymore, a sign income inequality is moving us closer to scenes from "other places" where the wealthy live sequestered from the dangers of being in public. Post-vaccine, restaurant patrons can be unmasked but employees mask up. Why?

Third, we all need to realize our health is our wealth. This could be our wake-up call. Americans are unhealthy. We don't eat nutritious food, because it's more expensive to buy and harder to find. Much of what Americans eat, at very low cost compared to food prices around the world, is based on the same ingredients used to fatten livestock for slaughter. I love bacon, too. Just sayin' let's accept reality. Our patriotic duty to fight COVID is to get healthy! We'd have a stronger military, too. We keep hearing about higher risk factors, but not in an encouraging way. *Get some cardio! Get that lung capacity up!* I have high-risk close family, so my message isn't "tough it out." I have clients with parents in nursing homes, terrified. I have a client whose father died of COVID. I know families concerned about their child with special needs post-pandemic.

Healthcare companies want us unhealthy. That's their business model. Surgery, medication, and consultation is all billable. If you're winded after walking a flight of stairs, you are a COVID target. Hunkering down, staying inside, and binge-watching aren't helping. I am aware of mounting research linking weight gain to trauma, stress, and genetics. This isn't fat-shaming; this is reality. Being unhealthy is dangerous and expensive. Seems like politicians on both sides want us afraid. As Nelson Mandela said, "Courage is not the absence of fear, but the triumph over it." *You can wear a mask, and be courageous. You can decline one, and still be afraid. It's not about safety. It's about identity and belonging now. Either choice has a social risk, too.*

We cannot swim upriver against the current for long. We created the present with our voting and shopping. We can escape the errors of our past by swimming toward our future. In lifespan theories of human development, some psychologists say that it takes a dramatic life event to change course. If things are comfortable, a person is unlikely to make change. More pandemics will come, so let's use this pain to reevaluate, innovate, and cooperate to get better. Throwing money and blame around in an unfocused way will get an unfocused result, like puddles on the pavement that evaporate instead of watering seeds for our future.

chapter forty

Black dollars matter

How can you, *a White man*, *tell a story about the Black experience? How can you, a so-called ally, write a book about culture and finance, and not try?*

I have heard it said that the only thing we truly own is our story. Agree or not, the power of a story is undeniable. It inspires or condemns, cautions or enables; pick any verb you like, and a story will bring it to life. Perception is reality, so the stories we tell ourselves and each other are powerful. For most of human history, all culture was preserved through story. So, what happens when two very different stories are presented as reality at the same time?

Ever lose a basketball or board game, and just couldn't shake the feeling the other team cheated? Or the refs were one-sided? You know that universally infuriating feeling of trying so hard and having it stolen from you? Sure, you could have played better or harder, but you could have won if the game were played fair. And you can't tell if your opponent really didn't cheat intentionally, or if they're hiding it well. Either way, they are acting like the winner, and treating you like the loser. Not outright mean, but by their smugness. It's hard to take. It's infuriating. No matter what happened during the game, the glory belongs to them, and they get the microphone to tell their story in the way they choose. They own both sides of the narrative. History is the story told by the winners.

That's what I imagine it's like to be Black in this country, or to identify as any marginalized group. The winners aren't always mean, but they don't acknowledge their cheating or outright advantage. The winners get the praise, and the opportunity to interview after the victory, and tell their side of the story. Being White myself, I can still be beaten by superior talent or effort, but I cannot deny the refs are on my side, along with home court advantage, and my opponents wearing ankle weights. Every time, the whole season. Winners like to think it was all grit, heart, and hustle (and God), and that's it. What a story. But win or lose, relative advantage always exists.

In the game of life and money, we have to play. As Americans, we are conscripted. Some like to pretend everyone started off on equal footing. I work with clients all over the country. As of writing this, about half are non-White. Regardless of skin tone, there are two approaches to the game that are described to me. Some see the awareness and use of money as an unpleasant necessity of life. This group presents themselves in different ways, but I observe their self-imposed distance, confusion, and distaste for the game of finance. They are inherently uncomfortable. I don't blame them, and because they're talking to me, they acknowledge they have to play so they're getting a coach.

The other group wants to play, and plays to win. I don't knowingly work with anyone unethical, but the fact remains they are considering all options to leverage their position. And unlike the first group, regardless of skin tone and income level, they show enthusiasm for strategy, progress, and opportunity. The former is grudgingly participating; the latter is competing.

How are these groups affected by the story, and the rules? In the game of money, the referees were also players. Still are. No wonder they won. It's so easy and tempting to talk about identity, which increasingly goes hand in hand with politics. Two academics, one White and one Black, wrote books that made complex topics accessible to a wider audience. Both focus on cause and effect in search for clarity in our modern world. So, let's leave identity behind, and talk about geography and history.

Europeans saw the "New World" as an economic opportunity. Prior to Columbus landing in the West Indies, Europeans realized they were able to capture Africans at gunpoint, and make them work for free, forever. They were able to because the Africans didn't have guns at the time. The gap in technology is explored in the seminal work by Jared Diamond in his book *Guns, Germs and Steel: The Fates of Human Societies*. A key piece of the puzzle is that Europe was divided into nation-states so tiny and evenly matched that their weaponry became the best in the world in their miserable struggle for survival. Meanwhile, civilizations in present-day China, South and Central America, Africa and the Middle East were way more advanced in every other way. And a money theme is that the powerful seek to maintain the status quo. They didn't innovate because they didn't have to.

When Europeans found the natural abundance of the Americas, and established a way to enslave and transport humans there, the opportunity to profit was glaring these f**kers in the face. The "triangle trade" of enslaved humans, crops, and manufactured goods was born. In colonial America and the United States under the Constitution, the money was just too good to stop enslaving people and stealing land. Stealing land was aided by the Europeans' immunity to all sorts of disease, which decimated Indigenous peoples in the Americas. They developed immunity, in part, by living in close quarters to livestock like cows and sheep, species which were domesticated in Europe, but not found on other continents. Poor Whites, then and now, worked for slave owners and landowners. But the entire economy, from growing cotton in the South to clearing tree stumps for farm fields in the North, was built on theft and slavery. Government policy encouraged "Indian removal" in the name of markets and God.

And it's easy to judge centuries later. For every materialistic progressive who throws around "decolonizing your mind" today, at least half would have done the same damn thing. If you had the chance to get a house in the neighborhood you wanted, for free, and were given a nanny, maid, and chef, for free, how would that improve your financial situation? And would it be enough that you'd do it? If all your neighbors were doing it … It wasn't against the law … In fact, the more slaves you had, the more representation you got in Congress, so it was encouraged.

Diamond's work is an example of environmental determinism: the study of how the physical environment predisposes states and societies toward development trajectories. More simply, geography created inequality. This brings an unsettling truth to the forefront: our destinies are deeply affected by random chance.

That's an unsatisfying idea. Our brains are wired to ascribe meaning, and find intent in everything. But the alternative, if people with less melanin had conquered those with more melanin even if all the other geographic factors were reversed, is … racist, and even less satisfying.

Environmental determinism says that the original referee in the game of power was planet Earth. One team was given a relative advantage for a few hundred years, and their jerseys happened to be White. We will see how long that lasts.

When I read that book around age 20, for the first time, I found a theory that moved past identity. Diamond won the Pulitzer Prize, but has been criticized as apologizing for past atrocities. I disagree. He didn't do that; people with his skin color did. But suspicion is warranted, because perception is reality. The rulebook matters. When the referees also play the game, they can change it when they're ready to take advantage.

For example, for centuries, the government has treated alcohol and marijuana very differently. It's clear that it is because alcohol has deep cultural roots in northern Europe, and the founding fathers didn't want to give it up. Fermented beer was safer than water for centuries. There is no evidence that marijuana is more detrimental to your health. But the story for decades has been that marijuana is a gateway drug for White suburban kids, who get a call to their parents when caught, and a threat to society with Black urban kids, who get thrown in jail when caught. The irony is that marijuana's medicinal properties no doubt helped Black folks cope with the trauma of being Black. Years later, as felons imprisoned for minor drug charges languish, White entrepreneurs, and their investors by proxy, are making a fortune selling weed legally, because now it's not against the law. The referees changed the rulebook when their capital was ready.

Ambition and power are innate in humankind. Human slavery existed in Africa and Indigenous America once consolidated power made it possible. When humans see a way to profit or gain advantage, we go for it. The distinction is: will that profit be at the expense of another? As we look back on the slave traffickers and owners of the past, we cringe and shudder. How will our descendants view our single-use plastic habit as the planet churns and burns with increasing intensity, displacing and taking lives? When I look for land in fertile, rural Wisconsin river valleys, and consider how my land will be worth so much more in the future as climate change refugees from Arizona and Indonesia alike flock to habitable land, and I can rent to them, I realize I am just another White man of means seeking financial gain by leveraging supply and demand. Land is a finite resource, so it appreciates in value, according to the rules of capital imported from Europe to the Americas. Indigenous peoples of America had ownership, but in a different cultural lens, one without fences.

The rulebook has changed for the better over time. The conversation breaks down when we don't acknowledge progress made and progress needed in the same breath. When the White male founding fathers gave every White male landowner the right to vote, that was considered woke AF by the standards of the day. The hypocrisy of "all men created equal" is astounding. *And* even granting the vote to all White male property owners was extremely progressive in 1789. Today, some Americans have an incredible advantage in earning and retaining wealth, *and* the "rags-to-riches" story is possible in America, while it is simply not in much of the world. Both are true. People can make good choices and evil ones in the same lifetime. No person is an infallible hero, and very few are irredeemable villains. It's not about identity; it's about choices.

The barrier to success has more to do with belief and optimism than ability. The key is an abundance mentality. But easier said than done. When we met at age 22, my wife, a Latina raised in the hood, instinctively believed that things wouldn't work out. I instinctively believed that they would. Why wouldn't they for me? I'm a well-educated, able-bodied, straight White male after all. The rules of play were designed for me. That's why sports and all forms of competition have such universal appeal: the rules are known, and therefore fair. The appeal is transparency.

Financial and legal systems are anything but transparent. After making it big in the 1990s, music artist and producer Jay-Z founded Roc Nation, an entertainment management company. With this step, he went beyond being a success himself to becoming a steward of others' success. He applied his knowledge of how the game of money works to others. He became a referee, not just a star player. With enough talent, anyone can make money, but to maximize, negotiate, and leverage, that requires more. When knowledge and trust are aligned, the partnership potential is infinite. If you can know your client's cultural experience, *and* know how the referees think, you can make some real progress. In financial services, advisors can earn trust with racial solidarity, and lose it with incompetence. And exceptional advisors are stymied from helping clients by mistrust in racial divides.

Jay-Z took some criticism for partnering with NFL owners on an entertainment contract through Roc Nation because the same owners sided against Colin Kaepernick's cause when he knelt during the national anthem to protest police brutality. But he understands who the referees are, and identified the table where decisions are made. He is willing to be uncomfortable as a minority there. He knows the NFL is big business with appeal across racial lines. He understands that bigger money has bigger impact, for good or ill. If the corner store owner puts up a Black Lives Matter sign, that's significant, and meaningful. If Netflix curates BLM content that is watched by millions of viewers, that has broader reach. He knows, as I have learned, that when you follow the money, you will find what folks care about. Has the most outspoken BLM activist on Twitter donated 1% of their salary to BLM groups? 2%? I'd be curious to know. Money changes hands often. It is a tool without a soul. Let's not assign a purity test for money like the one-drop rule. I'll take my government stimulus with anyone's signature on it because I can redirect it to any purpose I choose. Politics and identity create a distraction in the front room while the money shuffles out the back door. Purity tests aren't practical. Ideology is another form of privilege.

People have power, and money has power. Organized people with money are the most powerful of all. Lake Valley Camp, where a piece of my soul will always be, brought different racial groups together in pursuit of a better community, one built on emotional and physical safety that allowed children to thrive for a time, taking chances, and trying new things. That camp was funded with corporate retail profits, which became private philanthropy. The donor is a good man. I don't know if he's a "woke" man. What I do know is that he is the referee to the extent he wanted to be, because it was his money. The kids at camp, intrigued by the low-profile "owner," would have benefited from a Black or Brown role model. Some will read that and say it devalues the grit and generosity of the philanthropist, a man I got to know as uncommonly kind, humble, and classy. Not true. He worked hard and earned it … *and* all else being equal, it would have been harder had he been Black. Does his relative advantage diminish his impact? No, and he may have relative disadvantages not visible to the eye. After all, he did something meaningful when he didn't have to. Just like Jay-Z's company promotes legislative changes like prison reform. All dollars matter. He doesn't have to. Let's measure all by their actions.

When we focus on identity, we tell the story we want to write, and evade measurement. But racism and antiracism are an act, not an identity. The professor and author Ibram X. Kendi gave the reader a way to engage with race. Easier said than done; most content on race is passive or buried in the context of history. His book *How to be an Antiracist* lays the framework very plainly, which is not easy. Racist actions, beliefs, and policies are brushed aside as "I'm not a racist, therefore, what I did cannot be racist." Just like a family's financial well-being is never neutral, but always improving or declining based on the interest current, we as people make choices each day that are racist or anti-racist. As I sat in our yard one summer night in central Milwaukee, listening to police choppers overhead, and the city groan and ache with anger, I looked at the patio furniture I just assembled and wondered, *"Am I doing enough?"*

I did not attend any BLM protests in the months following George Floyd's murder. *Racist choice.* I did read Kendi's book. *Anti-racist choice.* And I did write this chapter. *And you've rewritten it five times since. Who do you think you are?*

Our local office held an open forum to share our feelings after the murder of George Floyd. Those who attended made an anti-racist choice. We aren't categorically racist or not. We just made a choice, one of billions in a lifetime. Just like we all spend money on people, places, and things. Every dollar spent has an effect of some kind.

So, why is this binary so triggering for so many White folks? Why does this topic provoke such anger in some? I attended a "White Men and Allies" all-day workshop put on by our firm around 2016/2017. The tensest moment was when a White male advisor in his fifties said, "Hey, we all have challenges to overcome," and doubled down. The professional facilitator, who was Black, said, "You have overcome a lot … *and* I have an additional challenge you don't have. I still acknowledge your hardship. Please acknowledge mine."

Some bristle at the notion they have "White privilege" because they don't identify as being privileged. And overall, many White people are not. We have *a* privilege. While Black people have the highest poverty rate as a percentage of population, more Americans in total are White and poor than Black and poor. You can have a rough, awful life, and be White. And you can be Black, and born into luxury with a loving family. It's all relative. Relative advantage. If we must soften "White privilege" to "relative advantage" to get more people to the table, I'm all for it. That's the goal, right?

This man was triggered by the statement that he was privileged. And yet, in his fifties, I knew he was doing pretty damn well financially. And even if he wasn't, all of us White folks benefited directly or indirectly from sweeping government handouts, from the GI Bill to the New Deal to the Homestead Act, which explicitly excluded African Americans from billions of dollars of government welfare. Even so, his tone and his body language indicated that he felt attacked. When one of my wife's co-workers tells her (a Brown woman) how hard it is to be a White woman, it's natural to scoff, but we can look for answers in mental health. When humans experience trauma, their responses will vary widely. When humans feel threatened, same thing. We get a fight, flight, or freeze response. Why proclaim "All Lives Matter" if your life feels valued already?

But tough shit. It could always be worse. You could be targeted and beaten by police. If you accept that being Black in America is traumatic to varying degrees, then the range of responses and behaviors to that trauma make a bit more sense. Anyone can feel threatened or have a traumatic event. On the other hand, I think the "liberal elites" find it very easy to put a BLM sign on the lawn. And because of their—I mean *our*—relative advantages, it is easier to extend grace to others, and lift them up. *And it's easy to judge.* The forces of globalization and urbanization seem to support us. We just aren't as threatened or as concerned we will lose out. "There's enough room for everyone to thrive," we say. "I can do well, and you can too."

Or if they aren't threatened, those resistant may have some money on the line: either they profit from fearmongering and racist structures, or they fear competition for minimum-wage work, or they just don't know our history. Or all the above. Throughout history, when people have been squeezed, they have looked for a scapegoat. I remember reading my social cognition textbook for grad school and muttering, "Identity threat, yup, that's happening … and oh that's happening too …" As a history major, I forget how Eurocentric intro level history is, that most people didn't learn history after age 16, and that many slept through what history they had as a dry list of dates.

History is really a collection of themes and characters, like in a novel. If you ask a friend to summarize the novel, they will give a version that supports their worldview. That's human nature. The Boston Tea Party story we learned as children? Some brave colonists (protestors?) took a stand against unfair British monarchy rule (oppressive law enforcement?) and sent a message by dumping tea into the harbor (senseless destruction of private property?) while disguised as Indians (who didn't have rights so framing them was no problem). See what I mean? Anger is an emotion felt by all exploited people.

Millions of people have left other continents to come here seeking a better life. Indigenous peoples were here, and then forced onto reservations. The Black Hills of South Dakota were the sacred heart of the powerful Sioux Nation. The fact that Mount Rushmore was built there is a huge insult. That's part of the story. Rebeca's parents fled civil war to come here with nothing. A key plot twist in that story was the funneling of arms from the US. They faced tremendous obstacles, including racism, in pursuit of the American Dream ... *and* they weren't captured in bed at gunpoint and enslaved. Her dad was hunted by the military and escaped. That's a different story.

Trauma must be acknowledged before it can be treated. Step one is to tell the story clearly, as it is. We celebrate White emancipation on the Fourth of July. Milwaukee County just declared Black emancipation, Juneteenth, a holiday. Sometimes the story is so obvious it escapes us.

Again, history is the story told by the winners. The losers are silenced unless there is a witness brave enough to share. George Floyd is not the first. He just had witnesses with phones, and that made all the difference. The advanced placement US history course I took in high school, and later taught, stopped right around civil rights and Vietnam when things get recent enough to be messy. Emmett Till was safely removed into "history," which happened to "other people," so can be mourned from a distance. Just as Emmett Till's open casket was a catalyst for that generation, the video of George Floyd's murder has been for ours.

Oh, history is being written now. Which means I am a character in the story. *Every business in America suddenly needs to make a statement. Black dollars matter.*

But when we choose not to be defined by our past, we can start fresh. What Kendi and Diamond gave me at least is a way to detach from my White guilt, which doesn't do anything productive, and engage with actions. In therapy, we shine a light on the pain.

My own story of White privilege shapes me, and it shapes many clients of mine too. The way I cope with White guilt is by taking anti-racist actions. I cannot change my past, and I don't want to. My childhood was wonderful. My parents valued education and extracurriculars, and encouraged my hobbies and interests, from sharks in first grade to lacrosse senior year. I went to a diverse public school. I lived in a safe suburb shaped by racist policies. It was a perfect place to raise a White family. With a little work, it would be a perfect place to raise any family. It's made for kids, basically.

My parents gave my sister and me every opportunity to thrive. They put us before themselves, weekend after weekend. I have such fond memories of my childhood and teenage years. "The world was my oyster" as my mom used to say. I could grow up to do anything and be anything. My public school education with advanced placement courses, my competitive high school sports career that forged character, our exposure to Chicago as a hub of commerce and culture, and the daily subliminal message of "my house is nice, my school is nice, the park is nice"—these nice things all let me know that I was destined for a life of nice things and opportunities.

If the suburbs were created through racist policies, an anti-racist education policy would be to separate property taxes and school district funding completely. No matter where you live, each child gets the same amount of spending per capita. Rural Nebraska, the Bronx, suburban Seattle, the same. We could adjust funding for teacher salaries and supplies to reflect the cost of living fairly, but imagine that ...

We do say everyone is created equal, right? Right? As it stands, this racist education policy is exclusionary based on access to real estate, which in turn is access to capital. The child's education depends on the parent's capital. *I can't decide. Is that the most American or most un-American thing ever?*

It always comes back to money. End of story. Invest equally upstream, then we may get a meritocracy. It's misleading to say racism is a product of ignorance and hate. It can be in individuals, yes. But racist power and policy is all about self-interest. It has been ever since the 1400s, when the Portuguese found a source of human slaves in West Africa to avoid buying slaves (of all skin colors) from Muslims. They just wanted to cut out the middleman, so devised the construct of race, and countless reasons to justify it. Follow the money, as the saying goes.

Since slavery ended, our foreign policy has focused on keeping cheap labor markets open to produce stuff to be sold in America. Outside of textbooks, free markets have never been free. We can just admit it, as a start.

I've seen the reception of my Black brother JB change in recent years. As my mentor early on, he was the only one I really trusted. I noticed how he was brief, or tense, or guarded with the firm at large. He wasn't the person I knew in private. In the early days, it was White men asking people of color, "How can we help you? What can we do?" I suppose with good intentions, but lazy. *They already have it harder, and now you can't even read a book or Google that?* In my experience with Black friends, they generally don't want to go to a party and hear a White person drone on about what being Black is like. But we've come a long way, one anti-racist choice at a time.

I had heard the phrase "old boys' club," but I didn't know what it meant until I first became a financial advisor. Now I heard JB speak with a different quality in that open forum after the George Floyd video came out, despite being asked to "speak for Black people" yet again. The difference was a collective acknowledgment of his lived experience. The story is changing, and that matters. These conversations are happening all over. We can't measure identity the way we can add up our choices. No demographic or economic category is good or bad. We are nothing more than the sum of millions of choices made up to this moment. We can always choose what happens next.

As for Jay-Z, he could buy a private island and chill for the rest of his life, but he is choosing action, venturing deeper toward power centers. Serena Williams, arguably the greatest athlete of all time, is getting into venture capital, historically an epicenter of current inequality perpetuating future asset gaps. If I measure clients' investment returns on a risk-adjusted basis, instead of a total return basis, should achievement in America be measured on a "race-adjusted" basis? Winning is still winning, but when a person of color takes a risk, like when a White survivor of trauma takes a risk, it's even more impressive. When the 2020 Milwaukee Bucks boycotted suiting up in protest, I was so proud. A risk, but money talks. Consumers have power. Black dollars matter.

Our ancestors took actions, and if we don't like them, we get to take new actions to counteract. Action is an antidote for guilt. I know that we all have hopes and dreams, fears and doubts. I've spent years grappling with my financial identity. I have also borne witness to, in hundreds of confidential interviews, our White assumption that things will go our way. I see White fragility in financial planning. The second bathroom that has to be remodeled? It's just not that big a deal. It won't make you as happy as you think. And if you looked different, your parents may not have helped you with the down payment anyway, made easier for them in part by racist government assistance in the past. It's not their fault, but it is still built on sins of the past. It's still generous of them. Be grateful the referees are on your side. Believe that a fair playing field will benefit all of us.

What are you doing? Trolling your less-woke high school acquaintance? Calling anyone with a critique unpatriotic? That's not helping. Focus on the problem and the antiracist actions you can take today. It's not about identity, but action. At the gym, I watch Fox and MSNBC side by side, and I can't look away, although I hate both. Political identity is red and blue. Our lives are purple.

As co-chair of our firm's Diversity and Inclusion Council, I don't have time for identity-based discussion in council meetings, like who's done more or who "gets it" more. We must focus on the actions and systems we can create to promote belonging for all members.

This isn't about redistributing the pie. It's about rinsing out the bad taste and getting a new, better recipe, one ingredient at a time.

chapter forty-one
to the "subs"

When I drive around southeastern Wisconsin with our kids, we talk about what's passing by: a dairy farm, a skyscraper, a playground. The middle one is obsessed with concrete boundaries. "Dada are we in Muhwaukee, Musconsin?" Our eldest quickly observed the pros and cons of urban and country living. Close to everything, with lots of different types of things to do and people to see. Peaceful around nature, with lots of room to run and play. That's pretty much it, right?

Since I was 18, I have lived in a city for 90% of the time. The other 10% was spent well off the beaten path in a beautiful valley at an overnight summer camp. From my little house there, the night was so … welcoming. As fireflies transitioned to stars, I could hear over the hills the shouting of happy children fade, and the hooting of owls take its place. The country is magical. Its natural rhythms bringing our souls back to a time when all humans lived in the country. While much knowledge has been gained since then, much wisdom has been lost as well.

Cities, for millennia a magnet for art and science alike, bring people together to create incredible things, but so often lose sight of ancient common sense. In cities, we are bombarded with stimuli, and as a result, generally become more accepting of difference. Or numbed by it. In the country, we grow so accustomed to how things have always been that the big wide world can pass us by if we lose all curiosity.

From the atlas view, the green expanse of the Cascades and the zoomed-in insert of downtown San Antonio are interesting to me. Improvisational travel is one of those things that makes me come alive. You know what's not as much? "The subs" as Roque calls them. That's where we live now, in the suburbs, where people and places alike are perfectly pleasant and purposefully predictable.

Because the suburbs are trying to get the best of both worlds, and in the attempt, fall short of capturing the essence of either city or country. They do, however, get just enough of both for kids to be healthy and active. Which is the main reason we moved. As parents, we value that pleasantness and predictability. We didn't want our kids run over in the street, or to look out our dining room window and see someone injecting heroin in a parked car 20 feet away. We don't plan to shield them from learning about the crisis of opioid addiction, including the role of big pharma. However, I'd like to pick my entry point for those life lessons.

In Milwaukee's inner-city neighborhoods, reckless driving is a problem. I don't mean aggressive driving; that can be found everywhere. I mean zero to 60, through a red light then a stop sign, and down our narrow residential street. Using the empty left turn lane or the parking lane to blow past at the onset of a green light. Passing within inches of the bumper in four-lane city traffic. Our old zip code 53215 is densely populated, and the intersection at the north end of the block is one of the two or three busiest in the whole city. Working from home, we would see a car accident from our window a few times a month.

The style of the reckless driver is what I recall from being 16, throwing caution out the window. These days, we add the distraction of screens to this irresponsible cocktail. So, why the issue? Like a 16-year-old, these drivers don't seem to consider what they have to lose. Like a 16-year-old, they are testing boundaries, thrill-seeking. Unlike teens, they are misplacing a need to display their dominance—in any way—after being totally numbed by the low-wage economy. How else can we explain an Audi with a bashed fender blow past me inches away from ripping the side mirror off? (Or to be fair, a man with an office job driving a fully loaded pickup with truck nuts hanging from the back?)

This is where we need to be careful. Some will say they ought to be criminally charged, not acknowledging the trauma those drivers have likely experienced. A grown man who drives in that way is not thriving. It's likely the car is the only place they can assert themselves; minimum wage and unemployment are emasculating. Others will say we need more "programs," and shift all responsibility to systems, not people. It's always both.

Living in poverty is not easy. When reading a book with our kids on the living room couch, and interrupted by a woman sobbing and shrieking at her man, who is trailing her with the car window open as she storms down the sidewalk, I am not angry. I am saddened by her suffering. I don't want to call the cops. I want to help but I feel helpless. When I was 23 and living with a roommate, I let a guy spend a winter night on our couch, after I watched him from the balcony staggering around drunk, crying out that he wanted to die. I watched him for about 20 minutes, and felt compelled to act. Now, with my family in the house, I would have to stay up all night watching this person. More likely I would call the police, who may handle it in any number of ways, as we have seen. If they come; they have their hands full with active crimes.

That stuff doesn't happen as much in the subs. Which is just what we parents want: a boring, predictable patchwork of homes, parks, churches, and schools that we can overlay with "activities." Once one becomes a parent, it's all about us before me. The freedom of just "me" was about ideology and identity, which now takes a back seat to the responsibility of parenting.

Our city experience wasn't predictable. As president of the Parent-Teacher Association (PTA) at our public school, the only thing Rebeca could consistently count on was getting mired in student traumas and district dramas. Despite wonderful, talented, committed, teachers and parents involved. My dad drove me all over the city trying to find our five-year-old after he was put on the wrong after-school bus. After four phone calls, we found him alone and terrified, surrounded by high schoolers at the start of this bus's next route, 40 minutes after he was expected home. This happened a few days after being hit on my bike, a week after Rebeca's miscarriage. *Why can't these simple things just work?*

City parents with limited resources often can't do more than make ends meet. Those with moderate resources (like us at the time) will find the PTA or parks department and try to leverage whatever free or subsidized resources we can find. Those with plentiful resources will go private: exclusivity, tuition, gates … What the liberal elite don't seem to understand is most people can't afford the doorman building and private school. Living in cities without money is not going so well.

Being at home with our two boys during COVID in 2020, I would listen to cars blaze by. "Close the gate!" I'd snap at six-year-old Roque, seconds after he left it open. "It's not safe! Your brother is out here!" His brother Rio, by now two, was just the type to run out that door onto the street. I imagined him on the pavement, with no way to take back my mistake. *You can't take it out on Roque. Your bike accident isn't his fault. You'll teach him to be afraid of everyone and everything. You valued your childhood innocence.*

And for Rebeca, working from home during COVID was an accelerator of this moving timeline. As a highly sensitive person, she is easily triggered by external stimuli. Her idea of an exciting Friday night is ordering from a new restaurant. *Now you're just accepting these threats to her mental health? Every day?* Living there was causing her anxiety. I asked her one day if she was ready to move, after a road rage incident in front of our house led to gunshots fired in the air during Roque's virtual first-grade class. I had asked her before, and she'd said, "It's fine that we live here" in so many words. This time, she said, yes, she wanted to move.

And two things happened. First, I felt an overwhelming sense of relief. Indecision is exhausting. Indecision pulls us out of the present. It drains our cognitive energy. I'm decisive with people, but financial decisiveness is my weak spot. Indecision has a cost of its own. I was tired of looking at houses and neighborhoods, and school district data and census info, and private high school costs if the public school choice lottery didn't go our way. *So, 529 limits for private high school ... Tuition today ... Monthly amount compounding nine years ... FML.*

Second, I had a baby due date as a deadline yet again, so I got right to work ... Which was as soon as possible without compromising intent. And when humans decide to do something no matter what, the universe/providence/God/psychology has a way of making it happen. People are at their best when pursuing goals. With a deadline (which was sort of winter, the February due date for our third child), I was activated. Instead of watching *Game of Thrones* (again) after the kids went to bed, I did research, and got ready to make an offer. By ready, I mean, confident enough to decide. After all, compensation—and home equity is a form of that—follows performance under pressure. Goal clarity gets results.

By wholeheartedly committing to buying a house in an affluent city neighborhood near the lakefront, we wound up in an affluent suburban neighborhood on the lake, one I'd never set foot in before. I never would have known to look here until I acknowledged that we weren't getting what we wanted in our price range in the city. By deciding to start, we learn about ourselves, and refine our goals along the way. In the end, there are no guarantees, and you must decide. It's easier to steer when you have some momentum already. The key is beginning and doing your best. Making decisions and following through to execution is a key mindset for financial abundance. We will make mistakes and have setbacks. It doesn't matter. Act decisively and imperfectly.

As it turns out, raising kids in a less chaotic environment is something that is kinda nice. Consider Pareto's Principle, better known as "the 80/20 rule," meaning that 20% of our actions yield 80% of the results. Applied here, 20% or less of "total childrearing" effort was required to move to a bigger house in a quieter, more affluent neighborhood. The 80% of results—what I'm hoping for at least—come from the attributes of a child-focused community, more affluent school district, and all the other resources found here. We don't have to "find programs," and separate all the choices offered in the city. We just have local ones with local kids. And that's that. And if there's something we want in the city, we're close enough to join.

This homebuying experience was so different from our first. We had a realtor, our old neighbor and current client. She was excellent. If you doubt what a professional can do, consider that her eye for interior design alone made our place look soooo much better. (Not kid-friendly, but great for showings.) She set a price point of $150,000, which she felt would attract buyers looking in a price bracket up to that and down to that. She was paid a fee on the sale of our home, as well as the purchase of the new one. And worth every dime, I'd say.

Capital organizes energy. The scarcity mindset would say: "Why pay a professional when it is a transaction I can handle myself?" In my observation, it's the For Sale By Owner signs that are in the yard the longest. Just like investing, the client should be paying for a favorable outcome, not a magical ability. We had never sold a home before. If I were responsible for finding a photographer, staging the home, and listing it on Zillow, we'd still be waiting.

And this time around, we were "good" clients. We were ready to go, decisive, and my steadily increasing income paired with Rebeca's new salary put us into a whole new price range. Banks wanted our business. We had a mini-bidding battle between lenders at the eleventh hour that didn't change the outcome but gave me a fantastic feeling of empowerment. Our loan was big enough that the banks would make some coin on us. It felt more like shopping for a car than asking for money. We leveled up our socioeconomic status, and were treated better because of it.

We all seek control in our lives. Money is one way to get more of it. Prejudice often begins when we misjudge and dismiss those seeking control—without success—as lacking the desire to have more control. That's the human experience, controlling what we can, making our peace with what we cannot, and discerning that key difference. Just a few months after we moved from our old neighborhood in the city, our seven-year-old asked from the backseat of the car, "Why are so many things broken in the city?" We were back in our old neighborhood. He had never thought twice about that when he lived among the broken things. His socioeconomic status changed too. I'm happy we improved our situation, but we never wanted to leave the city. I'm worried that he'll begin to judge those with broken things, but I'm no better. The trash strewn all over the street started bothering me more than it once had.

I tell myself as I tell you: it's alright to say that out loud. I've spent years "in solidarity" as a way of coping with guilt, or at least discomfort, with my privilege. I was in nonprofit work 110%, and felt good about my contribution. In the years since, I've spent untold hours trying to reconcile my personal beliefs about the nature of inequality with how I wanted to run my business. And I just like cities. They're a visual feast of human diversity and expression, architecture and food, activity of all kinds.

We went to a wedding a few years ago, before we moved, and happened to sit next to a successful author, coach, and speaker of color, well-known in Milwaukee and gaining national attention. We said we were neighbors of the bride and groom, and asked where they lived. She replied, "Oh we're out in Brookfield." That challenged my solidarity philosophy. She was like, "Nope, my family's not dealing with all that." *Am I holding Rebeca back?* I caught up with a few former students, now clients, after we moved, and they basically said they couldn't figure out why I, in their eyes a well-off authority figure, would have lived where we did. *Almost … disappointed in me.* I have since read in the book *Creating Money: Keys to Abundance* that the greatest gift we can give others is the example of our own life working.

By moving further out, we gave up: Montessori education through Milwaukee Public Schools, my bike commuting, walking distance to the lakefront, beach, coffee shops, and restaurants, even my vision of writing over a long lunch at my café table for one, like a Parisian. We kept everything else we wanted in a home for at least $200,000 less than we would have paid in the city. Which even at a low 3% interest on this mortgage, amounts to over $300,000 of savings by the end. We would spend every dime we had to maintain predictability and pleasantness in the city, just to reconcile some identity crisis.

Those from the hood will inevitably be accused of selling out when they move out. Whether out loud, online, or the inner voice, the naysayers know that getting out is scary, and they haven't done it. It's unfamiliar. In the hood, everyone is getting by, so really … anything goes. People passing by would just sit on that retaining wall I'd built. It was a nice seat in the shade, yes, but on our property, with their McDonald's or brown bag liquor. I just said hello and walked inside. We had teens on dirt bikes doing hot laps through our alley, fireworks in backyards, cars idling in the street doing who knows what behind tinted windows. It was vibrant and jarring, welcoming and confrontational all in one breath. *I do miss it.*

Now if my lazy ass doesn't get out and shovel the driveway 20 minutes after it stops snowing, I am the neighborhood deadbeat.

People take pride in their homes. And that's a nice thing. Now Rebeca can walk outside without being catcalled. That's a nice thing. I can walk the kids down the block to the playground without clenching their hands as cars blast by. That's a nice thing. We can walk or jog at night. That's a nice thing, too.

All these nice things, day after day, allow us to replenish and reinforce our self-worth. By not thinking about basic needs for security, we can repurpose that thinking time to growth and each other. Living in poverty is traumatic. Living comfortably is …a nice thing.

As a teenager, when Rebeca got a ride home from a friend's parent, she would deliberately point out a single-family home, across the street from her run-down apartment building, and walk up to the stranger's house and wave, and wait on the porch until her ride pulled away. Today, her nonprofit Core El Centro provides trauma-informed care. She doesn't need more trauma exposure at home. She's ready for some well-deserved suburban predictability.

We wanted a home that can grow with our kids. In our mid-thirties, we wanted a home big enough to have our parents stay here in their later years if they wanted. A full finished basement that could host a bunch of teenagers privately while still letting me saunter unexpectedly down the stairs to "check on something." A driveway with a basketball hoop. A space that promotes a healthy lifestyle while at home. For the next 20 years, 80% of my thoughts and emotions will be family-oriented. I let go of identity and considered the compounding effect of daily activities. *Maybe I belong in the land of boring dads.*

Humans deserve to enjoy the nice things during the 80% of life we want pleasant and predictable. The other 20% we should be in the city or the wilderness, the museum or the county fair, seeing new people and places in an unpredictable way. Sometimes the unpredictable is unpleasant, and seeing the unpleasant might make us angry, or motivated, or appreciative of what we have. Volunteering for that discomfort is less likely to happen when your home is nice. Habits, like dollars, follow the path of least resistance in the absence of vision, focus, and faith. Without that discomfort, a nice person may go from their nice house to their nice office to their nice lake house, and ease into a moratorium on new experiences, until they can no longer entertain a perspective different from their own. Their world becomes those nice places only. Our own choices reinforced by nice things, but less relevant by the day. *Your deepest fear.*

It's just so much harder to become the best version of ourselves within a chaotic environment. Which is why so many tales of success start with leaving the war-torn country, staying off the streets and in the gym, or getting out of the neighborhood. Successful people flee unpredictable environments. I heard this in an early advisor training in my first year, and I bristled at that assumption, since personally I'm so attracted to spontaneity and extremes. But even my road trips were built on a predictable foundation of basic needs met that I took for granted. I had spontaneity sprinkles on my consistency cake. I had a basic life plan, so I could improvise from there. By contrast, financial instability creates a culture of no planning, because planning is futile, which perpetuates instability.

The harder a person works to achieve their vision, the harder it becomes to accept removable threats to that vision. My core vision of being an involved and active father, and providing a lifestyle that my parents gave me, led me to the suburbs, a block away from a playground, tennis court, and forested creek instead of the busiest intersection in

Milwaukee. If I can minimize the risk of a traffic fatality, I will. Maybe control is not the goal. Yet if the basics are secured, there is no doubt a person can think bigger, take more risks. If our physical or mental safety is threatened at home, it's harder to thrive. Let's build on the basics: everyone deserves a respite at home.

As I write, nearly two years into living in our new home, you know what I appreciate most? That I don't wonder if I left the garage door open, that I don't wonder if the kids' bikes will be stolen from our yard, that I don't wonder if Rebeca feels safe home alone. She's at her desk with the blinds open now. Hard to put a price tag on that.

general merchandise

"This is what we spent on general merchandise. Here's dining out."

"Are you serious? You just went to Peru with friends. I'm not doing this."

That's not how this was supposed to go. I had spent hours categorizing all our transactions from the last calendar year into our finance app. I devised a visual infographic of sorts to compare spending categories visually, painstakingly measuring blocks for accurate scale on a 2' x 3' sheet of paper. How could this "first annual household budget meeting" go so comically wrong? What an epic fail.

You had a budget without a board.

Years earlier, as a new financial advisor, I was nominated to join a nonprofit's board of directors. "I'm on the board." It's a fun thing to say, and it felt good for my fragile ego, because in my younger days, "the board" always felt so omnipotent. A board of directors was something adults were on, and now I was one. I could name-drop "I'm on the board of _______," and get this immediate sense of purpose and pride. I was volunteering for a cause, which was good for the soul. A board (three at one point), three kids, a marriage, a business, and a book are probably too much at once, but when you love them all, it's hard to pull back.

If being on a board never occurred to you, you aren't alone. And to be fair, some professions and careers lend themselves to board membership more than others. You need some amount of flexibility with scheduling. The high school teacher and the surgeon are out most likely.

This illustrates, perhaps by coincidence, the second filter. The board member must be seeking exposure to and exchange of ideas with other people. The IT professional, the teacher, and the surgeon usually work within a system that does the recruiting, staffing, and security for them: the contracts, students or patients show up. On the other hand, attorneys, florists, executives, judges, realtors, and so on are often in the market for exposure. We can bring new connections and resources, which increase income for the organization. In exchange, we can offer pro bono advice or in-kind services that allow the organization to reduce flexible expenses, like payment for professional services or vendors.

Expertise is a form of volunteering. I bet you've been in a meeting before, good ones and bad. And I bet you've made some tough decisions before. I learned a lot about both in board meetings. I've seen the epic back and forth when the tension is palpable. I've seen the mundane where even the most well-intentioned attendee is stifling a yawn. From HR to PR, I've seen how multiple perspectives, diversity of skills, and shared commitment to the mission drive outcomes. I've realized the best practices in nonprofit board governance can work for you, and your household.

There is no reason why you couldn't gather a group of like-minded people with varying skill sets around a common purpose, for the benefit of all.

Think and Grow Rich outlines the concept of a mastermind group. This group is a collaboration of individuals that have complementary skill sets, and the same mindset or goal. By spending time with this group, you can leverage all these different abilities efficiently and wisely. You may have heard a present-day speaker or two riff on the concept: "You become the average of the people you spend the most time with." It is not easy to focus on a vision of buying your mom a house by age 30, when your five besties do nothing but party and blow through cash. Without focus, you will default to the average of what you see around you. In a board meeting, when a problem of strategy, capacity, or intent comes up, the more perspectives, experiences, connections, and skill sets are in the room, the more effective the shared "mastermind" is compared to any individual.

A person can know anything if they surround themselves with the right people with the right expertise. *Why should I know how to troubleshoot the heater when I have my father-in-law?* Do nonprofits have attorneys, graphic designers, financial planners, and CPAs on their full-time staff? Rarely, and not the smaller ones. But they still need these services, if only in small quantities. The right board member, with their unique expertise and network, can ascertain in minutes if something is a real problem, whereas the executive director could research that all week, and still be unsure.

Much of what a board (or your household) will do falls into three categories: promoting the mission and vision, budgeting and forecasting, and making tough decisions. As a board member, I am an ambassador and tell people about our work all the time. *Which reminds me . . .* I served on the Urban Ecology Center board for four years, and an advisory committee before that. The mission there—to connect people in cities to nature and each other—is so important to our family, and our lifestyle. That board is large and established, and I learned a lot about structure and communication. I'm currently board president of Project Kindred. Our mission is to disrupt the cycle of segregation by uniting and empowering diverse young leaders through transformative experiences. Children of vastly different backgrounds are growing up as one cohort, one that looks today like the inclusive future we seek.

Our first personal finance lesson to take from board governance is promoting the mission and vision. The development team charged with fundraising must be incessantly optimistic, even as they monitor and assess internally. Sometimes you just gotta go for it, without any guarantees. Board room decisions are toughest when they involve making commitments of financial resources based on *assumptions* of future income, as opposed to guarantees. In the finances of a nonprofit or a household, we have to chart the course, and start with the end in mind. The mission and vision for your household (and your nonprofit) must be compelling enough to make a short-term sacrifice worth it.

The fundraiser asks for support in a sea of unknowns. The benefactor gives under the same circumstances. In pursuing a worthwhile mission and vision, everyone will take that risk. What is your household's mission? Is it compelling enough to sacrifice a bit today for a brighter tomorrow?

By promoting the mission, we meet wonderful people we never would have otherwise: mentors, vendors, collaborators, and just all-around dope people. Believing in the mission gives us a social bond, a level of trust that we can build on. In my work as a board member and as a financial planner, I have a reason to reach out to tons of cool people, and get to know some of them pretty well.

Selling isn't a dirty word. Just sell something noble and of quality. And when you put it out there and risk rejection, you'll often get support in unforeseen ways. Through board volunteering, I've met people who became clients, and I've asked clients to join boards alongside me. The common thread is mission and vision. *What is all this hard work for?*

When the organization—or your household—loses sight of that, it will slowly devolve into busy work, and routines that don't motivate. More general merchandise without more general wellbeing.

I was in a board meeting once, and the focus was on the development committee and progress toward fiscal year targets. They had a spreadsheet with multiple categories for their fundraising pipeline. One category was "regular committed." This group had a high degree of reliability. Most people keep their commitments because it's hard to back out. Also, commitments become routine. Another category is "new donors," separated by anticipated amount of the donation, or their capacity to give. New donors are harder, because people tend to be risk-averse, and don't do new things easily. Another category was "past donors." The confidence threshold here was higher, because giving again would be congruent with giving in the past. There is already a relationship there to nourish and grow, versus starting from scratch.

OMG, this spreadsheet is exactly how I track my own revenue and clients. Truly, it was all there: timeline, confidence threshold, revenue. Deadlines for tax deductions influenced our calendars similarly. Which goes to show that selling is an action, not a value. The value lies in the outcome. Often, donors give only in support of a specific outcome near and dear to them.

On to budgeting, which is how we translate the mission and vision into a sustainable reality. Most people know the board keeps tabs on the cash monies. Yet many people hate budgeting in their own lives. Most things don't seem like a problem, until suddenly they are. By nature, many financial things aren't urgent until the ideal time has already passed. Granted, some people find it extremely cathartic. (And those folks tend to have a spouse who rolled their eyes when their elaborate spreadsheet was unveiled in their meeting with me.) The biggest hang-up is that we budget for routine expenses like our bills, but not car repairs or vacations, wedding season or birthdays.

Budgeting best practices are knowable, learnable, and applicable to anyone, though. At Lake Valley Camp, I would submit a budget proposal to the executive director every year, and he would reply with questions, comments, and concerns. Then I'd edit, and he would take it to the board for approval. I would track past expenses to make future estimates, budget for large expenditures already on the calendar, and assume that certain unplanned expenses would come up. If they didn't, great. I had to plan for the cost of leasing horses and vehicles for summer camp eight months ahead of time. There is absolutely no reason a family of four in South Dakota or a single person in San Francisco couldn't do the same thing. *Summer vacation next year, how much do we want to spend? Braces? Car replacement? What should we get done this year?*

The budgeting without the "board meeting" is not all that helpful. The couples I meet with have miscommunication, often because they have different perspectives and skill sets. This helps their relationship, but we need a board meeting to connect the dots. The analyst will analyze because that's what they do. What's the goal though? He knows every detail, and she wonders why he spends so much time tabulating. *Isn't the point of working hard to enjoy life?* But the meeting without accurate data isn't helpful either. The "big picture" half of the couple will say what they want, but "they don't know what it will take to get there." The board becomes the referee.

People might hate budgeting because most spending doesn't happen every month. Life is messy and unpredictable. Let's focus on patterns and intent instead of nitpicking every dime. (If you are in serious debt reduction mode, maybe nitpick if it helps. The first step to a healthy relationship with money is always awareness.) What did you spend eating out on average in the last three months? How do you feel about that?

You plan to spend $2,000 on a big vacation 10 months from now. Can you afford to defer (all saving, from the bank to the 401k, is just deferred spending) $200 each month from then to now? If not, why? Too much spent eating out? The vacation on the credit card again, how would that feel? Who would be negatively impacted? *Our donors and our children are trusting us to be responsible. If single, childless people spend recklessly, who cares? You did. Stop judging.*

Like an organization, a household has three options to improve cash flow We can earn more with a side hustle, passive income, or raise. We can reduce our fixed expenses by moving, downsizing or driving a more reasonable car. We can reduce our flexible spending by not taking that vacation or eating at home instead of going out. It's got to be one of these three, or a combination. *Last year, our family spent more than we earned. All these numbers, in every direction, are so much bigger than we're used to. We need to get a handle on this. But you're at least half the problem. And what about all your spending that you enjoy, but categorize as "for Rebeca?" Where does that fit in? Everything is so much busier than it used to be …*

This is the nitty gritty nuance of the board meeting. Sometimes we find revelations; sometimes hard truths are revealed. But at least we know this type of thing for couples should happen once or twice a year, quarterly at the most. There's a reason some mortgages require a tax escrow: if they came around once a year for thousands of dollars, a lot of people wouldn't have it.

The phases for an organization and a household are cyclical. Awareness comes first, followed by intention, and then automation. In your household, or your board, each meeting should progress through the phases. You can't be intentional without awareness. Intention is only found in relation to mission, vision, and values. Get the facts before the meeting. You shouldn't automate something without intention first. You need to know if something is worth it. *Sorry, kids, no Netflix till Ozark*

Season 3 comes out. And you've already seen every Storybots episode five times. You know the science by now.

Life isn't linear. Things ebb and flow. But budgeting and forecasting can be learned. The bigger the numbers, the more important a framework becomes. As our family grew, the number of transactions increased along with it. The number of "needs" addressed by less than $50 multiplied faster than our income. I couldn't identify all the transactions, let alone ponder their utility.

In a board meeting, the staff reporting will share the need for spending or explain the revenue, and the board interprets. Ideally, a finance committee does pre-work, and reports out the board as a whole, with materials sent in advance. This can be tense because hindsight is always 20/20, but the future is unknown. We must make predictions rooted in optimism and caution at once. For that reason, most boards will separate operations from development, split into two committees. I must exercise extreme caution, considering the employed staff and the donors are trusting the board's oversight.

The third role of the board is to act as a fiduciary, assuming a legal responsibility for sound governance and financial practices. Our executive director needs approval to spend outside of approved budget numbers, even though we "can afford it." *Rebeca and I never say no to each other. That's part of the problem. We used to out of necessity.* As a board member, it is difficult to know what's really going on day to day. We observe programs, get reports, review documents, yes. The 5:00 pm conference room talk doesn't capture the energy of the weekend program. Back at LVC, I struggled to capture my own work for Jim. And he was candid about how daunting it was to summarize our progress for the board. There is a lot of pressure on staff to condense lots of data into a digestible presentation. Board members are volunteers, making asks, and putting their reputation on the line for the organization.

Leadership is often lonely. A quality board brings insight and perspective. I've heard it said we can't live long enough to make all the mistakes, so we should learn from mistakes others have made. I've seen first-hand that one of the most valuable services a board provides is giving the organization's leadership a sounding board, a listening ear outside of the office, under the umbrella of formal commitment to the organization. In your household "board," an advertisement isn't a board member. Commercials and water cooler talk don't bear any liability.

In hard times, that element of pressure means it is not the same thing as planting trees on a Saturday. It's the table where decisions are made. I've seen board discussions in which everyone is searching their conscience for the best answer. I've seen board discussions that are out of touch because most members live in another community. It is agonizing to take the risk and make a commitment to fund new programs for real people and participants. Even more gut-wrenching to cut them. It feels like an admission of defeat. Especially when we care deeply about these people. *How can you possibly tell her she needs to spend less after how she sacrificed to get* your *career off the ground? But that doesn't change our deficit last year. But that's on you, too.*

A board left in the dark can't be effective. A board that meddles in the details gets in the way. A good board meeting has a clear agenda, shared well in advance, along with relevant materials, like budgets, program proposals, and so on. Staff leadership or decision-makers attend if the agenda pertains to them, so they have a first-hand account instead of relying on the executive director's account later. The meeting is moderated well, not favoring one topic or one person with too much time. All opinions and questions are encouraged. The routine is measured for accuracy, the goals are described, the concerns are voiced. Actions steps and key comments are recorded in the minutes. Decisions require a vote. Both sides know what comes later, what comes now, and what needs more discussion.

Facilitating a productive meeting is both an art and a science. Some critical statements come out, unplanned, that cannot be rushed. Holding a space for dialogue that is emotionally safe and confidential is not easy. And what could be more emotionally charged than how we fundraise or spend, save or give away our hard-earned income? That's why an outside perspective is so helpful. As a member of your household's board, I can share my professional opinion, on the record, but you ultimately decide. Responsible decisions cycle back to the budget, and often to mission and vision. There's a tough call to make. Can the budget sustain this course of action? Does this course of action align with the mission?

And that taught me what an annual financial review for a family should look like. How often do Rebeca and I put our lives on pause and discuss, free of interruption, what our short- and long-term goals are? We don't often have thoughtful talks on big purchases, but a series of short "I was thinking that…" interrupted by "can we go outside on the swing?" followed by "…did you finish the laundry?" That's incomplete at best. Without awareness of all the information, reflection on your intentions for the future, and a plan to automate and set boundaries till the next meeting, money talk between couples is prone to error.

In my reviews with clients with young kids, having a meeting with me gives them a deadline to reflect and generate questions in advance so our time can be productive. A successful year won't happen by accident. That meeting with me is all that nudges their finances from the important category to the urgent. If this type of format works for nonprofits and businesses with annual budgets of $100,000 to $100 million, why wouldn't it work for your family? When you're in your forties, why does spending on holiday presents and flights still surprise you every year?

I dreaded this budget meeting with Rebeca. *You're a financial planner. You're writing a book on finance and culture. C'mon.* In part, it was because I knew I could never be objective with her. I spent "for her" and she spent "for the kids." In part, it was because we had no tiebreaker, no arbiter of our inevitable differences. And because of our differences, and dare I say, love for each other, we couldn't say no. I chose to avoid almost certain but fleeting discomfort—an immediate argument about money—over potential but lasting happiness from long-term alignment, clarity, and financial balance. Humans make that mistake all the time. *I had a long day. Now isn't a good time to bring this up.*

A client of mine complained to me about how his fiancé was "wasting" her money by leaving excess in savings, and declared with gravity, "She really needs to start investing." He's a wonderful client and person: responsible, kind, hard-working, and devoted to his fiancé. He took my message to him in the past, and projected his own emotions onto her in a way that was counterproductive.

By being on his "board," I could provide objective advice from a distance, recommend that she talk with me, and he stay out of it, and ultimately show her that what he wanted was in her best interest. We found common ground this way. She didn't have to do what he said, but it helped to identify his money advice as a proxy for caring. Only he was persuading from an agitated state with an established position. That's how many romantic and work relationships are, but it's hard to see it when you're in it. A professional can observe impartially. Things are always subjective with our kids, significant others, siblings, and parents.

So, why didn't you follow your own damn advice?

I didn't follow any processes I learned from my work on boards or financial planning. I just put my head down, building up this budget meeting with Rebeca in the echo chamber of my head. Emotions compound, in any direction. One person's idea can take off, fed by confirmation bias in online searches, and nourished by an unchecked inner voice. *This is brilliant. I love the graphic. You're so insightful. She'll take this in immediately. It's so intuitive.* A board would have pointed out that I didn't have prior year spending for comparison, that Rebeca doesn't like visuals without numbers, that I just took a vacation of a lifetime without her. Yet "general merchandise" was unacceptable?

Her mission is to give and spend on friends and family without thinking about the price or bank balance. She's not high maintenance. She just had very little for the first 25 years of her life. After a two-year break, I dragged her right back into that. My mission, on the other hand, was to "achieve" a handful of big experiences and things for family, and to be minimalist or thrifty with everything else.

We ended up doing both at the same time. I pushed for a bigger house and nicer car. She was grateful, but would've been fine with less. She spent nominal amounts all the time without seeing the running total. Our financial situation just a few years ago seemed like a lifetime away.

I was grasping for control in a spreadsheet, when what I needed was to ask for help: from her, from a friend, from a professional, or all of the above. *If you want to go far, go together.*

Online crowdsourcing may provide ideas. It doesn't replace the value of having a board altogether. A good board, like a good friend, will say what needs to be said, and a richer conversation will result. You may not "need" it, but a mastermind group can help. The only price is vulnerability. You just have to decide if your long-term mission and vision are worth a bruised ego for a day here and there. The best ones always are.

finishing a book

After years of telling people "I'm writing a book," I went beyond the risk of being "that guy" who's all talk, and committed to hiring an editor and taking time away from my business to protect nights and weekends with family. With a possibility that…nothing would happen. A big risk. And the bigger the risk, the scarier it is. But hey, it's either important, or it's not.

Once I committed to finishing this book, it consumed me. Ideas would occur hourly almost. Images from the past and future alike would revolve in my brain. I would miss things my wife said in passing, I was so lost in thought. It became harder to enjoy myself, to make small talk with people, when my mind was whirring with behavioral economics 24/7. Harder to cheerfully talk with client after client about buying a house when I was writing a chapter about land theft at gunpoint being the starting point of American prosperity. For those holding the gun, that is.

The harder you work toward a goal, the harder it becomes to quit.

And the more divisive and conflicted the role of money in American culture became, the more I knew I had to finish this, that it had value. The more we pour into a dream, the more protective we become.

I committed to write this book when I was 30. My mom once said, "30 and 60 just seemed to matter in a way the other ages didn't."

I began writing to better know myself and process my thoughts. A new financial advisor at the time, in its infancy, this book resembled journal entries. I tend to encourage expression in others and repress my own feelings, so I thought it might be cathartic for me in addition to being helpful to others. Along the way, my passion and knowledge grew. And then I slowed down. I looked for reasons to delay, deleting calendar time for important work to make room for the endless urgent work, day after day. Why?

Ralph Waldo Emerson wrote in his essay *Compensation*, "Do the thing, and you will have the power." My perspective took years of education and experience to acquire. Now it was time to do the thing. Doing is hard. We must prepare for an opportunity, identify it when it arrives, and act despite fear.

Socialism and capitalism are economic systems that organize money differently. All people are socialist and capitalist. Admittedly, some lean way more one-sided than others. Unchecked socialism inevitably leads to corruption, even if socialism is democratic and not authoritarian. Unchecked capitalism inevitably leads to exploitation, even if markets are free and not monopolized. When basic human needs can be invoked for a market opportunity, we see the most insidious effects of capitalism: bloated military spending "for the troops," "college prep" claims from for-profit charter schools, endless "pro-America" fundraising for political campaigns, and whatever "out-of-network healthcare provider" means.

Only with an informed assessment of dollar value and human value can we blend these two systems for the benefit of all. The tension between human value and dollar value is nothing new. These values will never converge. All humans are priceless. If all money was priceless—or worthless—we would have no reliable reference or means of measurement. Detach from your dollars. They don't define you as a person. You define them through your choices. People tend to make errors of global attribution, meaning we falsely assume success in one area transfers to success in all contexts. Money is the easiest thing to measure, and in turn mythologize. Those with it aren't good at everything. Those without it aren't bad at everything.

On an individual level, we should inform our nation's young people about the nature of human value and dollar value so they can make informed decisions on everything from cars to careers. Month after month, I listen to clients who identify with "excess" human or dollar value sheepishly apologizing for lacking the other.

Not that they're helpless. We just hesitate to act without understanding how the systems work. And in that pause, we see a sponsored ad. In cultural finance, as in philosophy, the first step for a productive debate is to define our terms. Socialism and capitalism, interest and depreciation, assets and equity, legislation and contract, leverage and opportunity cost. You are playing this game whether you like it or not. Shouldn't you know the rules? They're buried in legislation, user agreements, legal contracts, and fine print of all sorts, but they are knowable.

Every time you spend, invest, or give a dollar, you are endorsing a person, cause, or product. No dollar is neutral. Every single one has a social impact, including the ones you keep. "Buy only what you use, use often what you buy" is a simple recipe for success, especially for the risk averse. This behavior changes the marketplace. Consider the demand for organic and fair trade in the past few decades. Or watch a mainstream comedy from the early 2000s: the sexism, homophobia, and tokenism of minorities will make you squirm. All that to say: in the free market, you have influence. You challenge the seller to earn your business. Change always costs something, which is why companies want to coast the current if they can, but they're built to paddle.

New wealth is created by meeting marketplace demand. Laws are the rulebook, and politicians are the referees. If we the people deem a source of wealth was created unfairly, or is excessive, then we need to change the laws. But focus: let's get the money out of politics first, and then see how many issues resolve themselves.

If you're anti-everything, you come off as a jealous whiner. Whining itself is a privilege not everyone has; stop long enough to thank a veteran. The United States, by way of conquering natural resources, creating a visionary democratic government, importing enslaved humans, and welcoming the ambition of generations of immigrants chasing the American Dream, has become quite wealthy. How ironic all that wealth has allowed us the freedom and luxury to complain about how terrible capitalism is. Capitalism gave us the ability and democracy gave us the right. These two systems can be frustrating no doubt, but they are flexible enough to reward via the system those that reform the system without breaking the system.

Don't just troll: run for office, read books instead of headlines, rewrite the rules. The financial rulebook is public record, but the wealthy aren't pushing it as required high school curriculum. For example, private education is millennia old and taught students how to be elite, to rule. Its much newer cousin, public education, with its American origins in building a docile workforce for the Industrial Revolution, teaches us nothing about money beyond balancing a checkbook to avoid debt, and how to acquire skills to get a job that earns more money. People decide what people deserve. We can invest upstream and build on the basics of education, healthcare, broadband, and transportation. Absolute power corrupts absolutely, so there's no time to waste. We the people, including you, fund corporate profits and the government. You may face well-financed cultural pressure to act like an employee. Start acting like the citizen consumer boss you are.

I didn't understand the compounding effect of investments and emotions alike until my late twenties. I've spoken about money like water throughout: the calm pond, the mounting pressure of a geyser, a slow steady river current, and tumultuous rapids. For mentees of mine, it takes a while to grasp the magnitude. What's 10% interest earned on $100? Ten bucks. $10,000? A grand. A million? 10% interest on a billion is $100 million. In a year. The owner will pay $20 million in capital gains tax by converting that interest into cash. Unless their accountants and lawyers can maneuver to the Cayman Islands, and bill them under $20 million to do it. And the earner starts the next year with same billion. Public services funded by taxpayers, like police, courts, roads, and government oversight, protect that wealth. Taxes are like an irrigation system, designed to move water to spots that are getting bare. And yet you don't have an opinion on taxes because that's boring. Well, most policy is boring. You don't have to nerd out on it, but I want you to know you are affected regardless. We have the power to define our own safety net, and our own incentives. It just takes more strength to redirect the current downstream.

Determination, passion, generosity, and love—like anything with infinite growth potential—compound when nurtured consistently. (Obscure hobbies will too. I've witnessed the passion for Pokémon compound in our house lately.) The impact of social media algorithms, trauma, or credit cards compounds with no help from us whatsoever. A compelling vision keeps you on track when you want to quit. What we think about and care for can grow exponentially. That's the big secret. So, choose your company and your habits wisely. What you think about and who you spend time with move you toward a destination with increasing momentum.

In the shifting sands of survival mode, it is difficult to build momentum in any direction. Those who do are even more remarkable. Define what success looks like for you. The compounding effect of thought and action will lead you toward it. Compounding is an accumulation of energy, like an avalanche. It is easy to change course early on, but gets harder and harder later. *If I don't finish this book, I'll regret it for the rest of my life.*

I know that even putting a vision on paper is a risk. The greater the risk, the greater the potential reward. As the years went on, I continued to make excuses for putting off this book. It was hard to focus with our kids around during the pandemic. *The essence of consumerism is … is … Mollyyyy, of Denali.* Part of it was we became more comfortable financially. Privilege can empower some to take bigger risks with a safety net, while it can lower the risk tolerance of others. *Life is good. Why rock the boat?* In the wealthiest nation on earth, when our basic needs are met, only fear and desire make us come alive. We find those only beyond our comfort zone. Writing this made me come alive at a time when I—*ick!*—entered my thirties. Coming alive makes financial hardship more tolerable. Becoming numb makes hollow consumerism more of an escape.

Financially, it was four steps backward to take one, two, five, or nine steps forward in the future. The human risk of rejection was harder to process … Being vulnerable had led to personal growth in the past, and what could be more vulnerable than writing publicly about my privilege, my mistakes, my issues? I was worried that people would think I was a prick, inflating the importance of my own commonplace experience. I was worried that I'd be judged for having a "White Savior" complex, trying to lift others up. I was worried that my litany of generalizations about people would be seen as arrogant. I was worried that taking this risk would undercut the financial planning practice, my "day job" that I was working so hard to build, and I might offend some of my clients. I was worried my parents would disapprove. But we all worry about things. Valid, but still an excuse. I committed because the pain of regret was becoming more stifling than the pain of growth. It's all risky in life anyway. I might die tomorrow.

My calling was becoming clearer, my connection to my purpose I felt deeply, and a repudiation of that would be hard to take. In my annual focus plan, I define what I do for others: (1) I connect the dots by reading and observing; (2) I coach and counsel people to align their actions with values to become their best selves; (3) I make complex ideas accessible. That's where my passion and skills converge. It took years of reflection to articulate that. That all pointed to writing. I can analyze a client's finances, but it's not what I do best. Arguably, I do it only as a byproduct of those three things I do best. So, why couldn't I finish this damn book?

After a lifetime of reading history, philosophy, educational policy, psychology, political science, economics, and more, people found my thoughts on finance in the context of culture interesting. Over and over. *I don't know anyone who else has my convergence of experience and perspective.* And the more I thought about how much I read, the authority I challenged, the books I read, the tone of the journal entries, and the other books I read, the more inescapable the need to do this became. I had been swimming against the current for a while. I didn't want to network for new business. I'd always rather read a book. *Listen carefully to that inner voice. You know this is what you need to do.*

As poet Maya Angelou said, "Do the best you can until you know better. Then when you know better, do better." We are all imperfect. This book isn't about advice. I just want you all to "know better" how we got here, and appreciate the opportunity you've been given: to write the future by telling your money how to behave. You really can create change from your dollars. Do what you will going forward. Don't be afraid of your unique ability to influence and achieve. We need you in the arena, doing your thing.

epilogue

For much of this story, my wife Rebeca is just out of frame, so to speak. We've been together since 2009, married since 2011, parents since 2013, and even worked together from 2016–2019. It wouldn't be right to speak on her behalf. One of the only things we truly own is our story.

In the fall 2009, we'd been together about six months. She was graduating in December, and I had just begun my second year with Lake Valley Camp full-time.

We had a looming conflict: stay or leave Milwaukee. This is a true test of the relationship: our willingness to compromise on a big thing, not just what to do this weekend. I was starting to feel claustrophobic. She was close with her family, and they were great. I had no complaints. But knowing how many Milwaukeeans never leave, I was getting a bit worried. I wanted an adventure, anywhere else. She wanted to work her way up through Milwaukee Public Schools and be Superintendent. So …

This divide loomed on the horizon, and over time we became

more guarded because of it, protecting ourselves. I wanted to go to Thanksgiving back home to see friends and miss something she was planning in Milwaukee. It was another tug that unraveled the relationship. We had a phone call, she said I wasn't committed to her, and I didn't argue. We took a break.

At the bar that Thanksgiving weekend, it was a big high school reunion. I could have gone home with a high school hottie—or so I thought—and came close to asking. I was back in college, baby! In the end, it felt hollow to even pursue. *You didn't break up to do this.*

Back in Milwaukee afterward, I hadn't spoken to Rebeca in a week. On Monday or Tuesday, I got a voicemail from her dad, just asking me to call him back. He was very polite, but it was terrifying, nonetheless. His politeness made it more terrifying. *What does he want?!* I knew that she had two older brothers who were protective, and I knew that she could get very angry, very quickly…But I had to call back. Avoidance was not an option.

When I did, he said that he respected me personally, that he understood both Rebeca and I had a lot to think about in terms of what we wanted from our lives. He would be happy to shoot some pool or something with me, if I ever wanted to, even if Rebeca and I weren't together. He quickly and masterfully extended an olive branch, relieved some pressure and, by not reminding me, reminded me of her and the shared life that we had already started together. I felt more at peace.

That weekend was uneventful. On Sunday, my roommate was out of the house. I woke up, never changed out of my pajamas, did some reading, some journaling, put on some type of melancholic drama (*Eternal Sunshine of the Spotless Mind?*). It wasn't a bad day. I'm more on the introverted side, so alone time and movies like that help me process my feelings and recharge my batteries. I did start drinking whiskey mid-afternoon, because …why not? I felt like I had before I met Rebeca.

Too much free time, not enough time developing. Satisfied but not challenged personally. Same old routine.

I got a text from Rebeca. It was our first contact in a week and a half. She said simply, "I have something for you. When can I drop it off?"

Mind racing. Immediately, adrenaline back. Not just because of the surprise, but because of the challenge. Rebeca challenged my habits, my assumptions, my opinions, everything. Had I forgotten that already?

I recalled the Tuesday night we met ten months earlier, after a mutual friend and my neighbor convinced me to go out with him (thanks, AD), and I left the movie, the couch, the beer in hand, and the pajamas. I remembered how embarrassed I'd been, wearing those horrid dad jeans I told you about. When we went on our first "date," we split the bill. She was thinking, "Where are his manners?" I was thinking, "She's a feminist, and I'm sooooo progressive." Six months later, she found that I could really poke some holes in her norms and beliefs, and I found that she made me realize I wasn't as well-rounded or enlightened as I thought.

I had spent the time since Thanksgiving going back to my old routine. Challenge at work, comfort zone everywhere else. If you'd asked me then, I wouldn't have said that I missed her. Even if I did, I don't think I was self-aware enough to realize it. If she'd never texted me, I think missing her would have surfaced a year later as a wave of hollow regret when I was living in Colorado or something.

What was she dropping off? *Was it a jacket I left at her house? Did she want to scream at me to get closure?* I had no idea. I said that evening would be fine.

The hours passed, and I started to wonder more. She rang the bell after dark. She was by herself. She had only a manila file folder in her hand. Nothing else. I opened the door, and she walked up to our floor without a word between us.

After that, I have a "flashbulb memory," which is a memory in which all the context is very vivid and detailed because of the emotional significance or surprise.

Rebeca gave me the folder, and said, "Read this. I'll be in the other room." I sat down and read it.

Inside, was a letter saying that she thought she knew what she wanted, and the path she was on. But knowing me had introduced her to new ideas, places, and people. She was willing to move away, and experience something new to be with me. Behind this handwritten letter was an application to teach English abroad, together, the following year. It was completed. The only thing missing was my signature, right after hers.

I looked at the page until she slowly walked back in.

"Yes. Yes, absolutely."

Since that moment, I have been 100% loyal to her in mind, body, and spirit. I think of that as our wedding day. She took a huge risk to save us. I could have slammed the door in her face. I could have said no. I could have said, "This is appreciated, but in the last week I've realized it's better we're apart." Her family told her not to do this. A woman isn't supposed to chase a man.

But she knew me better than I knew myself. When I saw that, I was all-in. Sometimes 1 + 1 = 3. Socially and financially, that's all we could ever ask. That night, I did realize how much I'd been missing during that week. I wasn't growing, alone with my own thoughts, doubling down on the things I already knew, already liked.

Fortune favors the bold. The bold aren't guaranteed success, but fortune smiles on them. Saying "I'll wait until I'm 30" or "we'll stay here for now" is not serving you. You either want something or you don't. If it's important enough, you'll find a way. If it isn't, let it go. Decide. We can't buy more time.

We like to compare in absolute terms. *So and so bought this. She has blank. He looks better than him.* But Rebeca judges me on how I do relative to my potential, not relative to others. That makes all the difference. The thing about money is there is always a connection between the amount of risk and the amount of reward. Nothing ventured, nothing gained. Every product, career, relationship was new to you once. Every time we try something new, there's a chance we'll fail. Succeed or fail, we grow if we learn and move forward.

Rebeca and I needed to break up to know what we were missing. Like in the movie *Inside Out*, Joy realizes that Sadness brings help. There is no true joy without sadness. There is no true appreciation without sacrifice. The greater the risk, the greater the potential reward. Investing 101, and true in our lives. Ride a bike across the country. Move across the world. Ask them out today. Bare your soul and see what happens.

Rebeca took a risk on me, and I strive to be a good enough "return" for her. I am forever grateful. She makes my life better, and allows me to take new risks, like writing about all this. I want to earn for her, to make her proud of me. This last story is about love. Love has nothing, and everything, to do with money.

Money is just a made-up thing after all. It only has value because we all agree it does. Every dollar, as a human construct, makes a change in the world through the spirit of its owner. It signals what lies within us. A loving person will spend, save, and give from a place of love. Love has unlimited supply. When a second child is born, you don't halve your love for the first. Loving is a risk worth taking. If you're a loving person who doesn't want to think about money, think again. You might find your money can spread love in more ways than you guessed.

acknowledgments

If nothing else, I hope my story emphasizes how interconnected we all are. When you've met so many wonderful people, and read so many fascinating books, it's hard to know exactly who did what. In the world and on the page, the wit and wisdom of human beings never cease to amaze me.

I will start with my parents: they took raising children seriously, and showed up every day to model consistency, work ethic, humility, and fairness. As a working parent now, I have more respect for their remarkable daily discipline. Perhaps it goes without saying, but a childhood free from financial concern is a gift. I learned their principles through osmosis. They gave us strict rules as kids, and firm consequences if broken. Mainly, they said what they meant, and meant what they said, which I know now isn't all that easy. And as an adult, not once did they question my autonomy in choosing a direction for my life, even as I made choices I suspect they never would have, like becoming a financial planner without a base salary. Yet, their example in treating people fairly is ever-present to this day.

Jim Flint was my boss as I came of age over nine summers and four years of formative full-time work at Lake Valley Camp. He showed me how to think outside the box to solve problems, and always plan. He demonstrated how to take calculated risks. But most importantly, he trusted me at a young age with big responsibility. Those experiences tested my limits and boosted my confidence.

I'm grateful to all the staff and participants at Lake Valley Camp from its founding in 2005 to when I left in 2014. It was no utopia, but we came closer to one than what we all had back home. Being a steward of that community's culture gave me a vision of what humanity can be, one that keeps me pushing in hard times to this day.

Thank you to my primary UW-Milwaukee graduate program professors, Dr. Jackie Nguyen and Dr. Chris Lawson. I signed up for their classes whenever possible. Their authentic enthusiasm for teaching, and curiosity about learning and development, gave me a framework to blend educational psychology and personal finance. This book isn't close to a peer-reviewed study, but you were role models, nonetheless.

My sister Nora Heaton and my friend MJ Atamian both helped me get from feverish ramblings to a workable outline, reacquainting me with concepts like "theme," which I hadn't needed since Ms. Lynda Appino's high school English class. So just to be sure, I asked for her opinion, too. These three insightful writers "got it" so quickly, and early on, when I doubted any of this made sense. A consultation with Chrissy Wiginton at Publish with Clarity nudged me further along at a critical time. Later, my developmental editor and book doula, Annick Ina, helped me cheer up and get to the point from the other side of the world. Her team pre-served my voice as the finishing touches came together. My friend and designer Robert Lenz created the cover and threw in the perfect title for good measure.

Shoutout to my brother James Bell. He gave me the gift of this career, which led to this book. We think alike, yet our lived experiences are so different. I am eternally grateful to have a thought partner who encourages me, and keeps it real with a good laugh thrown in.

I'm so appreciative of my teammates at the time, Lydia Priatko and Gina Pagán. Lydia kept my emails at bay, Gina made intros to publishing contacts, and both managed to politely listen to muttered musings of a writer on busy weekday afternoons. Thanks to them and all the friends, colleagues, and clients who heard me casually drop a few sentences about this project and showed enthusiasm. They made it harder for me to quit.

At the end of this project, I am grateful for the support of my managing partner, Steve Holter. He didn't come from money himself, and has gone out of his way, late in his career, to make a career as a financial advisor accessible to everyone that wants to put in the work. As a result, our office has become far more inclusive and diverse than the one I remember in my first year. Thank you to Michael Ortiz, our office principal, for volunteering to read the manuscript, even before he knew what it was about, let alone how long it was.

Through it all Rebeca's parents, Jorge and Anamaria, have always shown up on short notice to move furniture, bring food, or watch the kids. Whenever they're in town, so have her siblings Destiny, Ben, and Jorge Jr. Saying "we could use help" is enough, no questions asked. Help out of obligation is one thing; joyful help is another. We all get the same amount of time, and they offered theirs freely. Knowing family has your back is priceless.

Especially Anamaria, who has made so much possible for all of us. She fled the civil war while pregnant and started with nothing. At home, her family owned a successful restaurant. Here she took a bus across

Los Angeles every day to clean the homes of the rich and famous. Then a mall in Wisconsin. Now she cleans our house. And takes care of our kids. And she puts eggs and tortillas in front of me at just the right time so I can get to work. She never complains and never judges my priorities, even when I judge myself. Her four children have gone from Compton to human resources director, Army staff sergeant, tech entrepreneur, and nonprofit director. Her giving became our gain. Despite the hardship, she achieved the American Dream, sending money home to her family while she cares for ours here with humble service. I hope to honor her sacrifice by being useful to others.

And I appreciate our second language practice sessions in the car. Maybe one day I'll be this fluent. *Especialmente mi suegra, Anamaria, que ha hecho tanto posible. Huyó de la guerra civil mientras estaba embarazada y comenzó sin nada. En casa, su familia era dueña de un exitoso restaurante. Aquí, ella tomó un autobús a través de Los Ángeles todos los días para limpiar las casas de los ricos y famosos. Luego, un centro comercial en Wisconsin. Ahora limpia nuestra casa. Y cuida a nuestros hijos. Y pone huevos y tortillas frente a mí en el momento justo para que pueda ponerme manos a la obra. Ella nunca se queja de eso, nunca juzga mis prioridades, incluso cuando lo hago yo mismo. Sus cuatro hijos pasaron de Compton a director de recursos humanos, sargento del Estado Mayor del Ejército, empresario tecnológico y director de una organización sin fines de lucro. Su dar se convirtió en nuestra ganancia. A pesar de las dificultades, consiguió el sueño americano de todos modos, enviando dinero a casa para ayudar a su familia como ella ayuda a la nuestra aquí. Espero honrar tu sacrificio siendo útil a los demás.*

And for Rebeca, the Virgo to my Aquarius. Thanks for letting this increasingly absentminded writer leave his pages out on the dining room table day after day. I know it drove you nuts.

about the author

Brett Heaton Juarez is a financial planner with active client relationships across the United States. He draws on his background in education and social science to guide individuals, families, nonprofit organizations, and businesses to align financial choices with core values, and plan accordingly.

Brett holds a Master of Science degree in educational psychology and a Bachelor of Arts in social studies education. He is passionate about treating all people with dignity in the financial realm. He is co-chair of the Diversity and Inclusion Council of Northwestern Mutual's Greater Milwaukee Group, business member of the Wisconsin Veterans Chamber of Commerce, and board president of Project Kindred, a local non-profit building youth relationships across lines of difference.

Brett lives in the Milwaukee, Wisconsin area with his wife and three children. His free time is spent reading with a good cup of coffee, outdoor recreation in any form, and trying to get his kids to love those things, too. (Minus the coffee.) This is his first book.

9 7 9 8 9 8 8 4 1 4 4 0 7